WHAT PEOPLE AR

THIS SPACE (

Stephen Mitchelmore has, over the years, in his blog, This Space, shown himself to be one of the acutest critics of contemporary writing anywhere. I do not always agree with him, but his work always makes me think and often helps me to understand.
Gabriel Josipovici, author and critic

For many years, Steve Mitchelmore has been a source of both inspiration and envy: introducing me not only to new writers but also to new ways of thinking.
John Self, blogger at The Asylum

It would be fulsome praise indeed to announce that This Space contains some of the very best writing in the literary blogosphere, but it would be more true to say that it contains some of the very finest writing on literature I've ever read anywhere.
Mark Thwaite, Head of Online at Foyles and editor of *Ready Steady Book*

This Space of Writing is such a lovely, luminous thing in my reading life.
Jen Craig, author of *Panthers and the Museum of Fire*

I've been an avid reader of Stephen Mitchelmore's posts on This Space for well over a decade. He not only shows us what to read, but new ways to read. His insights and analysis always leave me inspired. This new collection is a reason to celebrate.
Todd Colby, author of *Splash State*

Stephen Mitchelmore is of the best minds of my generation and an inspiration.
Lee Rourke, author of *The Canal*

Stephen Mitchelmore was the first literary-critical blogger, and has remained the best. His blog, This Space, ten years in existence, and commanding a wide readership, contains exquisite long-form meditations on literary fiction of the kind only the blogosphere can allow. Gathered here, Mitchemore's essays show a cumulative power, developing a philosophy of literature in a manner that recalls Blanchot's *The Space of Literature*.
Lars Iyer, author of *Spurious* and *Wittgenstein Jr*

This Space
of Writing

This Space
of Writing

Stephen Mitchelmore

Winchester, UK
Washington, USA

First published by Zero Books, 2015
Zero Books is an imprint of John Hunt Publishing Ltd., Laurel House, Station Approach,
Alresford, Hants, SO24 9JH, UK
office1@jhpbooks.net
www.johnhuntpublishing.com
www.zero-books.net

For distributor details and how to order please visit the 'Ordering' section on our website.

Text copyright: Stephen Mitchelmore 2014

ISBN: 978 1 78279 980 1
Library of Congress Control Number: 2015943104

A CIP catalogue record for this book is available from the British Library.

Design: Stuart Davies

Printed and bound by CPI Group (UK) Ltd, Croydon, CR0 4YY, UK

We operate a distinctive and ethical publishing philosophy in all
areas of our business, from our global network of authors to
production and worldwide distribution.

CONTENTS

Something Less (or More) than Literature

An Introduction by Lars Iyer

Ten years ago, on his blog *This Space*, Stephen Mitchelmore quoted Adam Phillips's celebration of the marginality of poetry in Britain: "It's freeing people actually to be able to work their own way. People are only going to be poets now if they really want to be. There's no money in it and very little glamour."

> *But it is not just poetry that is marginal in Britain; literature itself now occupies that position – shut out by multinational publishing conglomerates, by the near-disappearance of maverick publishers and magazines in which to showcase innovative work, and by a secure and complacent press. But then, as Phillips says, being shut out might be liberating too.*

Granted, there remains a whole infrastructure to help the literary writer make sense of their endeavour: reviews, profiles and interviews in the broadsheets and, for the fortunate, lucrative publishing deals and well-attended launches. Not only that, new courses of study in creative writing are increasingly popular, leading to teaching positions and visiting professorships; there is a proliferation of literary festivals and literary prizes; and authors' rooms are photographed for the newspaper. And, in a time of the declining prestige of literature and the decimation of the earnings of writers, who would begrudge authors the chance to meet admirers at literary festivals, or to find reassurance in their profiles and interviews, or to backslap writer-comrades in the review pages and to be backslapped in their turn? Who would be so churlish as to deny that teaching creative writing is a great way to get by in these difficult times?

Yet this supportive infrastructure, which continues to makes sense of literary writing, tends to reward a certain kind of book – if it is not a money-spinner, written for marketers' projections of the common reader, then it must appeal to the judging panels of literary prizes, the contemporary arbiters of "good taste". Prize panels typically favour ostensibly "serious" and "profound" books, and are suspicious of what they suspect to be "pretension" – the heavy hand is in; the light touch, out. Hence the triumph of clunky middlebrow narratives, as technically accomplished as they are paranoiacally uptight, guarding themselves from doubt, from openness through writerly accomplishment and through the cynicism and irony that are the mainstay of our times. This quintessentially British literary "good taste" is one of Steve's great bugbears, being sure of itself to the point of smugness, and hardly so much as aware of the existence of other literary traditions, of literary works in translation, and of its own homegrown radicals.

It is therefore only by proceeding in the *opposite direction* to the literary market that the writer might discover an element of freedom. The problem is that such freedom is *difficult*, subjecting the author to the uncertainty so effectively disposed of by "good taste". The abandonment of the middlebrow gold standard of literary work is to be exposed to the predicament that has faced every genuine writer since Romanticism, who must work without the safeguard of a tradition and therefore without a model of what literary writing should look like. "Last year's words belong to last year's language / And next year's words await another voice" (T.S. Eliot). And it is not enough to shake off a whole order of good literary habits and good literary manners to find "another voice". The real challenge is to transform the freedom-*from* established norms and traditional securities into a freedom-*to* "make it new".

In *Whatever Happened to Modernism?* – a book that is a touchstone for Steve, and the subject of one of his richest essays (included below) – writer and critic Gabriel Josipovici assembles

2

a counter-history of literary figures for whom received ways of writing were inadequate to their needs, figures who felt called to write but had to struggle to discover how they might respond to this call. Told backwards, with the emphasis on what they achieved subsequently, the careers of Kafka, Proust or Mann – writers so important to Steve – can seem all too monumental. As Josipovici reminds us, however, these figures lived their writing *forwards*, experiencing "the daily struggle, the daily uncertainty, the daily need for artistic and human choices in a world where there are no longer any guidelines for such choices", negotiating, in their own way, the dilemma bestowed upon us by the infinite freedom to write that characterises our time.

But there is, I think, a difference between the great modernists and us. In our time, the prestige of literary writing has declined. The old elitist culture of high modernism, with its valiant vanguards taking a stand against bourgeois taste, seems ridiculous now. Literature can no longer be heroically opposi-tional when no one much cares about the battle. The reign of "good taste", championed by broadsheet review sections and prize-giving panels, is so triumphant that it appears entirely natural. Indeed, we may be understood to live at the end of literary history, coming after a time in which literary writing might be something you fight over, might have real stakes, might actually matter. The literary writer is a diminished figure, her struggle against the middlebrow and against the market now judged as the hangover of old snobbery. Literary heroism is out of date.

* * *

Samuel Beckett – another of Steve's touchstone writers – when asked why he wrote, answered, *"Bon qu'à ça"*: "It's all I'm good for", or, "Because I'm good for nothing else". The vocation of writing – once sublime, once glorious, the legitimate heir to

3

religion as the most dignified search for meaning – has degraded into a gratuitous compulsion, an imperative that is emptied of its content and objective. As Jeff Fort notes, Beckett's *Bon qu'à ça* "speaks of exclusivity ... but precisely in the mode of abjection and default", an abjection that is also *comic*, Fort continues, "precisely because we know what extraordinarily high stakes have been invested in the thing called literature, and in particular, what Beckett himself invested in it, which was virtually everything he had".

And when Maurice Blanchot – another constant reference for Steve – was asked "Why do you write?", this is how he replied:

> *I will borrow from Dr Martin Luther when, at Worms, he declared his unshakability:* Here I stand, I cannot do otherwise. *May God help me. Which I translate modestly:* In the space of writing – writing, not writing – here I sit bent over, I cannot do otherwise and I await no help from the beneficent powers.

Blanchot's writer is no Luther, sure in his faith and his mission. Rather, unsupported by the old grandiosity of literature and by the reassurances of tradition, Blanchot's writer is humble, almost derisory. Once again, there is comic bathos to Blanchot's pronouncement, when we reflect that his investment in literature was at least as great as Beckett's.

And yet, not even Beckett and Blanchot may do as models for the literary writer now. Because, for Beckett and Blanchot, there is a *joy* in the response to the push or draw of writing, even a kind of *hope*. To tell stories (of a kind), to posit worlds (denuded worlds) in which events happen, to write criticism (in Blanchot's case) which shows the author drawn into the uncanny and anonymous space of writing, is, for them, a kind of ecstasy. It is the ground of hope. "If he is 'good for nothing but' writing, it may also be that nothing is quite so good as writing", Fort observes of Beckett.

In one of his earliest posts at *This Space*, Steve writes:

> *There is one reason that keeps me writing: hope. The hope that I might be able to write what I need to say because it could not be said in any other way.*
>
> *That said, I am not writing.*
>
> *There is also the hope of reading, which is much the same: to find, at last, the narrative that allows me to breathe and to step forward actually; not vicariously through a character or the author's experience, but actually to step forward. The metaphor is the only means.*
>
> *That said, I am not reading either.*

What kind of hope is this, when the literary vocation has now shrunk, not merely to an empty compulsion, but to something that is, in the British context, even more risible than it was in Beckett's and Blanchot's France? For Beckett and Blanchot, there was at least still some prestige in the idea of literary writing. At least no superegoic voice was telling them to "come off it" in that all-too-British manner of deflating what is taken to be pretension.

One aspect of Steve's freedom lies in the "no" he delivers to a smug and parochial literary culture. But the other, higher aspect lies in the "yes" of his hope, which releases him to search for words adequate to the needs of his criticism.

* * *

Steve's writing on *This Space*, from which this collection draws, has attended, from the start, to the predicament of the contemporary literary writer – the writer for whom literature is in some way a *problem*. Such a writer is stranded in what Maurice Blanchot calls *"L'Espace littéraire"*, the "space of literature", a zone of dispossession and destitution, charged with strangeness and volatility. Indeed, this phrase of Blanchot – the title of one of his most famous books – could also be translated as *The Remove of Literature*, or even, more freely, as *Literature's Default*. It is significant that for the title of the present book, Steve drops Blanchot's word, "literature" altogether, as though the notion of literature itself were too prestigious, too imposing, for the uncertain and obscure practice to which he would attest.

There is another telling Blanchotian resonance in the title of Steve's blog. Combine it with the name of his Tumblr, and you have the phrase, "this space of resonance", used by Blanchot in a programmatic essay, "What is the Purpose of Criticism?" The critic, Blanchot argues, lets a kind of "nothingness" resonate in the literary work; the review is the "space of resonance" which shows how literary meaning is interrupted or sidelined – whether by uncertainties in the act of narration or by the outbreak of uncontrollable, transpersonal affects. For Blanchot, literary criticism can show us how literary works both posit structures of meaning – carefully rendered characters with which to identify and empathise, codified emotions, psychological depth, social expansiveness, detailed and convincing environments – and destabilise such structures. In this way, criticism responds to an element of literary works that is easily forgotten, especially when fiction is understood through the lens of realism. By letting the "nothingness" of the work resound, criticism shows us what lies beyond the shaping of meaningful events and the evocation of psychological depth. The apparent modesty of literary criticism – its secondariness with respect to its object; the fact that it remains occasional – does not, then, prevent it from becoming part of the unfolding of the literary work itself. The Blanchotian critic watches over what Steve has called "something less (or more) than literature" by attending to the *condition* of such writing, that is, to both the possibility and the impossibility of its meaning, holding these apart and tracing their interplay.

Steve has been watching over "this space of writing" since he began blogging at Spike Magazine's *Splinters* in 2000. Indeed, Steve has a good claim on having been the first ever literary blogger – certainly he is one of the few who has continued to publish for so long. After a period of contributing to the collective blog, *In Writing*, in which he developed a longer, more ruminative blogging style, Steve started his own, solo-authored blog, on which he has published an extended review-essay every month or so for more than ten years.

Part of the impressiveness of this tenacity lies in the lowliness of its medium. I once introduced Steve to an editor for a well-known publishing firm, telling her about *This Space* and its followers. "So you're a blog-o-naut", she snorted, terribly amused, before she excused herself to speak to somebody more important. Of course, times have changed. There is now a respectability to online criticism, even a kind of professionalism. But that is itself a problem – online magazines can become little more than review conveyor belts, doing nothing to exploit the potential of the form. However, in solo, long-distance blogging, you still have a chance of being, like Phillips's poet, answerable only to yourself and those readers who follow you.

This Space of Writing collects forty-four essays of varied length, culled from many more essays at the blog, and mostly focused on contemporary publications (including translations) of a very diverse range. Each essay was originally a dated blogpost, title in red, text in black, with photographs and other illustrations (some of which are reproduced below) breaking up the text, and followed by several (usually not particularly enlightening, and sometimes plain abusive) comments. There are hyperlinks, of course, and, at the bottom of the page, links to other literary blogs. But the essays are the thing: each one intense and demanding to be reread, often including what appears to be, but is never simply, personal anecdote, and characteristically touched with a rather dry humour.

* * *

What are the protocols of a typical Mitchelmore essay? His review of Richard Ford's *Lay of the Land* does not stop, as so many reviews of Ford do, by praising vivid characterisation and fine phrasing. Ford is certainly adept at creating a convincing and enjoyable "illusion of meaning", giving us characters to empathise with, psychological depth and social expansiveness, but for Steve, Ford's novels are more than "a report from the real world reflected through the craft of fiction", since they contemplate the problem of fiction-writing itself – the relation to life and the world that the act of narration entails.

Ford's *Lay of the Land* is part of a sequence of novels narrated by Frank Bascombe, whose writing career has stalled after the death of his young son. Bascombe gave up teaching creative writing on the ground that "the lie of literature and the liberal arts" is the spurious search for "transcendent themes in life". Bascombe, on Steve's account, means to stay with this world, to keep immanent. Yet the "desperate stoicism" of his narration, his "voice beyond defeat", bespeaks a great uncertainty. The drift of the narrative, restlessly recounting one inconsequential event after another, seems, as it proceeds, to answer only to an empty necessity to speak – a hope to step forward in writing, which never quite secures the means to do so. In this way, Bascombe's voice is thrown back on itself, on its enabling conditions, becoming a meditation on the difficulties of the act of narration itself, on the impossibility of shaping real life into story. Steve argues that what Ford shows above all in his novels is that "the nature of existence will remain unclear and will never be resolved into coherence". Immanence is broken, without, for all that, opening on a larger transcendence.

Alas, as Steve argues, Ford does not have the nerve to carry through this aesthetic vision, shoehorning "event glamour" into the final pages of *The Lay of the Land*. There is a terrorist attack, a narrative climax that is supposed to wrap everything up and make sense of what has gone before. Ford cannot resist the temptation, as Steve says, "to fabricate meaning, to provide a telos for the interminable". This is what makes his work so warmly received in the mainstream press – we want our fiction to make sense, to confirm the order of our world. But what Steve shows is that Bascombe's voice ultimately prevents this reassurance, since it gives presence to the empty and powerless insistence of what cannot be contained by coherent narrative. Thus, Steve reads Ford against his critics and against himself, affirming an openness in the Bascombe novels that makes them much more than fine examples of literary realism.

These themes arise again in Steve's provocative account of David Foster Wallace's suicide. Foster Wallace's human tragedy, Steve suggests, is the result of a failed literary ambition – a thwarted hope "that everything could be contained in a book, unified by narrative", that "a novel might become the world, exceeding the limits of the self". For Steve, Foster Wallace's 1088-page *Infinite Jest* was an attempt at just such a novel, a novel to make sense of the flux of the world. And his next attempt, *The Pale King*, destroyed its author, who died of his failure to write a book that could *be* the world.

A book can never be the world – the question of how to resist literary uprightness, literary closedness, is therefore crucial, certainly for Steve's criticism, which, of recent times, directs us to the volumes of Knausgaard's *My Struggle* as responding, more than any others in our time, to the challenge of the writer's freedom. Steve highlights the recurrence of pseudo-epiphanal scenes in Knausgaard's work, each of which shows "the promise and terror of an imminent revelation, which never in fact occurs". These "frustrated epiphanies, without message, each a scintillating blank", these "offerings of transcendence", point to no final realisation. They resolve nothing, add up to nothing. But, in their very accumulation over the vast stretches of

Knausgaard's prose, they progressively unsettle the sense that *My Struggle* is a simple autobiographical recounting. For Steve, Knausgaard eschews what Foster Wallace killed himself to accomplish, embracing instead a creative uncertainty, a "letting go" that his critics have missed in their praise for the verisimilitude of his work.

* * *

I am an absolutely happy individual, a man who is by nature taciturn yet determined; irritations last only a few hours apiece; after one of them I walk around outside, I read a well-turned sentence, I look at a painting of some German or other-European martyr qua philosopher, and I am once again in my element.

These lines, taken from a letter by Thomas Bernhard, for me conjure up the image of Steve in his "non-writer's room", laptop open on his desk, a book under review by its side, a block of Icelandic lava nearby, typing away, never irritated for too long by the latest philistinism of broadsheet criticism, by the vicissitudes of his beloved Portsmouth FC, by the horrors of neoliberal politics. I imagine Steve, sat bent over, as *absolutely happy* as the author I believe he regards as the greatest legatee of modernism, good for nothing but writing because there may still be nothing as good as writing, and because he is unable to do otherwise.

"The sea closes up, and so does the land"

I wanted to get an early copy of *The Lay of the Land*, the final book of Richard Ford's Frank Bascombe trilogy, in order to post a review to coincide with all the others. Now, sometime after the event, with the arrival of my copy delayed and all the full-page reviews read, absorbed and the consensus set, it seems there's nothing to add. The trilogy is "an exhaustive look at the inner life of an American Everyman" (*Slate*), not unlike John Updike's Rabbit series (*The Daily Telegraph*), the distinction here being Ford writes in a "richly textured, rolling and poetic" first person (*The Times*) contrasting with Updike's free indirect style, all of which combines to make Bascombe "our unlikely Virgil, guiding us through the modern American purgatory" (*The Washington Post*), though the final volume does become a little bloated (*The Guardian*) because Ford has "failed to give him a compelling story" (*The Telegraph*, again). And that's pretty much it really. Yet not one review asks the question I had hoped to address before everyone else, the question whose answer I think helps to explain the unique quality of this trilogy, the question burning into each and every page: why is Frank Bascombe writing this?

The reviews take it for granted that this is a novel like any other, only much better than most. But right from the start Bascombe consigns his literary career to the past. He won't be writing a novel again. What he is writing now will be something much less than that. It will be enough for him to speak in "a voice that is really mine". The manuscript of his first novel got lost in the post and, soon after, he wrote a collection of stories which were published and well received. The film rights were then sold for a lot of money. Using that foundation, he settled down to write another novel. Halfway through, his son died, and so did the novel. "I don't expect to retrieve it unless something I cannot now imagine happens." The ambiguity of that unimaginable something resonates throughout *The Sportswriter*. It suggests that the novel must find a connection to life that it now apparently lacks.

The implications of Bascombe's abandonment of creative writing have themselves been ignored by the experts. Recently, James Wood said "the major struggle in American fiction today is over the question of realism", yet from the reception of the trilogy one would imagine the struggle is over already. Writing is a report from the real world directed through the craft of fiction and Richard Ford has written such a book. That's it. Frank Bascombe, however, isn't so sure, and Wood's question is thereby placed not over realism, nor even over fiction, but writing itself.

Readers of *The Sportswriter* will recall that Bascombe puts the end of his literary career down not just to Ralph's death but also to "dreaminess", a rare euphemism for this plain speaker. It never becomes clear what dreaminess is exactly, as only its apparently harmless symptoms are ever described ("taking a long-term interest in the weather"). Despite this, Frank is clear that dreaminess is to be avoided. He reckons it precipitated the break-up of his marriage. Redemption of a kind, however, came with a job on a sports magazine.

> *If sportswriting teaches you anything, and there is much truth to it as well as plenty of lies, it is that for your life to be worth anything you must sooner or later face the possibility of terrible, searing regret. Though you must also manage to avoid it or your life will be ruined.*

Like many other readers back in the late 1980s, I was very taken with Bascombe's voice. Indeed, reading those words again prompts a nostalgic reverie. I recalled that it was like a layer of bluff and deceit had been removed from fiction. No more wild imaginative flights of fancy, I thought, no more card-shark plot teasings, no more broad canvases "taking on" the 20th Century.

Instead, here was a voice from beyond defeat. I was so taken with its desolate stoicism that I read the novel three times in as many years. There is an irony in such returns.

If there's another thing sportswriting teaches you, it is that there are no transcendent themes in life. In all cases things are here and they're over, and that has to be enough. The other was a lie of literature and the liberal arts.

I returned because Frank Bascombe's voice promised a transcendence of fiction. After all, it is fiction's basic promise: to give meaning to life. As one reads a book or watches a film, that is what one enjoys, the illusion of meaning. But sooner or later it ends and one is exposed again to blank freedom. One can divide readers of modern fiction into two groups depending on the response to this experience: those who "devour" books so that blankness is elided for as long as possible, and those who wish books could include that experience of the blank in the work itself. Richard Ford certainly includes it. Frank Bascombe's disillusion with the pleasures of the imagination defines the person he has become, the story he has to tell and the way he tells it. But of course his condemnation of literature is still literature and one of the most celebrated examples of recent years. It promises meaning still. The irony gives the trilogy its uncomfortable dynamic. In principle, Frank Bascombe could write on and never stop. Every moment of his day can be described in detail. Literature is Frank's useless freedom; he drifts, bobbing up and down on an endless ocean. To criticise him for bloating his narrative is insensitive to his predicament.

The search for land, where literature meets life, was the theme of Frank's lost novel he called *Night Wing*. He wrote it after lying in an army hospital bed thinking about "nothing but dying". It tells of a young southerner who "goes to New Orleans and loses himself into a hazy world of sex and drugs and rumoured gunrunning" – another kind of dying, another transcendence of the self. Frank then tries to live it himself, travelling on his disability money from the army. But, after staring at "women and the oil derricks", he goes to Mexico "to write stories like a real writer". Everything is about finding the real.

Despite his rejection of literature, Frank's regular resort to it demonstrates this chronic trust in writing. In the opening scene of *The Sportswriter* he reads Roethke's poem *Meditation* over his son's grave, yet stops after the first line. Later, he describes otherwise inexplicable meetings with mystic Mrs Miller, a "reader-advisor" whom he claims not to take seriously yet still pays to see. In *Independence Day*, he recommends Ralph Waldo Emerson's *Self-Reliance* to his troubled son Paul, who promptly rips out a page that impresses him. Frank's mixture of horror and acceptance is that ambivalence in one moment. After all, which part of the essay is going to help? The whole thing together or one sentence? Why be precious if it helps Paul? The boy's insensitivity is just an extreme version of Frank's ambivalence. While he reveres the text, he too wishes to rip the book to pieces.

It's an ambivalence that Frank sees all around him. There's his old poet buddy Bert Brisker who couldn't write anymore so "substituted getting drunk as a donkey, shacking up with his students and convincing them how important poetry was by bonking the living daylights out of them in its name". There's the deeply unhappy Peggy Connover floundering in her life while carefully constructing a Great Books course. And then, worst of all, there's Frank's Divorcee Club colleague, the sleepless Walter Luckett, writing a novel one minute, a suicide note the next. Even sportswriting is not immune. Interviewees expect the sportswriter to make things better "because they don't think it's got worse". All of which is soon played out in the great set-piece meeting with Herb Wallagher. After small talk, Frank finds that the crippled football star wants to talk about his own desperation with his condition rather than provide the inspirational, feel-good story of his post-football life. So Frank calls time:

> *"I've got all I need for a good story. And it's getting pretty chilly out here."*
>
> *"You're full of shit, Frank," Herb says, smiling across the empty boat dock. On the lake a pair of ducks flies low across the surface, fast and slicing. They make an abrupt turn, then skin into the shiny water and become invisible. "Oh Frank, you're really full of shit."*

As Herb cries for help from his wheelchair, Frank is eyeing the distant freedom of ducks, and very affecting it is too; Frank sees what Herb sees. But of course that poetic, dreamy observation has no impact on his behaviour. It's a purely literary moment. Frank's readers browsing the sports magazine, however, will experience something uplifting about Herb. For them literature's promise remains pleasantly in place. So rather than having abandoned the falsification of fiction, Frank has merely displaced it with sports. He's still dreaming.

Not that this is always a bad thing. Sometimes disengagement is necessary. Looking back to the time after their son's death, Frank and his wife found solace in the "irresistible" life offered in shopping catalogues; real life by mail order. Regret for the loss of that other life is detectable in one of the special treats of the trilogy: Frank's outrageous descriptions of people according to their lifestyle and consumer tastes. Most seminarians in Haddam are not Bible-pounders but "sharp-eyed liberal Ivy League types with bony, tanned-leg second wives ... who'll stand toe to toe with you at cocktail parties, drink scotch and talk about their timeshare condos in Telluride". His real-estate assistant Mike began his career "taking orders for digital themocators and moleskin pants from housewives in Pompton Plaines and Bridgeton". Consumerism is the new transcendence. If one has doubts over one's life or career, don't despair: "lease a new Z-car, buy a condo in Snowmass, learn to fly your own Beach Bonanza, maybe take instruction at violin making". It's also a major feature of his ambivalence. Envy and contempt compete for dominance in these oddly melancholic formulations. Frank watches the driver in "the red Mercedes with a Victorian manse in its future, or a high-roller suite at Bally's" and it's unclear whether he wants to be that driver or hates the idea.

It's one curiosity of the trilogy that we never witness Frank actually buying anything other than food and drink. He doesn't even express a consumer's temptation. Perhaps his most conspicuous possession – purchased between novels – is a Chevrolet Suburban, a large, bland car. Even if it is a utility rather than a lifestyle choice, he also climbs in to disappear into the world of activity to which it alludes. Not that he can disappear. Or rather, that disappearance implies only one thing. Frank gets a glimpse when, in *Independence Day*, he visits his girlfriend Sally Caldwell at her beach-side house. She's yet to arrive, so he stands on the porch and gazes at "the quiet, underused stretch of beach, the silent, absolute Atlantic and the gray-blue sky":

Here is human hum in the barely moving air and surf-sigh, the low scrim of radio notes and water subsiding over words spoken in whispers. Something in it moves me as though to a tear (but not quite); some sensation that I have been here, or nearby, been at dire pains here time-ago and am here now again, sharing the air just as then. Only nothing signifies, nothing gives a nod. The sea closes up, and so does the land.

This sounds like the dreaminess described in *The Sportswriter*, when fiction became a negative force, destroying his marriage. Then he had to stop writing and turn back to life. But here he is, ten years on, having ditched all creative writing, including sportswriting, still experiencing dreaminess. Frank defined it then, without definition, as a state of "suspended recognition". Perhaps it remains unrecognised. For how can one recognise death? Nothing signifies. "You don't seem to be somebody who knows he's going to die", Walter Luckett told him, and he was probably right. Frank has never been able to close the distance between himself and life. Life, and therefore death, is elsewhere. He looks back at his marriage as the time when he had a definitive connection. Now he meets his ex-wife and is "forever the hunch-shouldered, grinning census taker at the door; she, the one living the genuine life". Ann is a long-suffering ex-wife. Frank wishes they were still together. "You can't live life over again", she tells him. "Yes, I know", he replies. "I didn't know if you really did know that", she adds. And nor does he. But he says the opposite. After all, it would be impolitic to deny rational truth. Yet he feels that might indeed be what he's trying to do. The disjunction between his feelings and his behaviour is watched with pain or horror by readers. But what are his feelings after all? We're not sure. It's a question he asks himself. One weekend, close to living the genuine life, he escapes to Detroit hotel alone with the comely Vicki Arcenault. Surely this is where he can leave literature behind and live life to the full?

> *And I feel exactly what at this debarking moment? At least a hundred things at once, all competing to take the moment and make it their own, reduce undramatic life to gritty, knowable kernel.*
>
> *This, of course, is a minor but pernicious lie of literature, that at times like these, after significant or disappointing divulgences, at arrivals or departures of obvious importance, when touchdowns are scored, knock-outs recorded, loved ones buried, orgasms notched, that at such times we are any of us altogether in an emotion, that we are within ourselves and not able to detect other emotions we might also be feeling, or be about to feel, or prefer to feel. If it's literature's job to tell the truth about these moments, it usually fails.*

It's not a matter of living life over again for Frank but of living it in the first place. How can one live the life promised by literature, where things are clear, where people live undivided lives? He knows that "living life to the full" is a literary notion. But how can one let go of such illusions? Vicki dumps him because his dividedness emerges in his actions. He tells her that she is the love of his life, then goes through her handbag when she's asleep. He frames it as a desire to get closer to her but, for some reason, she sees it differently. She'd rather he behaved like the leading man in the romantic novel also in her handbag.

While all this makes for the traditional discomforting comedy of modern relationships, and could be read as merely that, it's also a painful revelation of mutual isolation and its implications beyond the local pleasure of reading. It's a revelation that depends on our uncertainty, our distance. In other words, even though Frank is narrating, we don't really know why he does what he does, just as he isn't sure why Vicki isn't so keen to marry him. Still, some critics remain unaware of the irony. Scott Raab of *Esquire* magazine puts the relative failure of the trilogy down to Ford's inability to convince us that Bascombe ever really buried a child. It's "too hard to forget that Richard Ford has never been a dad". So even though the novel undermines the hope of fiction, particularly realistic fiction, by making us experience its limits and becomes as much an obstacle to communication as a means – Ford has failed because the reader retains that hope!

To demonstrate literary reasons for his critique, Raab might have used evidence of real writers writing about real lost children. He might have even limited the sample to Frank's favourite writers.

In the death of my son, now more than two years ago, I seem to have lost a beautiful estate, – no more. I cannot get it nearer to me. If tomorrow I should be informed of the bankruptcy of my principal debtors, the loss of my property would be a great inconvenience to me, perhaps, for many years; but it would leave me as it found me, – neither better nor worse. So is it with this calamity: it does not

*touch me: some thing which I fancied was a part of me, which could
not be torn away without tearing me, nor enlarged without
enriching me, falls off from me, and leaves no scar. It was caducous.
I grieve that grief can teach me nothing, nor carry me one step into
real nature.*

Perhaps Raab will accept that Emerson lost a son even if the
author is describing an experience, a lack, shared by Bascombe.
That is, grief in a lack of grief; a lack we call, in this case, a trilogy.

The melancholy resolve of *Experience*, the essay from which
this famous passage comes, is a neat contrast to the healthy
confidence of *Self-Reliance*, the essay Frank recommended to his
living son. It's a contrast we can also see in the trilogy:

*People grieve and bemoan themselves, but it is not half so bad with
them as they say. There are moods in which we court suffering, in
the hope that here, at least, we shall find reality, sharp peaks and
edges of truth. But it turns out to be scene-painting and counterfeit.
The only thing grief has taught me, is to know how shallow it is.*

That's Emerson again but it could easily be Frank.

Stefanie Hollmichel has written a sensitive appraisal of
Experience for her blog *So Many Books*. What's instructive here is
the response from her readers: "Emerson waxes disingenuous",
insists one, following Scott Raab's scepticism. "I have great
trouble believing Emerson was not deeply and permanently
moved by the death of his son". Another observes that Emerson
seems to be writing two essays at once: "the ostensibly intellectual one that attempts to master experience, and the subterranean, grief-stricken one … It's like Emerson doesn't want to
admit how much experience can hurt and damage, because to do
so would be to render impotent the analytical thought that
means so much to him."

While that dual-essay observation is spot on – for Emerson

and for Ford – its suggestion of a subtle self-deception is not. That doubleness is the necessary means for its admittance into the essay and the trilogy. Emerson's words attest to the emotional poverty not so much of the intellect but of writing. After all, how might that subterranean grief manifest in words? He might gnash and wail with expressive heat to impress those who assume words have a direct line to the heart, but Emerson knows it would betray the cold discovery made as he writes and as we read.

> *[Grief] plays about the surface, and never introduces me into the reality, for contact with which, we would even pay the costly price of sons and lovers. Was it Boscovich who found out that bodies never come in contact? Well, souls never touch their objects. An innavigable sea washes with silent waves between us and the things we aim at and converse with. Grief too will make us idealists.*

While Emerson is accused of intellectualism, denying his feelings, buttoning himself up against reality, his critics, their emotions so much more in-tune with the real world, so safe from the impact of analytical thought, resist the implications of his painfully painless ambivalence. Their hope for literature must remain unchallenged.

The implications for Frank's resistance of Emerson's apparent failure are significant. If Emerson cannot convince writing in the experience of personal defeat, then what hope for Frank Bascombe or, more pertinently, Richard Ford writing fiction? Like Emerson, Ford has made his work subject to the experience of distance. He has gone further and displaced his voice into that of a fictional character. It's a brave decision as both he and Frank live in a culture where plain fact carries a superstitious aura. The incorrigible denial of Emerson's and Ford's creativity appears in a memorable set piece in the middle of *The Lay of the Land*. Frank has driven to meet Wade Arcenault, Vicki's elderly father, to watch the demolition of a convention hall. There are grandstands for the event-hungry public and the demolition crew put on a dramatic show for them. As they wait for the big bang, Frank tries to be polite when responding to Wade's harangues about finding himself another woman. "I guess we might as well think our life's the way it is 'cause that's how we want it, Wade".

"Haw!" replies Wade, "That's in your brain."
"That's where a lot of stuff goes on."
"Think, think, thinky, think. In your life it does. Not mine." Wade
gives my door a fearsome, dismissive bang shut.

That's Wade's creativity in that bang, right there! From our vantage point, we also get the allusion to events beyond Thanksgiving 2000, events that other novels have used to mitigate their dreamy separation. But it too is only a controlled demolition; it too courts suffering. Naïve readers imagine themselves impaled on sharp peaks and edges of truth as they watch reruns of jets flying into towers, but they're too forever on the grandstand chomping hotdogs. When Frank gets back to the car park, the rear window of his Suburban has been smashed. Reality is always off-stage, stirring the frustrated imagination.

The Lay of the Land began with similar noises off. Frank recalls his reaction to a news item about a murder. The story upsets his hard-won equilibrium. Once again we follow him as he tries to accommodate the idea of reality into his everyday existence. Each novel covers the same ground. The career-moves from novelist to sportswriter and then to selling real estate were merely attempts to make literature present in the world. If sportswriting mitigated literature's remove as a form of self-help, then selling houses turned books into bricks and mortar. Frank calls realty "the profession of possibility", something he could easily also call writing novels. In the early days of his realty career, "getting people into the homes they (and the economy) wanted themselves to be in (at least for a while)" meant a lot to him. But those parentheses indicate the usual shortfall. Nothing much has changed. He's still writing of "constantly feeling offshore" and "experiencing the need for an extra beat".

He now has to contend with prostate cancer; something that may have made its home in his body yet still remains an idea. His rambling narrative toward or away from coming to terms with his condition takes him through a Thanksgiving weekend. In the first two novels it was Easter and July 4th respectively; each of them holidays, an exposure to freedom. Ford's problem in the final volume is how to resolve that freedom without relying on the false meaning toward which the novel inevitably takes us. But significantly, Frank's wish to have done with the imagination isn't as strong as it has been. Now he seems keener just to speak plainly to his fellow Americans. His night-time reading is a collection of great American speeches. On the night before the big Thanksgiving meal, he wants to get into bed to read the Gettysburg Address "out loud to no one". His visitors keep him from that ideal. He's also writing a letter to the President, which he'll never send. Everything he does delays the conclusion: meeting a businessman to discuss investment in a "parcel" of land, visiting a lonely stranger as part of a "sponsoring" programme, getting into a feeble fight at a bar, driving up to the hospital where Ralph died. There are many more and all very engaging if you've invested time with Frank and want to find out what happens to him. Otherwise, it can all seem rather pointless, part of that branch of contemporary fiction relying on character-isation and fancy phrasing ("I idled down Seminary Street, abstracted and empty in the lemony vapor of suburban eventide") to make up for a lack of traditional action. Unfortunately, Ford doesn't have the courage of the novel's lack of conviction because, late on, he shoe-horns event-glamour into the narrative. There's a terrorist assault on the hospital and, later, a murderous robbery. This has almost happened before at the end of *The Sportswriter*, when Frank drove into the aftermath of a motel murder. Then it could be mitigated as emphasis of Frank's lonely remove from the world of action; here the events seem grafted on to punctuate the trilogy. They provide a temporary mask of plot to disguise the ambivalence which gives the overall narrative its unusual presence. At the end, having been through so much, and yet so little, Frank feels compelled to announce that the extra beat is "to live, to live, to live it out". Yet that too is a literary expression. For Frank, for Richard Ford and for us, the extra beat is writing. We have been here before. The sea closes up and so does the land.

The Necessary Alien

Tao Lin's gleefully titled first novel *Eeeee Eee Eeee* can be welcomed as a comedy about the empty and disjunctive lives of a Florida pizza delivery boy called Andrew and his various acquaintances (to call them friends would suggest mutual empathy). It can be enjoyed on this level alone, perhaps with a smirk and ultimate indifference. The characters in the novel would probably respond in this way themselves, if they could be bothered to read. But it is also something else. It is something else because it isn't exactly a comedy. Not that it isn't funny; it's funny on every page. But a comedy has the shape of a smile. It moves from one point, descends through another and ends with a return to the higher level. There is movement, there is resolution. Think of Dante's *Commedia*. There is no such movement in *Eeeee Eee Eeee*, and no resolution either. It remains instead with emptiness and disjunction. This is really why it should be welcomed.

Nothing happens in Andrew's life – unless getting fired counts as something happening. It happens on the first page. Or, rather, it doesn't happen. Andrew is late for work and is told to clear out by one of the managers. He gives the manager "a shit-eating grin" and carries on as normal, as if nothing had happened. There are many such non-happenings in *Eeeee Eee Eeee*. The manager then tells Andrew to drive co-worker Joanna home after a shift. "Don't rape her, or we'll know", he says. Andrew doesn't rape her, but the possibility lodges. It becomes part of the routine journey. As they drive, Joanna – "a phone person; a high-schooler" – says a turn was missed, so he makes a U-turn and a cop stops the car. Andrew gives him a shit-eating grin too and then:

has an image of himself drunkenly resisting arrest; being shot in the back of the head while running away. He is afraid there are

24

kilograms of illicit drugs in the glove compartment. He will fight the cop in hand-to-hand combat.

This doesn't happen either. He gets a fine instead and carries on. Almost all the action depends on the imagination. Suggestion animates routine and offers endless possibility. Andrew enjoys possibility. It eases him through an empty life. He is calmed when a co-worker says something about dying from eating too much pizza after sex with a prostitute. He feels calm when it feels like he's being filmed, starring in an independent movie. "Things must happen and explode because of being in a movie." But nothing happens. He's troubled by possibility too. He remembers taking a girl to see the film *Mulholland Drive* and how she kept saying she was having fun and that they ought to go out together again, to which he readily agreed.

Andrew saw her next a few months later, from across a street, and she averted her eyes. Did she avert her eyes? Maybe she was being polite when she said ten times enthusiastically that she was having a lot of fun. Maybe she was being sarcastic. Maybe politeness is the same as sarcasm.

It's possible, so it might be true. How can anyone tell? Did he even really mean to agree to meet her again? If he doesn't know what he felt himself, how can he know what she was thinking? It's one thing to let possibility animate one's empty life, another to let actuality dissolve in it. One means of giving life some meaning is to create a stable environment. So Andrew is writing stories about "people who are doomed"; people like himself. Doomed is the hyperbole necessary to give meaning to an empty life. Andrew is not doomed.

He will never commit suicide. He will never kill anyone, start a band, or commit suicide. His girlfriend in college once tried to commit suicide. Then she published a book. Andrew needs to publish a book. Publishing a book will not make him feel less fucked.

The book will create the stability life lacks, the lonely stability of the book. But it is still possibility masquerading as actuality. A book leaves the doomed world behind. I becomes he, fucked becomes less-fucked. It's why *Eeeee Eee Eeee* is written in the third person. It isn't Andrew speaking. If he could speak, his life would not be empty. He is left behind, still fucked. In his actual world, Andrew laments the absence of his ex-girlfriend Sara, whom one might call his real-life book.

She never thinks about Andrew; hasn't ever e-mailed or called. Andrew never e-mails or calls either, really, just has imaginary conversations with her almost constantly; his idea of her. Maybe he will e-mail her tonight. She will respond with a form letter. We thank you for your submission but are unable to see your work at this time.

Like his book about the doomed, Sara's presence offers the possibility of meaning. Her absence means emptiness, disjunction. He imagines calling everything in the world after Sara. He imagines every face being Sara's face. Everything would be as clear as a book; the kind of book with which we're all familiar. The author crafts a world of meaning pretending all the while it is actuality and denying that it is only ever possibility. For Andrew, without Sara, it's nothing, just doomed. "He wants to drive into a mountain and make the mountain explode. Florida has no mountains. Florida has no Sara. No Sara; no future. No marshmallows. Andrew stops thinking."

One aspect of Tao Lin's novel that I haven't yet mentioned is also what will draw most attention. Andrew and his various acquaintances share their blank world with talking bears, dolphins, hamsters and moose. They move around like any other member of the community. "Eeeee eee eeee" is the sound made by the dolphins when they're not talking to humans. Everyone in the novel thinks it is perfectly normal. And of course it is perfectly normal, in novels. Anything can happen in a novel. They have so much life and it's why we love them. But what's left behind remains fucked, which is why we should also resent them. Resentment appears in *Eeeee Eee Eeee* as its most mysterious character. As well as bears, dolphins, hamsters and moose, Andrew also occasionally encounters an alien, sometimes standing in a doorway, sometimes lurking in dark places, sometimes right there in front of him, and he's frightened. He's not frightened by the bears, so why is he frightened by the alien? He doesn't say. He can't because the alien is the absence of possibility, which is alien to his world, alien to the novel. The alien appears as the death of the imagination; the death of possibility.

While the alien threatens an unnameable fate, the animals seem merely to want to convey something about now. And although they can talk, they do not say it. Instead, a bear insists that Andrew climbs down a ladder into a hole in the ground. Eventually they reach a cliff above an underground city of dolphins and bears. Andrew views it from on high. A dolphin joins them on the cliff. Then more dolphins. So many dolphins that one is crowded off the cliff. As it falls it goes: "EEEEE EEE EEEE".

This may not be what the bear wanted him to see. He doesn't say. But that gleeful or distressed cry is the cry of the novel, and also the experience of reading it. We plunge into the breach that opens up between possibility and actuality. It is an exhilarating plunge. This experience alone sets *Eeeee Eee Eeee* apart from the lumpen literary scene. But then there is Tao Lin's bracingly deadpan prose with its ever-so-slightly obsessive repetitions of words and phrases – "killing rampages", "Jhumpa Lahiri", "Duane Reade", "Shit-eating grin". These resound meaning and meaninglessness across the apparently insouciant narrative.

Some, though, just make you laugh: "I wish I could punch Sean Penn in Sean Penn's face".

He is embarrassed for the pizza box. He folds it. 'Shit-eating grin.' He needs to stop. He needs to use his face to convey emotions to other humans in order to move sincerely through life – laughing in groups of three or four; expressing gratitude, concern, or disapproval about people, the weather, or food; and manipulating members of either sex to get them to love him, like him, or respect him. That is what a face is for.

Can that be done in a novel? *Eeeee Eee Eeee* appears to admit defeat by ending with a swift descent into whimsy. Andrew meets Salman Rushdie, the animals, an alien and the President of the United States in a café. Along the way they all claim to have read *The Book of Disquiet*, Pessoa's fictional diary of boredom and solitude. One might judge this a failure of nerve, albeit a knowing failure, while mitigating it with expressions of hope for Tao Lin's future "career" as an "important" writer. Except all this would be to evade the singular gesture of this unique novel, its rejection of the empty pleasures of fiction even as it indulges them; a gesture toward the gleeful or distressed cry of actual life. But which is it?

Metaphysical Ache

When Booker Prize judge Giles Foden brushed aside the challenge of JM Coetzee's *Diary of a Bad Year* as "a piece of radical literary theory" and because "theory is not fiction", I was prepared to let this go as an overstatement based on the novel's apparent aesthetic astringency. From glancing at reviews, the impression was that the novel consisted of self-indulgent essays written by a lightly disguised Coetzee figure with a cursory and slightly pervy sub-plot about his friendship with a much younger woman. I could appreciate how this might not appeal to consumerist demands, even those pretending to Literature.

However, now that I've read *Diary of a Bad Year*, Foden's judgement appears at best ignorant, at worst disturbingly intolerant. To say this novel is "a subversion of the whole commercial and promotional mechanism whereby books are distributed" is about as accurate as saying *The Last King of Scotland* is about the British constitution. Yes, the novel is indeed aesthetically astringent – the relationships remain formal, the opinions under-developed and on each page the narrative jumps from one voice to another – but these constitute much of the novel's originality as well as providing its emotional and intellectual ballast.

Diary of a Bad Year is an exceptionally moving investigation of what it means to have singular opinions in a plural universe. The short, diverse essays at the top of each page signal a diminishment of writerly power and might evoke a hollow echo if published alone. At least one reviewer sees this as a problem to the success of the book. Yet, if they were more fully developed, they would crust over what is currently an open wound, and it is this wound with which Coetzee is concerned. Success, in the sense defined by the reviewers, would be failure.

The writer character begins by making a distinction between freedom and democracy. He sees the handover of power to the state in liberal democracies as irreversible. Freedom is threatened for the sake of democracy and leads to another brand of totalitarianism. As readers we can agree, disagree or remain indifferent. This should go without saying. The point is: how might our response be included in such opinions? Or rather, how might the opinion appear if it tries to include the plural? How can we reconcile democracy with freedom? Such is the task of the novelist, hence the distinction, albeit narrow, between the author JM Coetzee and the writer in this novel.

The writer asks along the way: "Why can there be no discourse about politics that is not itself political?" We might wonder in turn: why can there be no novel that is not also *only* a novel – a work of masterful craft and imagination? The questions are essentially the same. To say the least, *Diary of a Bad Year* is as close to answering as any book published in recent years. The writer praises Harold Pinter's trenchant Nobel acceptance speech for its brave indifference to the scorn it would attract: "there comes a time when the outrage and the shame are so great that all calculation, all prudence, is overwhelmed and one must act, that is to say, speak". The same words can be applied to the form of the novel we're reading, in which calculation and prudence would have demanded "fully developed" essays and a "rounded" relationship between writer and muse.

Instead, Coetzee imagines two people of the world – Anya and Alan – with whom he has nothing in common. He lusts after the body of one, and perhaps for something else too. Below the essays, we read his apparently private observations on the couple and how he pursues the "metaphysical ache" Anya arouses in him by getting her to type up his dictaphone ramblings. At first this undercuts the writer's seriousness with the petty concerns of bodily existence. But then Anya's voice appears below his, engaging with his ideas, setting them against her assumptions and suspicions about his person, as well as discussing her own life with Alan, a philistine, commercially minded brute. This suggests the ache is more than prurient. You might say it is religious.

Then Alan's voice is added. The intertwining of each separate voice, how one influences the other and how the ideas find their way in the world, encourages us to think not of the specific greatness of the novel with regard to our own readerly demands, but of the possibilities for a different kind of discourse. Not one of self-isolating opinions but something more inclusive, even if isolation (and low sales) is inevitable.

In this case, we can think of a new kind of novel: one that resists both the spirit of impotent scorn toward which the isolated writer tends and the self-assured denial of prize-winning novels in which the freedom of the imagination is an unquestioned good. That someone considered fit to judge Britain's most prestigious literary prize did not notice any of this and indeed dismissed such an intrepid novel as "theory", suggests there is something very wrong at the heart of British literary culture.

Disastrous Repetition

The second chapter of Jeanette Winterson's novel *The Stone Gods* is entitled "Easter Island", after the island in the Pacific now known as Rapanui. Like Jennifer Vanderbes' 2003 feminist romance *Easter Island*, it uses the island's devastating history as part of a larger story. For both novels it is a microcosm of Earth in the time of the humans. The story is well known: Easter Island had sustained a population of many thousands at least until the late 18th Century when Captain Cook's *Resolution* arrived to find a barren, inhospitable land with a ragged population "few in number". What had happened? *The Stone Gods* suggests an answer by using the famous stone statues – the moai – as a metaphor of global industry. On her website, Winterson spells it out: "There is no environmental explanation, only a human one, chiefly the pointless obsession with carving stone gods... but read the story for yourself".

Reading the story as Winterson has framed it enables us to understand that Easter Island is a lasting presence rather than an isolated case. What happened to the island will happen to us; or rather, is happening to us. Just as deforestation apparently ended Easter Island's moai-building culture (timber was almost certainly used to move the statues from the quarries) and eroded the nutrient-rich soil, so our "pointless obsession" with economic growth will, if we fail to act on the signs, lead to a destitute time.

Although there's no evidence that Easter Island's decline occurred so dramatically, in *The Stone Gods* the women try to stop the men from cutting down the final tree. They fail, of course. The novel's four chapters – different from one another yet interlinked – might be a more sophisticated, if equally vain, attempt to prevent an identical fate. It is aware of its likely reception. Billie, the main character, finds an old manuscript on the London Underground (the Circle Line). It's called "The Stone Gods". She examines it: "A love story, that's what it is – maybe about aliens. I hate science fiction." Later, she hands it to her robot friend Spike to read:

> *"What's it about?"*
> *"A repeating world."*

Yes, a world that carries on regardless, unable to see the implications of its actions even as the implications loom like moai on the horizon. She thinks it is an entertainment; the truth becomes "science fiction".

After I had read *The Stone Gods*, Ursula Le Guin's review appeared especially cranky.

> *It's odd to find characters in a science-fiction novel repeatedly announcing that they hate science fiction. I can only suppose that Jeanette Winterson is trying to keep her credits as a "literary" writer even as she openly commits genre.*

This is doubly wrong: one character says it and says it only once. And, if my reading is fair, it's also a joke resonating with the theme of disastrous repetition. How many times will we turn exigency into a genre? Winterson diverts from the record too, with more interesting results. The nineteen-page chapter compresses and distorts Easter Island's real history. Cook's party did injure an islander but did not kill him. Nor did *Resolution* sail away immediately after. Not one row of moai on the coast stares out to sea; they all look inland and, contrary to what Billie observes, the plinths on which they stand do not contain wood. Also, after Cook has sailed, islanders are seen to be toppling moai, suggesting a loss of faith. However, such destruction occurred between the arrival of the Dutch on Easter Day 1722 and Cook in 1774. Very few moai were left standing by the time Cook popped by. In a cave, Billie is introduced to the

Rongorongo tablets displaying a written script despite the fact that this was not reported by visitors until almost a century later. Of course, setting out such deviations from fact is unfair because they emphasise the value of the imagination.

Later some moai's "unseeing eyes" are said to be fixed on the interior of the island yet, if they had not been toppled, it is very likely they would have had eyes of white coral with painted irises and pupils. I admit that this example is particularly unfair. Even when painted, we know they could not see anything; "unseeing" is not wrong. Yet still, the viewer has to make the intellectual leap to deny the illusion. And it's this uncertain space between instinct and intellect where the gaze of the moai becomes uncanny, even when the eyes are blank grey basalt; perhaps even more so. Where does it leave us?

> *It is as if, here, everything signifies some other thing: the Bird, the Egg, the flag, the writing, the winning, the winner, the Stone Gods, even the island, even the world are symbols for what they are not.*

Face-to-face with a universe of symbols, we await some other thing; something that is not. The inexpressive eyes of the moai make it felt but never allow us to see. Perhaps this is why they were toppled. It was an attempt to bring an end to the power of the imagination. Now, in the civilisation of the book, they have been raised again.

Non-Writer's Room

This is the room in which I do not write. The computer screen is open only to hide from sight the three books behind it. I prefer not to be reminded of my failure. The one book in view is Maurice Blanchot's *The Book to Come*, as I believe it adds an ironic counterpoint to my otherwise desolate non-writerly existence.

Resting on the Moleskine Ruled Notebook (Large) is a Pilot V7 Hi-Techpoint 0.7 Pure Liquid Ink pen. Both offer promise of annotating the undying torment of my profoundly literary imagination. On the open page you can see the beginnings of what might be the last poem I ever write:

Soya milk
Bread
Porridge

The lamp and the candle are never used because darkness enables me to forget the memories they contain. The lamp was stolen from a German friend. At the time, I wanted a reminder of his fine, civilised nation as I prepared to leave never to return, while the candle was a gift from a beautiful woman of that same land whom I haven't seen since she discovered I wanted to be a writer. It's a misunderstanding, I told her, and I could explain. But she had seen the discarded pen caps, the dense scribbles in notebooks and the hoard of unread books. It was too late. She looked into my blank eyes and left.

Above the desk on which I do not write are two pictures. On the right is a photograph I snapped whilst strolling in the Ninth Circle of Hell on the Sussex coast. On the left, almost out of sight, is a work entitled *Ruining* by an artist who has since taken up painting.

The only thing on the desk that I have yet to explain is the glob of Icelandic lava. I have no idea what it's doing there. Perhaps it was placed there as a curse to prevent me from writing. Iceland, I understand, is expanding.

The Work of Night

If the writer is, as Maurice Blanchot declares, a daytime insomniac, then the reader is a sleeper sunk in the other's impossible dreams. But what of the boundary separating reader from writer? If we recognise a space between them, between the sovereign self and the unavowable community of *booklovers*, between mastery and oblivion, does it exist in a purely metaphorical realm, an unlit border crossing with inattentive guards perhaps or a no-man's land littered with corpses and literary critics? Or could it be that the space is before us, for real, hidden in plain sight?

Thomas Glavinic's novel *Die Arbeit der Nacht*, translated as *Night Work*, might help to answer. I recognised his name from the 2007 German Book Prize so picked up the copy from the library shelf for a closer examination: "An ordinary man wakes up on an ordinary day to find that he's the only living creature in the city..."

A library worker had added a sticker to inform clue-blind readers that this is Science Fiction. However, Daniel Kehlmann's praise for the book opens this to question: "*Night Work* is a wonderful, big novel about ... the uncertain border between waking and dreaming". That would make it *Austrian* science fiction then, just as Kafka's *Der Verwandlung* is Austro-Hungarian science fiction. Indeed, the literal translation of the title *The Work of Night* implies that night is at work in the story as it was in Gregor Samsa's sleeping body. This is very much the opposite of sleepless agency implied by *Night Work* and it marks out the territory of the novel far more accurately than any other label.

By day Jonas works hard to explore his lonely situation. The bulk of his story is taken up with descriptions of his thoughts and behaviour. He looks around the silent city, he adopts an Alfa Romeo, he redesigns his flat. In this sense, the book is workmanlike realism, written in the third person, as if there is indeed someone else in the world who knows more. We're with Jonas as he awaits change, seeing signs in every minor scene, every leaf blowing across a path. But nobody answers his phone calls, nobody responds to the notes he leaves all over Vienna, and he sees nothing in the video recordings set up across the city. We are not rescued by a twist in the tale. Glavinic maintains the reader's fascination because the relentless lack of revelation infects every new situation with ominous promise. After 150 pages, with tension and exhaustion becoming indistinguishable, and with over 200 pages still to go, I feared he would lose nerve and introduce a grand explanation. There was no need. The original title is revelatory enough: what happens happens at night, in the dark.

What happens first is that Jonas discovers not the apocalypse but singular existence, distance from the world. On the first page, making breakfast, the bread-knife slips:

> He'd cut himself to the bone, but he didn't appear to have damaged a tendon. It didn't hurt, either.*

He holds his hand under the cold tap and inspects the cut.

> No one, himself included, had ever seen what he could see. He'd lived with this finger for thirty-five years without ever knowing what it looked like inside.

The unique presence of the inside of his finger and the unique experience of *witnessing* such unique presence heralds many other moments like this. In effect, his entire existence becomes a round of unique moments. By coincidence or not (and it makes no difference) indeterminate epiphanies like those experienced by Jonas also appear on the opening page of *My Year in the No-Man's Bay* by Glavinic's illustrious compatriot Peter Handke. This novel lists extreme experiences which seem to signal both something and nothing, including, as it happens, the accidental cutting of a finger to the bone. The narrator also rinses it under a stream of cold water: "Part of me was numb", the narrator says. "The other part carried on with the day as though nothing were amiss." They prompt him to become, or try to become, a passive observer and, in his work as a writer, to present the world as it is, bone-white. To write, what's more, against what until then had been a self-contained universe, itself a kind of death; a world without others. The work of the outside – something working *through* him – proved fruitful to his life as nothing else had:

> For me, nothing can sweep that fruitfulness from the world. From it I know what it is to exist.

For Jonas, the experience is similar except that he wants to return to the community of friends and family without losing his new-found land of the self. It means he must be there to witness it all. But how can the world and his witnessing coincide? There's a clue in the novel's epigram from Kundera's *Immortality* expressing the belief that there is no happiness in living. "But being, being is happiness. Being: transforming oneself into a fountain into which the universe falls like warm rain." Jonas' adventures can be seen as a rage to become that fountain, a channel through which all the world can flow.

In the first scene of Kundera's novel, the narrator is captivated by a single gesture of a woman which seems to remove forty years of bodily aging. "There is a certain part of all of us that lives outside of time", he observes. Jonas as himself, apparently alone, is deprived of time and is, though he may not be conscious of it, trying to maintain the timelessness of the gesture that is his life. In his wanderings around Vienna, he finds himself at a fairground shooting stall firing a few shots.

He hung up another target and slowly crooked his finger.

He had always fancied that you could die of slowness by prolonging some everyday action indefinitely – to infinity, or, rather, to finality – because you would depart this world while still engaged in that process. A step, a gesture, a wave of the arm, a turn of the head – if you slowed that movement more and more, everything would come to an end, more or less of its own accord.

His finger curled around the trigger. With surprising clarity, he realised that he must long ago have reached, yet failed to reach, the point of release.

Yes, the world would end of its own accord but he wouldn't quite be there. He'd be engaged always elsewhere in an endless, timeless action. This might explain why the novel appears overlong.

Whatever his fancy, Jonas remains subject to human time. He has to sleep. It is here that the novel becomes subject to the logic of its title. As he needs to witness everything, so he must witness the night. He sets up a camera to film himself asleep. What he sees is someone else, someone he calls "the Sleeper" engaged in actions his waking self cannot recall. An apparently unbridgeable division is recognised. The work of sleep undermines his conscious life to the extent that, by the time he is engaged in his most ambitious plan, he has more or less lost conscious control. He becomes both his biblical near-namesake Jonah down in the sides of the ship sleeping soundly as the storm rages *and* the terrified sailors above fearing for their lives. How can the two be reconciled?

So the shipmaster came to him, and said unto him, What meanest thou, O sleeper? arise, call upon thy God, if so be that God will think upon us, that we perish not.

Jonas as the shipmaster asks the same question, makes the same demand of his sleeping self. In the Bible story, the sleeper knows that he has been chosen and must sacrifice himself to calm the seas. Once overboard he is swallowed by a large fish and, three days later, vomited onto dry land to complete his worldly mission set by God. Jonas' sacrifice is more ambiguous. *Night Work* ends in a grand valedictory gesture in which he begins to die of slowness, begins to witness eternity. For the book itself, the point of release has been reached and has, as a result, failed, but necessarily. The reader is awoken, vomited back into the world. We have been subject to the work of the night. There it is, the book. A division is recognised.

*Translated by John Brownjohn

The Gift of Writing

Suffering is by no means a privilege, a sign of nobility, a reminder of God. Suffering is a fierce, bestial thing, commonplace, uncalled for, natural as air. It is intangible; no one can grasp it or fight against it; it dwells in time – is the same thing as time; if it comes in fits and starts, that is only so as to leave the sufferer more defenceless during the moments that follow, those long moments when one relives the last bout of torture and waits for the next.*

Cesare Pavese writing in October, 1940. Ten years later he killed himself.

Ten years in a sentence. Is this the gift of writing?

I had no intention of writing about David Foster Wallace, and I still don't. Instead, I want to try to answer my own question by writing about the response to his death. Not just the initial shock and disbelief of his fans, which is plain to see, but also the move toward his books since the dreadful news, which is not.

There are two sides to this movement. First, the everyday. For months in my local library, the sole copy of *Infinite Jest* had sat bright and squat on the shelf without a single withdrawal. Now it is in demand. I saw it on the "Reserve" shelf awaiting its claimant. Of course, there is no need to guess why it shares the fate of the latest celebrity autobiography and Booker-shortlisted politeness. And while it would be my default position to disdain the extra-literary reasons with which a book can attract the curious, in this case I wonder if it has less to do with readers seeking the testimony inferred by the 1088 pages of a novel than with an obscure need to comprehend the book's presence now that the author is dead. This is the second side.

It's easy to disregard. Alistair McCartney's response to the news at *Ready Steady Book* is to reassert the separation of author from his work: "from a literary perspective", he writes, "the suicide of David Foster Wallace, or for that matter, the suicide of any writer in the 21st century, is of no importance". He means of no importance to their writing.

> *[I]n these early days of the twenty-first century, the suicide of a writer does not mark their body of work, does not inflect it, in the same manner in which it did previously, during the epoch of Romanticism.*

He refers us to *The Savage God*, Al Alvarez's famous study of literary suicide, which describes why "between the 18th and 20th centuries, the suicide of a writer was a significant and meaningful gesture". Now, McCartney says, the significance and meaning of suicide extends beyond the realm of the literary.

> *[In] the 21st century ... suicide as a gesture has taken on an entirely different resonance, specifically because the arena in which it is conducted has shifted, or rather expanded, into the public realm, due to the activities of those individuals whom we refer to as suicide bombers. ... In this sense, suicide is no longer purely a private gesture, or one connected to art or creativity or personal suffering. It is also, and, as of this moment, primarily, a public gesture, and a political one.*

However one feels about the timing of such an argument so soon after the event – and feeling is very much part of the issue at hand – I quote this at length because it highlights a conflict embedded in general literary discussion about art in its relation to personal suffering. It's a conflict that suggests the epoch of Romanticism remains with us, unresolved.

When we think of Romantic writers we think of Wordsworth and Byron, Goethe and Hölderlin – writers working in heady political and intellectual times – and we respond much as Edmund Blackadder responded to his coffeeshop owner as she swooned in their presence: "Mrs. Miggins, there's nothing intellectual about wandering around Italy in a big shirt trying to get laid".

Yes, of course, the writer is vain and writing is selfish! The irony is that such knowingness is a product of Romanticism's resistance to the separation of art and life. Romanticism is a counter-enlightenment in which intuition, imagination, and feeling take precedence over rationality. The Romantics explored freedom beyond the conventions of the reasoning intellect, hence their formal innovation and their attractive personal and political adventures. Unfortunately, there was a contradiction at the heart of this project: the logic of such exploration meant ultimate personal freedom equalled the loss of sovereign individuality, a merging with the mass of humanity, with nature, with the sublime, with God; death, in other words. Science was perhaps a better career move.

Suicide then marks both a failure and a success. While it is the supreme act of selfish power, its result, if not its goal, is a loss of self, impersonality. Creativity is much the same. "This comparison of art to suicide is shocking in a way", writes Blanchot in "The Work and Death's Space":

> But there is nothing surprising about it if, leaving aside appearances, one understands that each of these two movements is testing a singular form of possibility. Both involve a power that wants to be power even in the region of the ungraspable, where the domain of goals ends.

Which brings this back to the goal of contemporary literature. David Foster Wallace is celebrated as a decidedly modern writer and, with *Infinite Jest*, he produced what might be the definitive modern American novel. But, according to a bibliography, it was his final full-length work of fiction. What happened? *Salon* reports that he had suffered from clinical depression. Could this be the answer? It's not a subject about which I knew much until Stephen Fry's documentary *The Secret Life of the Manic Depressive*. I assumed depression was always one-way: down. However, Fry describes its two sides: hypomania and troughs of desperate, self-hating inertia and anxiety. The first includes outbursts of fecund creativity, the second, a wish to die. Oliver Sacks describes the *literary* symptoms in his review of Michael Greenberg's memoir:

> *The onset of mania is sudden and explosive: Sally, the fifteen-year-old daughter, has been in a heightened state for some weeks, listening to Glenn Gould's Goldberg Variations on her Walkman, poring over a volume of Shakespeare's sonnets till the early hours. Greenberg writes: Flipping open the book at random I find a blinding crisscross of arrows, definitions, circled words. Sonnet 13 looks like a page from the Talmud, the margins crowded with so much commentary the original text is little more than a speck at the center.*

In a hypomanic state, there's an unshakable fascination with meaning, the possibility of meaning, there's a belief in achievement, in encompassing everything, the visible and the invisible. One idea sparks another and then another making it impossible for the individual to rest. Keith Gessen loves Wallace's essays for their stability on such a high wire:

> *He writes such long sentences, they are filled with so many ideas, you don't think he'll ever get back to the point, the point has been lost, and then he does, and it's incredible. It's incredible and then you never forget it.*

Whether or not Wallace had manic episodes is not a question here. Whatever the clinical facts, his work displays, in its size, scope, ambition and worldly success, an energy and optimism unique to his nation's literary life, and unique to its demands. The incredulity of his fans at news of his death supports this impression. *Infinite Jest* embodies a certain hope; a hope that everything could be contained in a book, unified by narrative; that with enough talent and hard work, a novel might become the world, exceeding the limits of the self, a hegemonic power against the regions of the ungraspable. All this is apparently contradicted by the manner of his death.

So what of the darkness spoken of by his friends and family? "Suffering from near-crippling anxiety", *Salon* says, "Wallace found himself unable to write". Perhaps the literary tragedy, which remains a human tragedy, is that he could not produce a work that maintained itself in the actuality of such suffering. It may be instead that the margins of the novels and stories he left will grow wider and we will see it there. The movement towards his books in the library evokes a longing for such a space, a space in which something appears. His death would then indeed inflect his work.

Another decidedly modern writer suffered a similar torment to Wallace. "For years I had taken refuge in a terrible suicidal brooding", he told one interviewer. "Every morning on waking I was inevitably caught up in this mechanism of suicidal brooding." But, as explained in Thomas Cousineau's book *Three-Part Inventions*, from which these quotations come, Thomas Bernhard displaced his suffering with a surrogate, a prose companion who crosses the line he, the writer in the refuge of writing, will not reach.

When I write about this kind of thing, about this kind of centrifugal situation that leads to suicide, I am certainly describing a state of mind that I identify with, which I probably experienced while I was writing, precisely because I did not commit suicide, because I escaped from that.

This is not to say Bernhard escaped; he also killed himself. But, such is the gift, it was writing that kept him alive.

* Translated by A.E. Murch

Review 6, Book 1

In planning this review of Dag Solstad's *Novel 11, Book 18*, I found two files containing notes for two more, both unwritten. The lists of ideas and quotations revealed wasted hours and renewed the hopeful pangs each had begun in me. I had believed the angels in Cees Nooteboom's *Lost Paradise* offered an unusual commentary on the strange call of fiction – something reviews routinely bypass or belittle. I wanted to pursue the call in this direction; reviewing is so much unnecessary repetition otherwise.

And then there was the diaphanous presence in Adam Thirlwell's *Miss Herbert*. The eponymous friend of Flaubert's is said to have translated Madame Bovary before anyone else, but the woman had died young and her work had disappeared. It leaves us, Thirlwell says, "a heavenly shimmer" of the perfect translation; something we'll never see. Again, there was a sense of something beyond reach, an unexpected residue. Thirlwell relishes the playful juxtaposition of contained narrative and surging life. Miss Herbert's absence is "not a story", he says, it is "real life", and leaves it at that. Indeed, his relaxed attitude toward the space between fiction and vanishing life is a constant throughout the surprising length of his book. There is never any anxiety at fiction's inability to close the distance. In my imagined review, I had hoped to show how Thirlwell's brief comment burnt a black hole through the bright surface of postmodern literary mastery.

By happy coincidence, *Novel 11, Book 18* lightly satirises my earnest concern to stalk the unseen. It is itself about the gap between our hopes and ideas and actual experience of life. The story concerns Bjorn Hansen, a Norwegian civil servant. His life is described from a distance, as if in a clinical report written in free indirect speech (hence perhaps the filing-cabinet formality of the title). For instance, his name is always "Bjorn Hansen", never only "Bjorn" or "Hansen". We're told he has left the mother of his two-year-old son to be with the wonderfully named Turid Lammers. Why he has done this seems to be as unclear to Hansen as it is to the report. He drives to Turid Lammers' house in a town 45 miles from Oslo, moves in, and continues his life as if nothing had happened. We never hear from the abandoned wife and Turid Lammers never says a word. However, it is at the latter's suggestion that he applies for a local job. He even joins the local amateur dramatics society in which she is a star performer. They live together for many years. Everything is apparently stable. There are no snags. At least, nothing untoward appears in the report.

This brief summary of the first half of the novel might seem inadequate but it is not much less than one gets reading *Novel 11, Book 18*. You might guess that there is something missing, and you'd be right. Something is missing for Bjorn Hansen too. The expected fullness of a meaningful existence with the love of his life has not materialised, at least not according to his expectations. The contingent banality of suburban affluence in a peaceful land is not enough. In a rare moment of reported speech, he tells a doctor that: "Nearly everything is totally indifferent to me. Time is passing, boredom is everlasting."

"I find myself [here] by pure chance. [...] But if I hadn't been here, I would have been somewhere else and have led the same kind of life. However, I cannot reconcile myself to that. I get really upset when I think about it", Bjorn Hansen said, once more shaken in his innermost self by the fact that he was really expressing himself in this way in the presence of another person. "Existence has never answered my questions" he added. "Just imagine, to live an entire life ... without having found the path to where my deepest needs can be seen and heard!"*

The angst would be comic if it were indeed angst in itself.

Instead, it is comical because it is emotion carried in the hunger for angst, for the reality afforded by the tag applied by public discourse rather than something unique to him, Bjorn Hansen. Bjorn Hansen seems to have realised that he has cultivated experience in order to make life lifelike according to the definitions of this discourse. Did he abandon his family merely because it was a decisive event? It seems so. When Turid Lammers flirts with fellow actors, he feels that he could go mad out of jealousy. Isn't this the real thing? Bjorn Hansen asks the same question and discovers the problem: "Had he not renounced everything in order to cultivate the temptation [of jealousy] in all its intensity, for what was left, after all, except this intensity?" Yes, this is the experience that might rent the fabric of life, but it has little or nothing to do with Turid Lammers and everything to do with Hansen's "profound yearning for something irrevocable".

The second half of the novel follows Bjorn Hansen as he seeks the irrevocable with more focus. It's a quest in which we, as readers, have a share. Will this novel begin to provide the shapely conclusion we expect? Until now we have had a serious lack. For instance, after leaving Turid Lammers, Bjorn Hansen is living alone in a flat when he receives a request. His grown-up son Peter, whom he hasn't seen in 14 years, asks if he can stay with his father while he takes a course at a local technical college. Bjorn Hansen is thrilled by the idea. It sounds like another opportunity to discover real life. When the 20-year-old look-a-like stranger arrives, it is immediately clear that he is a peculiar and obsessive character. This gives a rougher texture to the novel. So what is the truth behind his strange behaviour and the decisions he makes that perplex his father? We never find out. Peter moves out with all the questions unresolved. This is the pattern throughout the book only this time it is felt more keenly. Bjorn Hansen himself moves on and continues with his plan to make real his idea of the irrevocable. Other novels might have led Bjorn Hansen into a crime ring or a murder mystery or have him discover some dark truth about his son. Instead Solstad gives him an at once upsetting and hilariously muted fate that changes nothing.

It is encouraging that the reviews for *Novel 11, Book 18* have been very positive. Perhaps more translations of Solstad's novels will be commissioned. However, to demonstrate what real literature is usually up against in mainstream reception, take a look at the review in *The Telegraph*. Alan Marshall falls back on public labels such as "the existential novel" for this uncomfortable take on modern unhappiness. He complains that "Hansen's relationship with his son seems to open up another possibility for the novel, away from the rather stale, existential plotline", as if this were not about the meaning of possibility itself. "It's a strange failure of imagination", he says, "posing as an act of imagination". It is strange precisely because Bjorn Hansen is seeking to make real his imagination; to make it fail as imagination.

We leave Bjorn Hansen as he lives the dream, only now he wishes that someone could see him do so, to notice what he has done. The unseen continues to haunt.

* Translated by Sverre Lyngstad

The Book to Come

Roberto Bolaño's 2666 is an obsessive and world-shifting epic. When I read it, I will be completely absorbed by it. It will be all I think about. It will affect my daily life in ways I can't fully understand, and when I finish it I will have come to profound revelations about the nature of existence.

There's a reason for Kirsty Logan's future tense on *The Millions* website: she's describing the joy of a certain kind of book, one that:

> *contains all possible characters, styles, genres, turns of phrase, metaphors, speech patterns, and profound life-changing revelations. An unread book exists only in the primordial soup of your imagination, and there it can evolve into any story you like. An unread book – any unread book – could change your life.*

She goes on to imagine the possibilities of a handful of other novels she hasn't read. Apart from *2666*, I haven't read them either. Yet, even though I have read all 893 pages of the British edition and was absorbed enough to believe I would not forget each highway and byway of the long journey, I find that now, looking back from beyond the final page, all the roads have concertinaed to form an impenetrable block.

Roberto Bolaño's *2666* has not affected my daily life, it has not caused any profound revelations, and the world remains unshifted. But for the complete absorption, everything of which Kirsty Logan dreams about *2666* didn't come to pass, unless, that is, for all of its characters, adventures, ideas and slow-burning narrative tension, for all of its richness of colour and texture, the revelation is that the nature of existence will remain unclear and will never be resolved into coherence, not even in the most lengthy work of literature with all of its innumerable interconnections and possible all-embracing overall design.

Of course, if this is the revelation, it is certainly *not* profound. As well as the encyclopaedic power to capture life, the aura of modern literature is borne on the promise of such revelatory exegesis in which something more will emerge, so one is bound to be disappointed. The persistent presence of an aura explains the range of readerly reactions from obsessive dedication of those who see revelation in the mathematical system underpinning Dante's *Commedia* to Book Groups chatting about "issues" in the latest Jodi Picoult unit.

A banal point perhaps: the reader is always seeking more than the book itself. After all, it is a form of information storage and retrieval. With the incommensurability of modern literature, the violence of interpretation becomes necessary if it is to mean something other than an increasingly minor branch of the entertainment industry. It certainly needs to be forgotten in order to read. If we begin reading knowing incompletion will be the ultimate experience – perhaps even disharmony and disunity – then what are we reading for? We begin with the idea, as Kirsty Logan suggests, of the novel we are about to read as the Platonic Form of its kind, an ethereal presence in which all stories coalesce and conclude. Here it is, in our hands! So when I say: "I've read Roberto Bolaño's *2666*", do I know or care what I am referring to other than the same possible book Kirsty Logan has imagined? As I announce my reading, a whiff of cultural oneupmanship begins to circulate. It alludes to secret knowledge, new power over those who have not read it and potentially over those who have read but have not comprehended its message. But I don't have that knowledge or power. What have I missed?

Nabokov said that the second reading of a book is always the first. The first is a blind reading. You have to read the book a second time in order to have read it once. So perhaps I should re-read Roberto Bolaño's *2666* in search of a subtler experience in which the disparate details begin to reach out to one another more clearly and the revelations become more profound. However, if Heraclitus is right, then that second reading is impossible. The second reading will always be the first and, if Nabokov is right, blind. The second reading will always be the book to come, and I have not read Roberto Bolaño's *2666*. I will never read Roberto Bolaño's *2666*.

Everything Passes

The first thing that strikes one about Gabriel Josipovici's *Everything Passes* is its austerity. Unlike the majority of contemporary novels, it offers little in the way of framing information; no names, no faces, no times. It begins:

> *A room.*
> *He stands at the window.*
> *And a voice says: Everything passes. The*
> *good and the bad. The joy and the sorrow.*
> *Everything Passes.*
>
> *A room.*
> *He stands at the window.*
> *Silence.*
> *He stands.*
> *Silence.*

Readers of contemporary literary fiction – even those who relish what Nick Hornby calls "opaquely written novels" – are unlikely to feel at home here. It is as if writing is denuding itself. Where is this room? Who is "he", why is he standing at a window? And who is speaking? So few words, so many questions. Isn't it the job of fiction to fill in these blanks?

Given this beginning, there is an inevitable impulse to seek genre distinctions and so gain purchase on the smooth surface. "A novella" is the simplest label, though there are very few novellas like this. "Narrative poetry" perhaps; the short lines and caesura certainly suggest that. Yet the prose style does become more expansive later on, so perhaps it is more accurate to compare it to a piece of music; a string quartet perhaps. Josipovici has himself said the inspiration for the novel was to make a writerly version of Schoenberg's *String Trio Op. 45*. Also, the rhythmic repetitions of words and phrases provides the mesmerising experience of music. This direction of enquiry offers more clarity because, as questions of context and meaning are raised in music, they are answered at the same time, soothing the listener, diminishing anxiety, even if the music is by turns anxious and mournful as is the string trio.

> *He stands at the window.*
> *Cracked pane.*
> *His face at the window.*
> *Greyness. Silence.*

> *And again the room.*
> *The window.*
> *He stands at the window.*
> *Silence.*

In listening to music, the reader is plunged into a world without distance or contradiction; feeling and movement are everything. Could *Everything Passes* then be affirming Walter Pater's submission that "All art constantly aspires towards the condition of music"? Answer yes and, for 18 pages, the issue is settled. The unidentified man at the window is met by memories of a woman no longer present and by visits from his fussing children. It is as if the novel is developing a theme framed by the voice telling him that everything passes; a theme of memory and its permanence in what passes, our everyday lives. In this way we can place the novel as part of literary fiction, an idiosyncratic part – an experimental part perhaps – and thus more readily assimilated. We can then hurry back to the mass of more detailed novels in which backstory and expressive words fill in the gaps left open here. We may deem it a worthy failure too because, if *Everything Passes* aspires to the condition of music, doesn't its form admit to an inherent failure?

What happens on page 18 provides the answer. A literary scholar called Felix interrupts the stream of memories to begin a conversation over a cup of coffee with his girlfriend Sal. He talks about how Rabelais had recognised the consequences for authorship by the advent of prose fiction. Until then authors knew their audience: for example Chaucer read to a royal court and Shakespeare wrote words to be spoken out loud before London theatregoers. He also cites Dante who, in *Purgatorio*, meets an old friend Casella. Three times Dante tries to embrace him but, as a spirit, he is incorporeal and Dante's arms meet only themselves. Dante then asks if it is possible for Casella to sing one of Dante's poems he sang on earth. Felix sings it to Sal:

"Amor che ne la mente mi ragiona"
cominciò elli allor si dolcemente,
che la dolcezza ancor dentro mi suona.

The answer is that the narrative is as isolated as the man at the window, as bodiless as Casella. The interruption indicates a determination to face the issue. What Felix's scholarly musings in a café then turn us toward are the consequence in the loss of this connection with an audience. It is a loss of community, of a guiding tradition and the loss, thereby, of writerly authority. It meant Rabelais, one of the first modern novelists, "was the spokesman of no-one but himself. And that meant that his role was inherently absurd. No-one had called him. Not God. Not the Muses. Not the monarch. Not the local community. He was alone in his room, scribbling away." Nothing has changed. Sal listens.

— *How did it go again? she asks, looking at him across the table.*
— *What?*
— *The Dante.*
— *Love that discourses in my mind (that's the first line of his old*

poem), he then began so sweetly that the sweetness still within me sounds.

He smiles at her: — Che la dolcezza ancor dentro mi suona, *he says.*

Despite the subject matter of the conversation, this is more what we expect from an English novel. Except it is the subject matter that turns *Everything Passes* from what might be dismissed as a mood piece into a challenge to English fiction. The sweetness sounding in Dante has an equivalence in the voices streaming through the man at the window. Opposed they reveal the duality at the heart of fiction: an experience that stills our daily disquiet yet also delays our progress, just as it delays Casella and Dante from climbing Mount Purgatory. Together they constitute our experience of art – its joy and its sorrow – whether it is poetry, music or fiction. Yet it is only poetry and fiction that can reflect on its own status and include this reflection in the experience. It's nothing new and radical. We see it in the scene with Casella, a 14th-Century poem.

It's no coincidence that Sal asks Felix to repeat Dante's own repetition of the song (that is, sung first in Purgatory itself and then in his poem of the same name). In it she is prompted to recognise the love discoursing over the café table. So, by describing Rabelais' recognition, Felix has opened a space in which communication becomes possible. His own isolation is implicated in his scholarly proposition, yet it also offers a promise of its end: Sal has become his audience, his community. Very soon after, she agrees to marry him. Here the distance between art and life – which is also the distance between Felix and Sal – is given measure. However, we must now realise that the conversation is also streaming through Felix as he recalls a happy time in the wretchedness of Sal's absence. He has lost his community, perhaps driven it away with a selfish focus on his own scholarly concerns, or perhaps the ultimate failure of communication, and thereby of art.

Everything Passes then is not so much a metafiction reflecting with postmodern knowingness on the elemental opening 18 pages than an Orphic gaze into the underworld of art and our inner lives. In exploring the issue within a novel, Josipovici implicates itself and our reading in the same process. The voices we hear resonate uncannily in our mind, offering the possibility of genuine expression and dialogue outside of all constraints imposed by the genre of the novel, yet also threatening to reinforce them with yet another beginning, middle and end. It is difficult to distinguish between the pathway and the cul-de-sac. To do so, we have to read, listen and write again. For the man standing at the cracked window things begin to look brighter as, toward the end of the novel, he finds release in creative life, only to make a discovery that seems to reverse all progress. *Everything Passes* risks such failure as no other English novel dare fail.

The Birth of Art

Art is primarily the consciousness of unhappiness, not its compensation.
Maurice Blanchot, *The Space of Literature*

What does Blanchot mean by this? We all know that art consoles us. It is why we return to it, flee to it; this awesome space in which we make our own intimate refuge. Blanchot seems only to be colonising the universe of art to express the post-trauma of post-war Europe. What about the art throughout human history, from prehistoric cave paintings to the plays of Shakespeare, to the rich novels of our time, how can all this be the consciousness of grief?

The same question arises when scientists, or in this case evolutionary psychologists, claim all art stems from mate choice in prehistoric culture. They say art is a happy by-product of sexual display, much like a peacock's tail. The animal demonstrates how healthy and powerful he is by using a surplus of energy to create the enormous folly of its tail. The peahen chooses to mate with the male that will most likely produce strong, healthy offspring. The more extravagant the tail, the stronger and healthier the male.

We ask: is this, then, the ultimate meaning of art? When Michelangelo painted the Sistine Chapel, was he keeping an eye out from on high for some skirt down below? Well, it's not as simple as that of course, as the example indicates. A theory of art such as this might be persuasive about unconscious motivations for the production of art, but it doesn't tell us much about the art itself, or indeed our experience of art.

This is not a modern experience. We can go back right to the beginning to examine it. In a review of George Bataille's book on the cave paintings discovered by chance in Lascaux in 1940,

Maurice Blanchot says that despite the understanding that the paintings come from a world of "obscure savagery, of mysterious rites and inaccessible customs", the paintings themselves are "strikingly beautiful" and "prodigiously clear". He says that the paintings evoke a "free spontaneity ... that is carefree and without ulterior motive, almost without pretext and joyfully open to itself" (with no trace of grief). Could it be that we are witnessing, as Bataille claims, the birth of art?

Blanchot doesn't doubt there are hundreds of years of paintings behind the current paintings on the walls, but what we see is always the beginning of art just as each work of art is the beginning too; a perpetual birth. We become aware of something that wasn't there before. While Blanchot admits that this thought is an illusion, he says it is also true: "It reveals to us in a perceptible manner the extraordinary intrigue that art pursues with us and with time".

What is this extraordinary intrigue? Whatever the answer, it is elided by science. If we compare Blanchot's expressive response with a random search of online writings on Lascaux, discussion of the paintings is almost entirely archaeological: do they reveal that Homo Erectus was "already setting traps, digging pits to capture elephants and rhinoceros"? The search for knowledge invariably overruns and obscures wonder before these works. The paintings become tools for explanatory use, much like the flint stones scattered on the floor used to slice animal flesh.

Yet, as Blanchot says, it is precisely the realisation of knowledge and control that was brought about by the paintings. By interrupting the everyday task of survival to create images and to celebrate the timeless time of being unconsciously part of the natural world, the creators began to separate themselves from other living species. Art became power and weakness: power over nature but also realisation of the inability to return to that pre-conscious state. The worker broke away from utility and became an artist. Appropriately, Blanchot speaks of the singular individual:

> *This void separating him from the natural community is, it seems, what revealed death and destruction to him, but he also learned, not without pain or misgiving, to use this void: to make use of and deepen his weakness in order to become stronger.**

We can see this in all art, in every branch of the arts: the use of weakness to become stronger, to become completely other than nature by virtue of the inability to become one with nature. It is a transgression against the natural order that Blanchot says is at the heart of becoming human.

While sexual selection might well have contributed to the technical facility and impulse to adorn the cave walls, what the adornment reveals is something else: a mutation beyond the graphs of evolution. It is not measurable, as the time of the void's appearance will always be obscured because the time's absence is the void itself. The cave paintings celebrate the power of this transgression but also retain a memory of the distress and horror of what it means: "the disconcerting thought that man does not become a man through all that is human in him".

Blanchot ends his essay by drawing our attention to the human figure in the Shaft of the Dead Man, the only such representation in the cave, comparatively feebly drawn and unadorned by colour:

> *The meaning of this obscure drawing is ... clear: it is the first signature of the first painting, the mark left modestly in a corner, the furtive, fearful, indelible trace of man who is for the first time born of his work, but who also feels seriously threatened by this work and perhaps already struck by death.*

So when Blanchot says that "art is primarily the consciousness of unhappiness", he is referring to this feeble yet indelible trace. It is present for us now. It is the strange apprehension of presence we sense before art; a non-experience that nevertheless occurs. We find the art in art not in technical aptitude, not in political or social or psychological content, not in the *tour de force* of a personality or techniques of self-effacement – all perhaps consoling in themselves – but in the experience of art brought utmost to the fore.

* Translated by Elizabeth Rottenberg

The Huge Difficulty of Dying

In 1938, living in Paris and short of money, the little-known writer Samuel Beckett agreed to translate the Marquis de Sade's *Les 120 journées de Sodome*. He confided in his friend Thomas McGreevy about concerns for his career if he was associated with such a book even though he believed it transcended its reputation.

> *The obscenity of surface is indescribable. Nothing could be less pornographical. It fills me with a kind of metaphysical ecstasy. The composition is extraordinary, as rigorous as Dante's.*

Soon after, of course, the war began and the project was abandoned. Beckett escaped to an unoccupied zone while de Sade's novel proved to be an insufficient realism. For this reason alone it is difficult to comprehend let alone accept the implications of Beckett's appreciation. It would mean that the pleasure he took in reading unrelenting descriptions of sexual violence and cruelty was in effect no different to that gained from reading Jane Austen, another of Beckett's favourites at the time and, by his own account, no less pornographical.

What's more, his rapture and comparison of de Sade to Dante suggests that compositional rigour manifests divine power. As readers, we are close to omnipotence, elevated from the trials and duties of worldly existence, able to create and destroy at will. Literary pleasure is thereby in itself independent of human community; a singularity become universal. Even as it evokes fraternity, the unique gift of art tends toward tyranny. What is to be done?

One of those attracted to the gift was a young Franz Kafka. Aged 21, he sought to resist the ease of solitary power. Writing to Oskar Pollack, he expressed a self-destructive literary manifesto:

I think we ought to read only books that wound and stab us. If the book we are reading doesn't wake us like a blow on the head, what are we reading for? So that it will make us happy, as you write? Good God, we would be just as happy if we had no books and the kind of books that make us happy are the kind we could write ourselves if we had to. But we need the books that affect us like a disaster, that grieve us deeply, like the death of someone we love more than ourselves, like being banished into forests far from everyone, like a suicide. A book must be the axe for the frozen sea inside us. That is my belief.*

Is *Les 120 journées de Sodome* such a book? Perhaps. But where does this need for axe-like books lead us? Eighteen years later, having written many of his greatest works, Kafka recognised the darkness in the initial romance:

Writing is a sweet and wonderful reward, but for what? In the night it became clear to me, as clear as a child's lesson book, that it is the reward for serving the devil. This descent to the dark powers, this unshackling of spirits bound by nature, these dubious embraces and whatever else may take place in the nether parts which the higher parts no longer know, when one writes one's stories in the sunshine.

This is why Kafka ordered Max Brod to burn his manuscripts rather than out of extreme literary scrupulosity or modesty, though these too were close to the writer. Kafka, like Beckett, had counted upon literature to nourish an otherwise emaciated life: "Writing sustains me", he says in the same letter, "but is it not more accurate to say that it sustains this kind of life?"

If Kafka is right and writing is in unwitting service of the devil, then what is the alternative: not writing? What would it mean for the individual striving for what is apparently beyond words to turn away from art yet still seek to defrost the frozen sea? An answer is presented in Jonathan Littell's novel *The Kindly*

Ones. What has so far been received as an historical fiction examining the psychology of genocide is also, and perhaps more significantly, a reiteration of Kafka's revelation.

When Maximilien Aue introduces himself he is a respectable business and family man, a manufacturer of lace somewhere in France. Before that, however, he says he was a Nazi intelligence officer working inside Hitler's imperial war machine. In order to remain alive and free he has had much to conceal. Now, as we begin to read this book, he is a writer too. What has caused the break in cover, the end of silence? At first, Aue claims to want to reveal "how it happened" and that this will be an edifying story, "a real morality play" in which we will learn something about the Holocaust. Yet, as we prepare ourselves for the long repetition of a story we know so well from other sources, the warning from history, the ease with which respectable men become savage killers, Aue moves further back:

> *If after all these years I've made up my mind to write, it's to set the record straight for myself, not for you. For a long time we crawl on this earth like caterpillars, waiting for the splendid, diaphanous butterfly we bear within ourselves. And then time passes and the nymph stage never comes, we remain larvae – what do we do with such an appalling realization?***

This then is a personal story rather than Aue revealing his universality. As is soon made clear, he is no Everyman; nobody ever quite is. Even at this later stage in life, Maximilien Aue is still himself alone, crawling through life, waiting to fly. Suicide, he admits, is an option and he imagines a hand grenade against his chest: "And then at last happiness, or in any case peace, as the shreds of my flesh slowly dripped off the walls". But no, he hasn't chosen suicide despite its promises. He's writing instead. Why? It was a question asked in their own lives and in their own ways by both Beckett and Kafka, and both were appalled yet still compelled to continue. In Aue's case, the answer has a history as long as his life: "Ever since I was a child", he says, "I had been haunted by a passion for the absolute, for the overcoming of all limits". From that time, he dreamt of becoming a great pianist with "cathedrals at my fingertips, airy as foam", and then wanted "above all else to study literature and philosophy". But circumstances conspired and he became a doctor of law instead. Undisclosed at first is another outlet for his passion, perhaps because it involves a deeper heartbreak.

The only person he has ever loved, he says, is his twin sister, Una. Their incestuous relationship ended before adulthood yet persists in Aue's inner life. He dreams of returning to the time when they were inseparable, swimming as one in the sea, their parents absent. She dominates his thoughts and behaviour. He claims to have had exclusively homosexual encounters since solely in order to submit to penetration, to be Una even as he remains himself; a repetition of transcendent love. Of course, this threatens serious repercussions in the ranks of the Nazi Party, which regards homosexual behaviour a crime. Yet the Party plays a similar role in Aue's life. Its ideology also presents itself as a form of overcoming, a transcendence of the limits of the self, an ascent into the *Lebensraum* of the world at large. To achieve this it too demands submission to the penetrating will of another, the Führer. Aue is prepared to do whatever it takes, whether this means transgressing Nazi law or following its orders to the letter.

His narrative is arranged in seven long chapters each with a musical title. It opens with *Toccata*, a rhetorical flourish, and then continues with *Allemande I & II* in which Aue is posted to the Crimea and, as the title suggests, links arms with his fellow Nazis to pursue occupation and suppress resistance. This includes arranging and carrying out mass executions of local civilians. As readers, we experience these through Aue's eyes alone – we are not introduced to Jewish victims but see them from a distance, almost as if Aue is writing one of his official reports. Their suffering is beyond description. Yet, rather than mollify the reader's anguish, Aue's objective narrative style deepens it. We have no sentiment to assist us beyond the experience. Despite also feeling disgust, Aue claims to have got through the experience himself by holding to the belief that the massacres are necessary for the long-term Nazi goal. However, it should be emphasised that such events against civilians are relatively rare in the novel and that *Allemande I & II* is taken up mainly by the intrigues of SS politics and his research projects into the ethnicity of the various populations in the Caucasus. The latter involves long, engrossing digressions with no violent disturbances. It means that when, after eighty pages or more, we return to the clearings in which thousands of Jews are to be slaughtered, we are provoked into feeling the dizzying absence of inevitability, the removal of the comforts of teleology. It is a peculiar horror considering it is a familiar subject in our culture.

Indeed, there are many passages in the book in which terrible things happen that serve no apparent purpose beyond their cumulative power. Many events are not resolved later in the novel and so leave the reader stunned and seeking some kind of release from meaninglessness. For instance, Aue joins a patrol in which a Ukrainian peasant woman is shot by accident. However, before she dies, her unborn child is saved – cut from her womb and wrapped in a shawl – by a German soldier, only then for an indifferent officer to dash the baby's head against a wall, furious that effort has been spent on a peasant's life. One expects a lesson to be drawn, for ramifications, but the telling of the event is all that remains. Despite Aue's ability to distance himself, this ease of killing does begin to have an impact. His body insists on vomiting and expelling diarrhoea. Also, his mind begins to pursue an understanding:

This was what I couldn't manage to grasp: the yawning gap, the absolute contradiction between the ease with which one can kill and the huge difficulty there must be in dying.

What can he mean? As a Nazi, such difficulty is surely beside the point, which is the destruction of Germany's enemies. In defending his intellectual concerns, Aue insists it is vital "to comprehend within oneself the necessity of the Führer's orders", otherwise one is "nothing but a sheep, a slave and not a man". There is a contradiction here too as rational consent to such necessity must also lead to the same condition; it is in the nature of submission. The problem that has been revealed is that submission is always incomplete; there is always the yawning gap. Submission is as impossible as death:

[E]ven with the rifle at the back of your head or the rope around your neck, death remains incomprehensible, a pure abstraction, this absurd idea that I, the only living person in the world, could disappear. Dying, we may already be dead, but we never die, that moment never comes, or rather it never stops coming.

Aue cites a need to understand the abstraction as the reason for not requesting a transfer to more traditional war zones. He prefers to remain to seek the "sensation of rupture" brought by the executions, the "infinite disturbance" of his whole being. All the same, like any addiction, the more he attends, the less he feels. If we set aside the impulse to dismiss this as Sadistic delight, we can see that Aue too is enduring the huge difficulty of dying. So why is he fascinated by this space opened between life and death?

While searching for a cure or an answer, Aue expresses admiration for the capacity of the Nazis' adjudged enemy to internalise its beliefs. "When the Jew submitted to the Law, he felt that this law lived in him. National Socialism had to be that too: a living law." Such measured respect for ancient religion over fresh ideology is telling and will resurface elsewhere. It suggests in effect Aue's only means to achieve the desired state is to take Nazism toward its logical fulfilment: that is, to accept obliteration. It means he must die alongside those being killed. But how? It's a question that runs deep throughout the novel.

Later on in the Caucasus campaign, it becomes clear the issue extends beyond the particulars of the war. Aue is leading Jewish men toward a forest clearing where his soldiers are preparing a trench. Before the slaughter can begin, they find that the Soviets have been there before. Already there are mass graves in the forest. Wherever a new trench is begun, more bodies appear, each with a bullet in the neck. The officers are agitated, the soldiers dig another trench and the Jews look on and wait. Here is the absolute contradiction in a literary tableau: the living and the dead confronting each other, both intimately close and infinitely distant; neither close nor distant enough. The reader, already discomforted by the horror of the scene and, if not certain, then aware of its likely accuracy to the historical record, is now as impatient as the officers for it to be over. The reader becomes a Nazi and the horror is thereby situated beyond disposable titillation. That said, the scene does seem to be too convenient, too literary, an adaptation of the historical record into a drama for the more discerning voyeur. The scene might also stand as a correlate of *The Kindly Ones'* literary bloodline: yet another work of fiction about the Nazis devoured by a greedy market, yet another distressing reminder of the Shoah, as if this work of leisure is also disturbing graves in order to kill nameless thousands yet again. Surely there something pathological in the demand for such cruel repetition. Setting aside repugnance in the forest, it does remain necessary to the reader's experience of this infinitely terrible time before and after an event, a time in which dying persists. It might also be asked: how can the absolute contradiction be recognised by the reader without the means also appearing contrived and distasteful?

The length of the novel, however, works against such impressions. A reviewer might seize extraordinary scenes such as this to present the kernel of the novel, but it is an unfortunate deceit. The primary experience of *The Kindly Ones* is similar – even at less than a third of its length – to that of Proust's *In Search of Lost Time*. Proust's novel cannot be reduced to the scenes involving the Petite Madeleine and the uneven paving stone. One could not add even the lesbian Sadomasochism at Montjouvain and the debauchery of the Baron de Charlus without losing the intense sensibility of the narrator, nor how our exposure to these four headline events is framed by the rest of the novel in which innumerable characters and events propel the reader forward in fascination. This is why reading the novel is necessary to move beyond its superficial context.

In his search for lost time, Marcel recovers it by chance. The power of an event or an experience is recovered or unveiled for the first time when he least expects it; intellectual control is subverted. Yet, whereas Proust's novel maintains intellectual control in presenting these revelatory moments, Aue's search for lost life demands that the narrative style itself changes to accommodate the meaning of that loss. After the cool, objective style – presented in telling clarity by Charlotte Mandell's translation – Aue continues his task of dying by divesting himself of mastery just as he divested himself of control in sexual encounters and in military service.

From the relative comforts of Ukraine, Aue is "sent to join those already dead" at the siege of Stalingrad. He is not so much frightened as intrigued. The conditions are terrible: lice live under uniforms, food is scarce and diarrhoea once again punctuates daily existence. Aue explores the frontline and experiences for the first time being under attack. Suddenly realism descends into pages of dream-like reveries involving Una and dirigibles. This is where the novel seems to be shedding its documentary narrative progression, testing the reader's expectations and patience. When we are returned to a controlling consciousness, the narrative is thereby infected with the danger of its loss; we are now always on the edge of darkness. It descends again during a period of recovery from the surrealist ordeal as Aue visits his mother and step-father in the south of France. Soon it will overwhelm him as well as the novel.

After the miasma of the front line, Aue retreats to Berlin and becomes deeply involved in Nazi bureaucracy. He has meetings with Himmler, Eichmann and Mandelbrot, a grotesque fictional player right out of Kafka. He attends a musical soiree at Eichmann's home and watches as the bureaucrat plays the violin: "his eyes rivetted to the score; he didn't make any mistakes, but didn't seem to understand that that wasn't enough". From here, despite the calm of imperial offices, that lack of understanding takes its toll. Aue's life and Germany's war begin to unravel. Illness and Allied air raids encroach on the social whirl and a traditional romance with a local girl is threatened; the vengeance of the Furies – the kindly ones of the title – is revealed.

One last time Aue encounters the huge difficulty of dying by visiting first an underground factory and then Auschwitz itself, both populated and run by the living dead. Given leave by Himmler's bomb-damaged ministry, he turns his attention to Una, "the thought of whom never releases me and leaves my head only to seep into my bone, the one who will always be there between the world and me". He travels to Pomerania where she and her crippled composer husband live. But their mansion is empty and thereby becomes a stage for Aue's final attempt to submit, to close the distance. It's a bizarre chapter particularly as the reader had been very aware of the Russian advance and expecting Aue's escape to be the focus of the narrative.

His return to Berlin maintains these expectations but by now it is too late and the kindly ones have swamped Aue's mastery, turning a sub-plot mystery into a Kafkaesque comedy. It is a difficult loss for the novel to bear and gives the impression of a failure on the novelist's part. There is one particularly unlikely scene involving the Führer himself that ends any doubt. It is clear we are at the end, when the huge difficulty of dying is finally over. Only not quite. Even as the kindly ones wreak their power, there is an excessive moment, a residual space in which dying never comes. We recognise the condition; it has been with us all along and has never been silent. Indeed, the absolute contradiction sustains Maximilien Aue and inaugurates his narrative. Had he not fallen into the yawning gap between life and death, he would not be writing this account of the war and we would not be reading it. The reader, his accomplice, is thereby also sustained. But then what kind of sustenance is it?

* Translated by Richard & Clara Winston
** Translated by Charlotte Mandell

Life Performance

Nick Cave's *The Death of Bunny Munro* is an impressive performance. Two features stand out. The first is the pleasure it takes in words and vivid descriptions: Bunny Munro is a man of the world, a cosmetics salesman on the move and he's always swigging from a bottle of whiskey and emitting "furious tusks of smoke" from his Lambert & Butler cigarettes. It's a lifestyle that takes its toll: his eyes are always "granulated", yet he maintains his appearance: the curl of hair on his forehead is always "pomaded". In order to read his watch, Bunny "trombones" his wrist out of its sleeve. And Bunny never closes his mobile, he "clamshells it shut" or "castaneted the phone". Of course, this is very reminiscent not of Cave's darkly romantic songs but of Martin Amis in his moneyed pomp. Had Bunny Munro contemplated a haircut, he would no doubt instead have considered "a rug rethink". This is why *The Death of Bunny Munro* has a conspicuously anachronistic quality.

While the novel is set in the city in which I live and describes the fiery destruction of the West Pier in 2003, it also evokes another Brighton, one trapped in the cartoon era of the early 1980s during which in another city John Self trampled triumphant for a time, flapping his flares into non-existence. Perhaps this is only a stylistic effect, except Bunny Munro is also himself a throwback. His seedy swagger and unrelenting, unobstructed appetites reawaken Lazarus-like an extinct species. Bunny has just spent the night with a prostitute while his wife is suffering at home with an unspecified psychological condition requiring medication. Scenes like this pepper the novel and are rarely less than uncomfortable. A review could well fill itself by adumbrating the most hair-raising with discreet relish. However, the highly-worked prose is their true significance. It emphasises the strain under which Bunny places his everyday life; an intensity so great the threat of collapse becomes inevitable (though of course inevitability in a novel is itself inevitable). This is why the prose style is more than spice added to the high entertainment of Bunny Munro's dissolution. It is a necessary part of the story. This is the second feature: for Bunny, and for readers following Bunny, everything is outside; the trombone, the castanets, the tusks of smoke, granulation and pomade are all projections of Bunny Munro's self. As Bunny lives, his actions in effect sublate his paltry, transitory self into the world, just as a musician – perhaps one playing the trombone or even castanets – is sublated into music. For this reason, Bunny Munro has no inner life to report or, rather, his inner life animates the world. Soon it becomes almost impossible to distinguish between the two.

Bunny is an aspirant solipsist; this "man of the world" seeks to be a tautology. His nine-year-old son, also called Bunny Munro, "thinks there is something about the way his father moves through the world that is truly impressive". Yes, he moves as if he is at home in the world; as if the world is a function of his ego. The novel we are reading is both a manifestation of this condition and its controverting action. Shocking events occur throughout these 278 pages that demand Bunny's active remorse yet Bunny's projections are also attempted rejections of the self. His responsibility has no ground on which to settle.

Bunny's incipient solipsism is threatened by the stirring opening sentence: " 'I am damned,' thinks Bunny Munro in a sudden moment of self-awareness reserved for those who are soon to die." This is Beckett's *Malone Dies* with Catholic supplements. Already, the world is revolting against his selfishness and will not cede. But the realisation passes and Bunny is immediately back to picturing a disembodied vagina – another repository for his self-projection – and glugging a bottle of vodka from the minibar. When he has to deal with the apparent suicide of his wife, he tries to contain his responsibility in his hurried escape.

He takes his son on the road – the concert tour meaning is relevant here – and we see things from the boy's perspective. At first, the son's point of view works against his father's domination of the narrative, yet, as we know, he shares his father's name, so he too may be a projection of Bunny Munro. They travel across town to meet his dying and thoroughly unpleasant grandfather, who also just happens to be called Bunny Munro. The centrality and repetition of "un" in their name suggests the eventual negation of all selfhood, as well as the misery of its inheritance. And of course the triune of Bunnys also alludes to the Trinity. Perhaps the Holy Spirit is embodied by the youngest Bunny. His fascination with learning from the world – he studies an encyclopaedia on the road trip – is not as blatant an indication of the possibility of redemption as the toy figure of Darth Vader he places on the dashboard is of the threat of genetic influence. But the symbolic content is a given from start, as this is a narrative borne on the struggle between Bunny's deranged imagination and the world. The death of Bunny Munro would then be the end of the struggle.

The end of the struggle would also mean the end of the novel. Death is preceded by a final night, a final performance on the road, in which Bunny walks on stage and makes a humble apology to an audience composed of those he has ill loved. Bunny is thrilled, suggesting that his life has really been only one long performance and this its apotheosis. Therefore any remorse he shows on stage also serves his self-regarding posture; it's still all about him. In this sense Nick Cave's stylised performance is necessary to its subject; the spotlight after all cannot illuminate anything beyond the stage. This is the fulfilment and insufficiency of *The Death of Bunny Munro*. If, as this novel demonstrates, life and art constitute a performance, then Nick Cave's is entertaining, memorable and stimulating. Only after the experience do we note that the performance of death is – in life and in writing – a striking absence.

Against Science

When Jonathan Gottschall argues in the *Boston Globe* that "literary criticism could be one of our best tools for understanding the human condition" if it would only embraces science, he admits that he's not the first to argue for a marriage of the two cultures. However, he goes further than CP Snow by calling for literary scholars to adopt "theories, its statistical tools, and its insistence on hypothesis and proof" instead of "philosophical despair about the possibility of knowledge". Scholars, he says, "should embrace science's spirit of intellectual optimism". "In some cases", he adds, "it's possible to use scientific methods to question cherished tenets of modern literary theory".

He first addresses the "shibboleth of modern literary theory" that "the author is dead".

> *Roughly speaking, this statement means that authors have no power over their readers. When we read stories we do not so much yield to the author's creation as create it anew ourselves – manufacturing our own highly idiosyncratic meanings as we go along. This idea has radical implications: If it is true, there can be no shared understanding of what literary works mean. But like so much else that passes for knowledge in contemporary literary studies, this assertion has its basis only in the swaggering authority of its asserter – in this case, Roland Barthes, one of the founding giants of poststructuralist literary theory.*

He then debunks this "cherished tenet" with results from scientific tests. Except anyone who reads Barthes' essay will find that the "radical implications" are only that. Nowhere does it say that we manufacture "our own highly idiosyncratic meanings as we go along". Nor does it deny the possibility of a shared understanding. It's ironic, given Gottschall's evident contempt for Barthes' swagger, that his refutation relies on a reduction of a complex essay to a "statement" and his own idiosyncratic extrapolation of the final passage of the essay:

> The reader is the space on which all the quotations that make up a writing are inscribed without any of them being lost; a text's unity lies not in its origin but in its destination. Yet this destination cannot any longer be personal: the reader is without history, biography, psychology; he is simply that someone who holds together in a single field all the traces by which the written text is constituted.

It's just about fair to imply from this that "authors have no power over their readers", but Gottschall is presenting it as an expression of Reader Response theory. The destination of writing cannot any longer be personal. What else do we share but impersonality? Rather than test "statements" with scientific method, it might have been better for Gottschall to call for more intellectual history in literary scholarship (not least for himself). *The Death of the Author* is part of a deep movement in Western culture. It reaffirms modernist resistance to Romantic notions of mastery begun in Proust's *Against Sainte-Beuve* (beginning: "Daily, I attach less value to the intellect").

Just as Gottschall isn't the first to cede authority to utility and rationalism, Barthes wasn't the first French literary thinker to distance the author from his work. Fourteen years before his famous essay, Maurice Blanchot published *The Essential Solitude*, an essay on the literary work's neutrality. We can see where Barthes is coming from because, as Christophe Bident outlines in his essay *R/M, 1953*, he writes in parallel to Blanchot. *The Essential Solitude* begins by distinguishing the author's solitude from the social world:

> In the solitude of the work – the work of art, the literary work – we

discover a more essential solitude. It excludes the complacent isolation of individualism; it has nothing to do with the quest for singularity. The fact that one sustains a stalwart attitude throughout the disciplined course of the day does not dissipate it. He who writes the work is set aside; he who has written it is dismissed. He who is dismissed, moreover, doesn't know it. This ignorance preserves him. It distracts him by authorizing him to persevere. The writer never knows whether the work is done. What he has finished in one book, he starts over or destroys in another. Valéry, celebrating this infinite quality which the work enjoys, still sees only its least problematic aspect. That the work is infinite means, for him, that the artist, though unable to finish it, can nevertheless make it the delimited site of an endless task whose incompleteness develops the mastery of the mind, expresses this mastery, expresses it by developing it in the form of power.*

Power is what Gottschall and those sympathetic to his call remain in thrall to. In their case it is the understandable desire for "relevance", a respected academic career and a book-buying public ready to afford criticism the same market-share as popular science. However, for Barthes and Blanchot (and Heidegger before them) the focus remains literature itself.

[T]he work of art, the literary work is neither finished nor unfinished: it is. What it says is exclusively this: that it is – and nothing more. Beyond that it is nothing. Whoever wants to make it express more finds nothing, finds that it expresses nothing. He whose life depends upon the work, either because he is a writer or because he is a reader, belongs to the solitude of that which expresses nothing except the word being: the word which language shelters by hiding it, or causes to appear when language itself disappears into the silent void of the work. The solitude of the work has as its primary framework the absence of any defining criteria. This absence makes it impossible ever to declare the work finished or unfinished. The

work is without any proof, just as it is without any use. It can't be verified. Truth can appropriate it, renown draws attention to it, but the existence it thus acquires doesn't concern it. This demonstrability renders it neither certain nor real - does not make it manifest. The work is solitary: this does not mean that it remains uncommunicable, that it has no reader. But whoever reads it enters into the affirmation of the work's solitude, just as he who writes it belongs to the risk of this solitude.

There is a reason for these overlong quotations. Blanchot's writing – its unique and relentless patience – is performative rather than didactic. Neither information nor wisdom is being imparted but, as Barthes says, it is writing "borne by a pure gesture of inscription" tracing "a field without origin – or which, at least, has no other origin than language itself, language which ceaselessly calls into question all origins".

Barthes, sharing Valéry's optimism, heralds the absence of authorial control as the birth of a new freedom, a new quest for the key to all mythologies. This headline-grabbing opportunism is perhaps what draws attention to Barthes and obscurity to his secret sharer. And it enables Gottschall to present a caricature of his own misreading of Barthes' essay and to believe it is guaranteed by means of extra-literary verification. Even his expression of appreciation for literature – "stories represent our biggest and most preciously varied repository of information about human nature" – indicates a patronising tolerance for literature only as fodder for the mills of science. "Without a robust study of literature there can be no adequate reckoning of the human condition." But in what way is "the human condition" already transfigured by the unnatural force of art? Unfortunately for Gottschall and his Monday-morning optimism, science, like religion, is just another system of expression; a literary genre.

* Translated by Ann Smock

The Shadow Cast by Writing

[A common scene?]

One day in the summer he was climbing a steep path toward a busy crossroads when, in an absent-minded daydream experienced by anyone walking familiar streets with only boredom and solitude to share, he saw among the cars, bicycles and pedestrians the profile of a long-lost friend. It has to be a daydream, he thought, identical to the one back then, when they were still close. He had glimpsed her on the same street, except that time walking towards him and beside someone else. A shock enough for him to take refuge in the darkness of an adjacent arcade, reeling from the revelation and hoping that neither had looked ahead, only to discover a few seconds later, as they passed, that it wasn't them at all. So, he thought, this time it has to be an illusion, only now there is no need to hide. It isn't her.

And what if it had been? No matter how well-attuned one is to the light, I think, life remains hooded by such fictions. They shadow the mundane present; stories overwritten mostly, sometimes flaring for a few hours, sometimes days, sometimes branded for years in a synaptic loop. Together they form a consciousness veiled by invention, hallucination and stupefaction. A good reason not to live, I think, if the alternative were not so much worse: a life exposed to the light. And then she turned toward me and smiled.

We chatted for five minutes, perhaps more. At the time, I knew it wasn't much. We exchanged small talk about work and health, queries about long-lost mutual friends and about our current activities. It really wasn't much. We carried on to our destinations in opposing directions, slightly diverted, nothing more. What happened next is the source of what is written here.

Next is five months later, in the cocoon of winter. Late one night I began writing at the top of a blank page, and I began writing about that meeting. As I could not quite remember the conversation, I let the pen find the words. Except, rather than the words themselves, what emerged were memories of the physical shifts and gestures between us; the awkward corners and delicate pauses in conversation. Spaces grew around the words and resonated with the past we shared. Was this the person I had met, or even the same person I knew back then? The questions surprised me. Was I imagining it? After one and a half pages, the writing ended. I've written nothing like it since and perhaps never will.

[Moving beyond fiction]

This summer, the one and a half pages of notes became a fetish for me, offering the possibility of a more elemental form of writing, one that dissolves well-attuned habit and reveals an alternative life; not, that is, a different life but the one waiting to be discovered. Why else would a few hundred words scratched out in a brief, forgotten time stir me while all the intricate ideas, elaborate plans and laborious executions leave me blank and disconnected? On what does the appearance of its alternative depend? Chance alone it would seem.

While it would not be presumptuous to dismiss such writing as occasional autobiographical digressions carrying its charge in the singular impact it has on the writer, this would obscure what needs to be isolated as unique to writing. But how can it be maintained or codified into a public form?

I was reminded of these questions as Geoff Dyer and Lee Siegel added to the surge of voices condemning the worldly disappointments of contemporary fiction and instead advocating creative non-fiction. Both arguments rest on the notion of the novel as a means of narrating events in the empirical world and of engaging readers with company, information and meaning.

The novel may be the apotheosis of "characterisation, observation and narrative drive" but now it has a more knowing equal. Given the examples offered, it's no wonder the war reportage Dyer celebrates appears more vital, exciting and relevant, while Siegel's call, couched in tabloid sneer for literary fiction to be more commercial and realistic in order to "illumine the ordinary events of ordinary lives", also seems fair if we assume that war and peace are the poles between which real life spins; a roadside bomb and a divorce spraying shrapnel into flesh and spirit. So how can the writing that stirs me – haphazard, unworldly – respond to these rousing condemnations?

First, we have to recognise the limits of the prevailing distinction between fiction and non-fiction. Both Dyer and Siegel appeal to cultural relevance to justify the relegation of contemporary literary fiction. For one, war is "the big story of our times – the al-Qaida attacks on New York and the Pentagon, and the subsequent wars in Iraq and Afghanistan" mean that "long-form reporting ... has left the novel looking superfluous"; while, for the other, a fast-tracked biography of Barack Obama is "overflowing with sharp character portraits", has "keen evocations of American places" and is, moreover, "a ripping narrative". Both cite novels from the past as exemplary and now impossible because, according to Dyer, "the time has passed" when "human stories contained within historical events ... could only be assimilated and comprehended when they had been processed by a novel". Siegel makes perhaps the more telling observation that novel writing has become a profession rather than a vocation, thereby producing novels in which "carefulness ... cautiousness [and] professionalism" are considered desirable literary attributes rather than "existential urgency and intensity". Certainly these latter qualities are to the fore in war reportage and in Janet Malcolm's article cited by Siegel but, from the evidence supplied, they appear to rely on familiar techniques of genre fiction. The old-fashioned quest to tell a story drives these books rather than anything beyond themselves, a connection, for instance, with what escapes the rhetoric of style and technique. Indeed, Dyer says one war book is "like a traditional third-person novel" giving "the chaos of events ... narrative shape" with "scrupulous observation and phrasing" spiced with "damaged lyricism" (a soldier's ruptured skull echoes an earlier description of the moon). In raising voices against the new type of book, Dyer first offers the straw man of an unnamed "fiction lobby" who say it's "too soon to tell" if the novel is out-dated, and, second, the fact-checking culture of the *New Yorker*. Deviation from the latter – a "willingness to digress" from strict factual accuracy – seems to be the only border war reportage shares with fiction. The "new" form involves arguing for this small creative licence. It is appropriate that, at the end of the essay, Dyer introduces a more challenging voice of opposition in the form of Martin Amis' thirty-year-old critique.

Amis claims that the non-fiction novel, as practised by Mailer and Capote, lacks "moral imagination. Moral artistry. The facts cannot be arranged to give them moral point. There can be no art without moral point. When the reading experience is over, you are left, simply, with murder – and with the human messiness and futility that attends all death." The essay is an old one, and the point can now be seen to contain its own limitation and, by extension, refutation. We are moving beyond the non-fiction novel to different kinds of narrative art, different forms of cognition. Loaded with moral and political point, narrative has been recalibrated to record, honour and protest the latest, historically specific instance of futility and mess.

Dyer is right that Amis adds little weight to counter his argument. Moral point is an inevitable consequence of all writing. However, its lightness may be deceptive because Dyer's dismissal appeals only to taste over judgement and immediacy over vintage. I would suggest Amis is wrong, instead, only because the new books seek to eliminate art (if not craft), or at least our perception of it, and this would be, in its ambition, the very height of art and, thereby, the height of morality, even if it is a studied amorality. "Art always throws off the appearance of art", according to Adrian Leverkühn in Thomas Mann's *Doctor Faustus*, and we should remember who helped guarantee *his* art throw off its appearances.

Despite the respectable ambition, it's hard to see how these invariably America-focussed war books are in any way "moving beyond" anything or in any way different from the careful, cautious and professional fictions of which Lee Siegel is so contemptuous. Their "existential urgency and intensity" emerges first from their subject matter and then, more significantly, from a fiercely limited perspective. Death lurks around each corner; soldiers can live or die in the next sentence. Unlike in the novel, the author here has no control over life and death. In this – perhaps paradoxical – way, war reporting has erased chance from writing. Paradoxical because, while chance fills the lives of the soldiers, it is erased in the telling: everything is necessary, already written in nature. This is of course a particularly thrilling reading experience – the illusion of extreme chance while one is safely removed, at rest with a book. While these narratives may appear to represent a "different form of cognition", it is merely a symptom of the triumph of genre. The only essential difference Dyer offers between it and Kathryn Bigelow's fictional confection *The Hurt Locker* is in its credibility. One we know is fiction because it is presented as such even if, in the telling, we are persuaded to believe otherwise, while the other is presented as truth "with multiple layers of dreadful, unresolved irony". But how can we know which is credible and which not without first having been convinced of non-fiction? Most of us have not, after all, been soldiers in the front line. The issue is one of trusting the sincerity of the author. What is happening here is the familiar trajectory of a loss of suspension of disbelief followed by a knowing cynicism eager to be seduced again. Except, the only thing that has changed is that the magical force of fiction has been renewed elsewhere, in light disguise. Behold, the Emperor.

[A realm beyond light]

I began with a run-of-the-mill story of memory and imagination skewing an ordinary experience and then how its reconstruction in words changed the perspective, enabling the writer to loosen the self's armour of habit, perhaps opening it to danger, perhaps to relief. While I recognise its banal nature, I think it offers an insight into a more worthwhile, time-independent distinction between fiction and non-fiction or, better still, between formal adventure and storytelling. Next I need to describe more respectable examples.

It is well known that, after initially resisting the idea, Henry James used a notebook to develop plots for stories and novels. Often these ideas were taken from anecdotes heard in drawing rooms or salons. *The Turn of the Screw* is a famous example, taken from an outline given by the Archbishop of Canterbury who himself was only relating a story told by "a lady who had no art of relation". The notebook repeats the outline and adds that the story "is all obscure and imperfect" yet recognises "a suggestion of strangely gruesome effect in it". Such obscurity may have convinced a lesser writer to abandon the story or to develop it to the point where it becomes a familiar ghost story. Indeed, the editors of the notebooks insist this latter project is all the writer intended. James does neither. He makes the decisive move to have the story told "by an outside spectator, observer", in this case the governess who takes a job in the house where the events unfold.

But why decisive? In his short essay on the notebooks, Maurice Blanchot uses *The Turn of the Screw* as an example to show how the development in the notebook of the obscure and imperfect aspects of the story led to its unique qualities. By deciding to place a step between the narration and the events in the form of the governess's letter, the plot of the story becomes the lucidity and obscurity of the governess's experience. James uses the distance between the real words and the real world to create the ambiguity of the children's innocence ("one of his most cruel effects"):

> ... *an innocence which is pure of the evil it contains; the art of perfect dissimulation which enables the children to conceal this evil from honest folk amongst whom they live, an evil which is perhaps an innocence that becomes evil in the proximity of such folk, the incorruptible innocence they oppose to the true evil of adults.**

The complexity of this ambiguity may be easily correlated to the narration of writers embedded in an occupying army among the ghostly, recalcitrant servants of Afghanistan. The governess becomes the imperial force invading an alien land, seeing danger and evil everywhere except in itself. In fiction, however, the reader is astute enough to recognise the governess may not be reliable:

> *It is she who talks about [ghosts], drawing them into the imprecise space of narration – that unreal beyond where everything is apparition, slippery, evasive, present and absent – that symbol of a lurking Evil which is, according to Graham Greene, James' subject matter and is perhaps only the satanic core of all fiction.*

The implication of these observations is that what we think of as "plot" undergoes a change. From being considered merely the thrilling sequence of empirical events orchestrated by a masterful author, plot is now the coercive presence of narration itself: "a presence seeking to penetrate the heart of the story where [the governess] is an intruder, an outsider forcing her way in, distorting the mystery, perhaps creating it, perhaps discovering it, but certainly breaking in, destroying it and only revealing the ambiguity which conceals it". The plot of *The Turn of the Screw* then is "quite simply James' talent", that is:

> *the art of stalking a secret which, as in so many of his books, the narration creates and which is not only a real secret – some event, thought or fact which might come to light – nor a simple case of intellectual duplicity, but something which evades elucidation because it belongs to a realm beyond light.*

James is a peculiar case in literary history because his fiction was written at the height of the Victorian era and then over the cusp of the outbreak of Modernism. He lived in an era, as Blanchot says, "when novels were not written by Mallarmé, but by Flaubert and Maupassant". Except Mallarmé was writing then and, as Peter Brooks has made clear in *Henry James Goes to Paris*, James was infected by his time amongst the radical artists, however long the virus lay dormant. The attractive question for us is: are we living through a similar shift toward "different kinds of narrative art"? If there are indeed "different forms of cognition", then Geoff Dyer and, most prominently, David Shields in his *Reality Hunger*, are merely outriders for a new literary epoch.

[Masters of war]

Of course, it could be that they're just unwitting conservative backsliders unable any longer to tolerate the perennial challenge of the imagination. But how would this manifest? Perhaps in one of the most notable aspects in Dyer's piece about war reportage: its circumspect phrasing; this passage in particular:

August sees the publication of Jim Frederick's Black Hearts, which investigates the disintegration, under intolerable pressure, of a platoon of American soldiers of the 502nd Infantry Regiment in Iraq's "triangle of death" in 2005-06, culminating in the rape and murder of a 14-year-old Iraqi girl and the execution of her family by four members of the platoon.

The focus according to this summary is on the soldiers exposed to "intolerable pressure" rather than the monstrosity of their crime or the suffering of the victims; that is, it is much like the bigger picture of the war according to official inquiries and polite opinion: a tragic procedural error for want of better management planning. One or two comments to *The Guardian* website where Dyer's essay appeared have already pointed out the warzones featured in these books are "home" to many and books about *them* are conspicuous by their absence. What is their experience, what "intolerable pressure" leads them to defend their sovereign lands with armed and political resistance, just as they did with our enthusiastic support less than thirty years before? Isn't this also "the big story of our times"? The nearest we seem to get is a brief mention of Lawrence Wright's *The Looming Tower* in which "complex and developing individuals" bear "the weight of larger historical drives or circumstances". Except this is a straightforward work of history, hardly a radically new kind of narrative art. So then the issue becomes: how might a writer begin to approach "the enemy" with anything like the same embedded empathy as displayed for those with the "acronym-intensive argot … worldview of the USMC"? It's a huge, intractable issue, perhaps necessarily so. For Dyer, however, "the biggest question mark about this [epic, ongoing, multi-volume work in progress] concerns the way in which it is illustrated".

[Shadows and shimmerings]

In these eye-level narratives, the moral point that Martin Amis regards as missing is the moral point precisely. Their evasion is as necessary to the books as it is to the military action itself. In their forensic attention to detail and narrative drive, they match the military's unflinching prosecution of executive orders. I'm reminded here of the standard efficiency and disinterested perception of Maximilien Aue, the narrator of Jonathan Littell's *The Kindly Ones*, as he pursues military orders. The reader of this book is forced to confront the contradiction of a deeply cultured and vigilant man with whom we are compelled to identify who also takes an active role in mass killings. Aue is aware that this is part of a necessary career path, even if he claims to find it unpalatable. Whilst massacring perceived enemies, he claims the alibi of the search for knowledge. As *The Kindly Ones* is a novel, the narrative is able to implicate itself in its evasions by opening onto the consequences; the writing done by evasion. It has this in common with *The Turn of the Screw*: a luminosity terrifying for the shadows it casts.

The ambiguity of knowledge and ignorance, innocence and guilt, good and evil, plays its part in some of the great novels that Geoff Dyer, David Shields and others regard as supplanted by non-fiction. As I've described, Blanchot argues that the plot of *The Turn of the Screw* is the very stalking of a secret elucidated in a realm beyond light which, because it is thereby also beyond darkness, still irradiates each sentence. It means the story is potentially as evanescent as the ghosts haunting the governess. It takes a special writer to follow the chimera shimmering on the horizon without losing touch with it or his readers. Blanchot aligns such fragility with the plot of Kafka's *The Trial*, and includes a perfect formulation of the novel's soul: "The story of a man pursued by his own conscience as though by some invisible judge before whom, precisely because he is invisible, he cannot justify himself", which, he concedes, "can hardly be said to constitute a story, let alone a novel", yet it is for Kafka the essence of his life: "a guilt whose weight is overwhelming because it is the shadow cast by innocence".

Writing manifests both innocence and guilt; "a sweet and wonderful reward" he tells Max Brod in a letter, "the reward for serving the devil". Joseph K's adventures are then comical and disturbing in equal measure because the narrative moves between darkness and light without him or the reader being able to judge which is which. It is a story borne on its own anxiety for solace and closure. So, with this in mind, we can wonder again how non-fiction war reportage might partake of the apparently unique power of fiction to countenance the turning of the screw. Perhaps, if the genre in which they are constructed is, as Dyer explains, determined by a culture of magazine journalism in which "current events", the "big story of our times" and "characterisation, observation and narrative drive" replace the shimmering and shadows, it is a literary oxymoron and thereby inconceivable. If it isn't, then asking the question, merely wondering aloud, is perhaps the first step on the path.

Writing of the kind I have raised to compare with war reportage also seems contingent on breaking certain silences and privacies. It often emerges from morbid isolation uncongenial to the security of public discourse to which Dyer and Siegel appeal. While we know about Franz Kafka's loneliness, Blanchot notes that James was like all artists in that he profoundly mistrusted himself – "Our doubt is our passion and our passion is our task" – and wished only to be able to let go in order to enter that realm beyond light. Instead, distance became the necessary passion and in turn it generated the narration which enabled the cruel effects of *The Turn of the Screw*. It is also an effect of the "essential loneliness" James expressed in his letter to Morton Fullerton: a loneliness "deeper about me ... than anything else: deeper than my genius, deeper than my 'discipline,' deeper than my pride, deeper, above all, than the deep countermining of art." Yet he also appreciated his notebook as a magical arena in which chance rather than facts and experience enters the creative process. As he wrote in his little book, his became "the deciphering pen", and he experienced what Blanchot calls "the pure indeterminacy of a work"; a time full of possibility and hope; perhaps even an end to loneliness. For some, however, writing which enters and maintains itself in an abandoned space disturbed only by ghosts can no longer be justified. They turn instead to narratives "recalibrated" to accept the rewards underwritten by empire.

* Translated by Sacha Rabinovitch

Intimacy and Distance

There is undoubtable pleasure in beginning to read the story of another's life. Whether it is in a novel or in the more formal context of a biography, we enjoy both the tremor of an imminent adventure and a profound sense of security. No matter what befalls the characters or the subject, however unfortunate they are, however cruel, brave, silly or dull, we are enveloped in the silence of a book, luxuriating in its unique serenity. After all, we know what is happening because we know what will happen in the end. Yet, while this peace is pleasurable in the simplest sense, it is also haunted. This is what makes it unique. In reading stories we reconcile contradictory forces.

As Sartre pointed out in *Nausea*, when we read a novel, we identify with the protagonist because we too face an imminent adventure, only, in the case of the novel, it has already occurred. It wouldn't be a novel otherwise. In reading of another's life then, our own becomes a narrative and afforded the same comfort of meaning given to a book by its necessary enclosure. Meaning is given by the end of possibility just as a mirror is afforded meaning by its dark backing. So, in one place we have both the sense of infinity and its signifying limit. A novel is therefore pleasurable only for as long as it can maintain this reconciliation, hence the lingering disappointment at reaching the final page and the relief of beginning again. Except the haunting extends beyond the book. Away from the page, never convinced by stories for long enough, we still wonder what meaning our lives may have. While many turn with relief to the invisible books of religion, science or ideology in which meaning illuminates every distant corner, writers of fiction and their publishers pursue the reconciliation with a confidence guaranteed only by unease; a commercial foreboding of tenebrous insignificance. Some writers exhibit the unease more openly by examining the space between art and its creators.

The really important things in any biography are what someone thinks and feels and not what he has done.
–Glenn Gould

In recent years, biographical fiction has become almost a distinct publishing trend. Since the 1990s, there have been several novels in which the lives of real writers and artists – that is, historical figures – are the main subject. Colm Tóibín's and David Lodge's novels about Henry James are two prominent examples. There is also JM Coetzee's *The Master of Petersburg* and *Summer in Baden-Baden* by Leonid Tsypkin, both of which feature Dostoevsky as a protagonist. Notable others include Gert Hofmann's novel about the aphorist GC Lichtenberg, Penelope Fitzgerald's story of Novalis and Joanna Scott's *Arrogance*, about the painter Egon Schiele. There are surely many others.

If this is a sign of anything, it is that the mystery of the intimacy and distance between life and art has been noticed and is being addressed, even if its expression is misunderstood and misrepresented by the gatekeepers of reconciliation. They assert that writing about writers, art about art is at best an entertaining sideshow, at worst a form of navel-gazing – albeit someone else's navel; an absorption that is also a desertion of the socialising role of art. Each argument is valid if one has a particular under-standing of the place of creation. However, if one has another, that art is, for example, a fundamental dream, an enabling illusion, then such demands only reaffirm the distress of harmony and the comforting rupture in the experience of fiction. So do these novels about artists merely seek to erase the distance between author and work, to describe the life from which it emerged and thereby explain both? Is the disenchantment of art all we have left to enjoy?

Another recent novel about a composer – Jean Echenoz's

Ravel, an exquisite, light-hearted summary of the final ten years in the life of the composer of *Boléro* – offers a negative answer to both questions. The time constraint in the novel is significant, particularly as it begins separated from time. Whereas Proust's *In Search of Lost Time* begins with Marcel in the timeless space of bed, *Ravel* opens with the regret of leaving another warm embrace.

*Leaving the bathtub is sometimes quite annoying. First of all, it's a shame to abandon the soapy lukewarm water, where stray hairs wind around bubbles among the scrubbed-off skin cells, for the chill atmosphere of a poorly heated house. Then, if one is the least bit short, and the side of that claw-footed tub the least bit high, it's always a challenge to swing a leg over the edge to feel around, with a hesitant toe, for the slippery tile floor. Caution is advised, to avoid bumping one's crotch or risking a nasty fall. The solution to this predicament would be of course to order a custom-made bathtub, but that entails expenses, perhaps even exceeding the cost of the recently installed but still inadequate central heating. Better to remain submerged up to the neck in the bath for hours, if not forever, using one's right foot to periodically manipulate the hot-water faucet, thus adjusting the thermostat to maintain a comfortable amniotic ambience.**

Yes, better to remain. Leaving the bath is not unlike returning to the world after reading a novel; if we are not uncertain on our feet, we still shudder in the cooler air. But we know that time will not relent and we have to make a journey. It's also significant that this opening does not quite specify who is in the bath. This immediately involves the reader rather than involving a separation from the subject of the novel. We are, as it were, in this bath together.

Echenoz follows Ravel as he dries himself and then delays his departure with preparatory rituals. He cleans his teeth, shaves, plucks his eyebrows, pares his fingernails, combs his hair, chooses which clothes to wear – he has an enormous wardrobe – and then goes around the house switching off appliances. The precision and swiftness of description is itself a bath-like repose. Time intervenes only when he leaves the house and "icy air suddenly buffets his backswept and still-damp white hair". One word and suddenly we realise Ravel is not young. This is a fine example of Echenoz's gift for inconspicuous concision: "white" here makes the presence of another life felt with an intensity that also passes by as a simple description.

No doubt Ravel feels the presence too though we are never told. Not being granted access to Ravel's inner life is also one of the novel's great pleasures. Glenn Gould may be correct, only not knowing what someone thinks or feels can also be experienced by the subject of the biography. Assuming what they think and feel through their actions is the important mistake. It then becomes a matter of allowing for what we or the subject himself cannot know to resonate. Echenoz does this by sketching a translucent surface. While Ravel remains "Elegantly aloof, icily polite, not particularly talkative", we realise he may also be aloof from himself, not quite there except in what he can display to the world, particularly in his music. It may be why he is so keen to dress well, to reveal himself as only covering up can do. Before a concert, he mislays some patent-leather shoes and refuses to perform until they are found. Does he know why?

By the time the novel opens, Ravel is already world-famous for his music. He has left his bath to journey to the harbour to board a transatlantic ship for a tour of the US. He is fêted and fussed over by everyone, though all he seems to be want to do is to lounge in solitude watching the landscape from an observation deck, perhaps to contemplate his next composition. When he is forced to socialise, such as at the Captain's table, Ravel entertains everyone with his tales of driving a military truck near Verdun in 1916.

One day, his vehicle broke down and he found himself on his own out in open country, where he spent a week à la Crusoe. Taking advantage of the situation, he transcribed a few songs from the local birds, which, weary of the war, had finally decided to ignore it, to no longer interrupt their trills at the slightest blast or take offense at the constant rumbling of nearby explosions.

Ravel is of course much like the birds. Weary of the worldly turmoil, he steps aside to write music. In the midst of a copyright dispute over music for a ballet, Ravel decides on a whim to write something entirely new: "it's only a ballet, no need for form strictly speaking or development, practically no need to modulate either, just some rhythm and the orchestra. The music, this time, is of no great importance. All that's left is to get on with it."

Back in Saint-Jean-de-Luz, early in the morning, here he is about to leave for the beach with Samazeuilh. Wearing a golden-yellow bathrobe over a black bathing costume with shoulder straps and coiffed in a scarlet bathing cap, Ravel lingers a moment at the piano, playing a phrase over and over on the keyboard with one finger. Don't you think this theme has something insistent about it? he asks Samazeuilh.

And this is how *Boléro*, his most famous composition, came into existence, at least here. No dramatic revelation as to what personal secret inspired this work – it was only a commission.

To those bold enough to ask him what he considers his masterpiece, he shoots back: It's Boléro, what else; unfortunately, there's no music in it.

Amusing anecdotes like this – and the novel is delightfully full of them – may give the impression that *Ravel* is a mere confection. We may assume it can now be left to monographs and official biographies to lay the heavy meat on the scales and to win serious acclaim for helping us to understand Ravel in his musical and historical context. But this would be to deny what makes reading *Ravel*, and indeed listening to Ravel's music, an uncanny experience.

After composing *Boléro*, Ravel is seriously injured in a traffic accident and retires from public life. A brain injury means he forgets how to perform simple actions such as signing his own name and, more dangerously, how to swim. He is found floating far out to sea. At a concert of his own music, Ravel turns to his neighbour: "That was nice, he says, really nice, remind me again who the composer is. One is not obliged to believe this story." Echenoz's insouciance may be offhand yet here it reverberates with the essential mystery floating this novel. It began in the bath with the absence of time and now ends with the absence of Ravel from himself and his music.

* Translated by Linda Coverdale

The Double Pressure

Reading David Shields' new book – but in what way is it a book? – is a frustrating experience. As demonstrated by the previous sentence, on almost every page of *Reality Hunger* the reader is interrupted by responses, doubts and questions. "Every artistic movement from the beginning of time", it begins, "is an attempt to figure out a way to smuggle more of what the artist thinks is reality into the work of art". Why, one asks, half-aware of the question because one is trying to get into the book, does he use "artistic movement" rather than "artist"? The answer is soon clear: he is seeking to galvanise a new artistic movement by expressing his own concern with the relation of art to reality. It has an impact on the form and content of the book, so much so that it fails to become a book itself yet, as a consequence, ends up enacting part of Shields' manifesto. What remains betrays it.

Reality Hunger's immediate resort to journalistic cliché establishes a workman-like, common-sense approach to its subject. It not so much smuggles reality as coshes writing over the head and replaces the body with a waxwork doll. And it doesn't stop. Why does he use the empty phrase "beginning of time" when its more appropriate, *realistic* alternative is the "beginning of art" – so that we immediately think of, say, the caves of Lascaux? Cave art is of course a beginning separate from any "artistic movement" or even any notion of art and surely would be Shields' ideal, yet it goes unmentioned. The absence of art known to those cave people and then obliterated by the paintings is like the absence of time in that it erases the conditions in which one is able to talk about it, thereby implicating any reflection on art's supplementary character, the character of which is Shields' subject. Moreover, to raise the opposition of art and reality immediately raises the question of what both art and reality are in themselves. *Reality Hunger* does present ancient literary references – Homer, Thucydides, the New Testament – yet few rate more than a paragraph's attention. Entry 23 provides the following insight: "The Tale of Genji: an eleventh-century Japanese text about court life". This is on the level of Woody Allen's speed-reading of *War and Peace*.

Cave art would be a good starting point. Perhaps, however, it is a poor example because its production in the want of natural light, its exertion of ritual pressure and its generation of the intense vertigo of time, is not the kind of reality Shields hungers for. He is keen on the notion that art has "retreated ... from the representational into the abstract", which would mean emerging from the caves into the light of day, away from art. To descend back, however, and, by the flickering light of burning torches, to witness the forms on the cave walls, reveals the poverty of such an opposition. If the caves reveal that art's presence enabled humanity to discover its unique power over life and death, a fundamental question follows: in what way is a work of art distinct from human reality? If the work of art is itself part of the world, an addition inseparable from phenomena, then the idea of smuggling is not only bafflingly superfluous but counterproductive. Shields' smuggled art would then be reality disguised as reality. Without this illusion, the task left for the artist/viewer is to have a relation to art that is distinct from his or her relation to reality. It would not be enough to claim membership of an "artistic movement".

Starting again

As this review has not got beyond the opening sentences of the book without asking crippling, unanswered questions, it will struggle to move any further unless it starts again. So, let's go back to the book and Shields' explicit statement of purpose:

My intent is to write an ars poetica for a burgeoning group of inter-

related ... artists in a multitude of forms and media ... who are
breaking larger and larger chunks of 'reality' into their work.

Reality Hunger comprises a collage of quotations and Shields'
own work is designed to enact the manifesto because very large
chunks of borrowed text constitute the bulk of the 208 pages.
While this is promising in theory, the raft of "artists" cited on
page four as examples doesn't encourage one to herald Shields as
the Andre Breton or Wyndham Lewis of the 21st Century. It
includes American radio shows, cable TV comedies, and films of
such avant-garde credentials as *Open Water* and *Borat*. Literature
is slipped in toward the end when Billy Collins' poetry is
admired ahead of the "frequently hieroglyphic obscurantism of
his colleagues" – though they're not frequent enough to warrant
a name check let alone an example from the poetry – and, finally,
a prose work: Dave Eggers' playful memoir. In fairness, this
wince-inducing list of parochial and commercial ephemera may
not be all Shields' own work. We have the quotations to consider.
However, this is clear only after one has read the book or been
alerted by other readers. If one reads from cover to cover without
looking ahead, then each of the 617 numbered entries reads as a
statement, an assertion, as part of a developing narrative forever
delayed or contradicted, rather than a mere collection. One is
bound to react with enthusiasm, impatience or hair-pulling
frustration as one agrees or disagrees along the way. After the
book has been read, the by-now-bald reader comes to this
author's note:

This book contains hundreds of quotations that go unacknowledged
in the body of the text. I'm trying to regain a freedom that writers
from Montaigne to Burroughs took for granted and that we have
lost. Your uncertainty about whose words you've just read is not a
bug but a feature.

It turns out the note to page 4 cites an article by a Soyon Im in *Seattle Weekly*, but it still doesn't explain who made the uninspiring selection within the note itself. That said, it does explain the regular bouts of déjà vu. Entry 49 is a paragraph from Philip Roth's famous essay about the writer's embarrassment in the face of American newspaper reality. *Reality Hunger* shares in that reality in that it defies approach, at least in terms of critical summary. One can read half a dozen entries and have a dozen responses, all clamouring to be expressed because Shields refuses to explain or explore the implications of each entry. Entry 48, for example, cites Cynthia Ozick talking about William Gaddis's *The Recognitions*: "it was already too late" she says "to be ambitious in that way with a vast modernist novel". Shields comments "It's difficult to overemphasize how misguided her heroic (antiheroic) way of thinking is". Why is it misguided? Shields has already lamented a creative freedom that "we have lost" so we can presume he thinks ambition is never too late, yet rather than wring one's hands, wouldn't it be instructive to investigate why we have lost that freedom? Elsewhere Shields declares that "Art evolves", so might Ozick's comment be sensitive toward that evolution? We'll never find out reading this book. Overemphasis would do ahead of self-contradictory sound bites. Shields' apparent support for vast novels is also contradicted by other quotations:

> The Corrections: *I'd say: I couldn't read that book if my life depended on it. It might be a "good" novel or it might be a "bad" novel, but something has happened to my imagination, which can no longer yield to the earnest embrace of novelistic form.*

So he (rather than we) has lost something; something has happened to him. What reality is this? The reader hungers for it. (To confuse matters the notes link this entry to an interview with Richard Serra in which, as far as I can tell, Franzen's novel is nowhere mentioned.)

Energy of delusion

Perhaps we need to start again, again. Shields' key components for his new artistic movement include: "deliberate unartiness: 'raw' material, seemingly unprocessed, unfiltered, uncensored, and unprofessional". He wants to encourage: "Randomness, openness to accident and serendipity, spontaneity; artistic risk, emotional urgency and intensity, reader/viewer participation; an overly literal tone". He doesn't provide immediate examples except to add, in parentheses: "(What, in the last half century, has been more influential than Abraham Zapruder's Super-8 film of the Kennedy assassination?)". Influential to whom and to what artistic end? American culture perhaps, yet there is nothing deliberate about this film, nothing "seeming" to efface: it is definitively unprocessed, unfiltered, uncensored and unprofessional. The assassination itself could be said to be as equally influential in the same parochial sense. In itself, skull bone and brain matter flying across the boot of a car has nothing to do with art unless we recognise that reality is borne on human agency: that is, the influential aspect of the assassination is not its reality – which perhaps only JFK could be said to have experienced (though the meaning of experience would then be under question) – but its distance from our grasp. Inherent, necessary distance would explain the looping repetition of the Zapruder film across half a century. In brutal contrast, the innumerable angles in the coverage of the 9/11 attacks still do not lessen our distance or tighten our grasp: the distance remains as fascinating as ever. Something happens to our imagination as we witness everything from art to atrocity: we recognise distance. No amount of "raw" material makes any difference except, perhaps, to delude the consumer of the latest angle of attack. The critic, of course, should be the first not succumb to such delusion. Shields, however, is drawn to it like a moth to the film of a flame. Entry 69, attributed to Saul Steinberg, is the dynamic beating the wrongheaded heart of his manifesto:

> *There are two sorts of artist, one not being in the least superior to the other. One responds to the history of his art so far; the other responds to life itself.*

Two sorts and, by now, we know which we're meant to favour. Yet both respond only to distance. To ask what life is in itself is already to open an abyss. It's not a question that troubles this book because it knows that life is what is "actually occurring in the world" independent of the viewer. To achieve all Shields' favoured elements then one must discharge agency, which is strictly impossible for the artist; appearing to discharge agency is agency by stealth. So what Shields wants instead is for the artist to efface agency, to risk nothing but being found out. His undue focus on the James Frey controversy – innumerable entries are dedicated to this singularly American phenomenon – reiterates the inconvenience of the question: "I'm disappointed not that Frey is a liar but that he isn't a better one".

Going through literature

The secret or mystery of art that *Reality Hunger* cannot resolve without denial goes back to its keenness on the false opposition of representation and abstraction. One of its most curious blind spots is a persistent misrepresentation of modernist fiction – that "retreat … from the representational into the abstract" again. Entry 14, apparently quoting a conversation with Jonathan Raban, claims Henry James is responsible "for much of the modernist purifying of the novel's mongrel tradition".

I see writers like Naipaul and Sebald making a necessary post-

modernist return to the roots of the novel as an essentially Creole form, in which 'non-fiction' material is ordered, shaped, and imagined as 'fiction'. Books like these restore the novelty of the novel, with its ambiguous straddling of verifiable and imaginary facts, and restore the sense of readerly danger that one enjoys reading Moll Flanders *or* Clarissa *or* Tom Jones *or* Vanity Fair – *that tightrope walk along the margin between the newspaper report and the poetic vision.*

Much of *Reality Hunger*'s unwittingly conservative nostalgia is condensed in the whiny repetition of "return" and "restore"; one can sense the regret and the wish to get back to a golden age when readers and writers flourished in a literary Garden of Eden untroubled by the beasts of Lascaux. Yet how do the four exemplars of literary modernism, which describe all aspects of life and more, and which contain all kinds of risk – Joyce's *Ulysses*, Proust's *In Search of Lost Time*, Kafka's *The Trial* and, more recently, Beckett's *Molloy*, *Malone Dies* and *The Unnamable* – present as acts of purification? Perhaps it is precisely the *and more* in this sentence that is objectionable; each approaches areas we can't quite call reality. It is particularly revealing that the conversation with Raban identifies a "newspaper report" as an ideal for a writer of fiction. Shields is the son of journalists and it informs his literary values and assumptions. Entry 66 quotes Rachel Donadio: "Today the most compelling energies seem directed at nonfiction". A statement one would *never* expect from a journalist at the *New York Times*.

The purest form in modern literature is surely that of genre, which by definition pre-packages reality. By no coincidence, the feature fiction review in the January 21st 2010 edition of the TLS is a long article arguing that "the crime novel and the thriller have a more direct power than their literary cousin to depict a society's ills". It's no coincidence because every month similar articles appear in the popular press, such is the sublimated urge to mitigate or disguise the purity of craft. But of course criticising genre is a literary faux pas of the first order. Best to stick to blaming the most radical artists who have no "artistic movement" to protect them.

What's at stake?

It is not that purity of form and control over material isn't a strong feature in most of the great modernist novels: despite Marcel's fascination with train timetables as he imagines returning to his love interest in Balbec on the Normandy coast, Proust does not – as one expects Shields would hope – reprint the actual published documents. Instead, *In Search of Lost Time* introduces reality by arranging for its absence to be long forgotten and then experienced again in habit-shattering fashion. This is why the novel is over three thousand pages long. The novel moves through literature rather than evades or effaces it. It moves toward what habit enables us to forget in order to know it again as if for the first time. In many ways Proust embodies everything Shields calls for, only attention to randomness, accident and serendipity are the gears turning at the centre of Proust's work.

In mitigation, there are several entries mentioning Proust without misunderstanding and Shields does seem to appreciate the value of the novel, but Entry 182, attributed to Bonnie Rough, is an abrupt reversal:

In Proust, for example, who is to me at base an essayist, nothing ever happens. The only obstacles are that someone might rebuff someone else or someone might get sick or grow old, and even these are usually hypothetical obstacles. People get educations, travel, buy paintings, go on diplomatic missions, but the events are for the most part meetings between various people (or simply sightings of one person by another, sometimes thanks to a stroll or a ride in a carriage) and what these meetings bring out, on a psychological level, about life itself. How can a work be considered fiction when there's no plot? Philosophy, perhaps, or criticism, but not fiction.

As this is clearly part of a larger piece we should not be hasty in responding with astonishment to the assumptions packed into this passage. But is her final question meant to lead to an explanation of why *In Search of Lost Time* is fiction and claim that here she is playing devil's advocate? Given that she believes Proust is "at base an essayist", we can assume the question is rhetorical. Perhaps Shields includes it as a corrective to the others in line with the lack of filtering demanded by his manifesto, or perhaps because throughout *Reality Hunger* he celebrates the "lyric essayist" and to believe Proust is "at base an essayist" is not to be blind to the lesson of his novel. Yet Proust's writing career reveals the necessity of the novel's status as fiction. It is more than a label. Had it not been fiction, his first novel *Jean Santeuil* – a conventional bildungsroman – would have been published, *In Search of Lost Time* left unwritten and Proust consigned to comparative literary oblivion. So what is at stake when the question of fiction is raised: is it merely a definition of genre?

The double pressure

Shields has a surprising and relevant epigraph for his book: "All great works of literature either dissolve a genre or invent one". It is taken from the first page of Walter Benjamin's essay "The Image of Proust". Surprising because Benjamin is otherwise glaringly absent from *Reality Hunger* – his essay "The Storyteller" is not quoted at all; a perplexing omission – and relevant because this is also true of Proust's great work. But only half-true. Alone it exposes the innocence of Entry 182's reading. Except, the sentence in which this line appears is truncated and leaves out "It has been rightly said" at the beginning and "that they are, in other words, special cases" at the end. Great works as special cases is an important idea. Each great modern work is a special case because it has been made from bottom up, not bolted onto the frame of genre. There is nothing "at base" from which to build except experience itself: experience of reality and experience of its absence. It is made, that is, from inside the distance between imagination and reality. What then is at stake in specifying that *In Search of Lost Time* is fiction is awareness that his novel attends closely to the pressure exerted on the space of writing; the double pressure of imagination and reality. Without opposing and supporting pressure, neither reality nor the imagination can have any vital presence in works of art: one is death, the other deathless. By writing imaginative fiction, Proust becomes able to open up his work to what haunts it, the outside, the unknown, perhaps "reality". In order to do this, he did not need to include chunks of undigested material into the work.

Perhaps *Reality Hunger* can be said to do the same in its own way given that it includes so much that is not David Shields' own work and so much that contradicts so much else within the work. Yet the restricted content – no inclusion of literary works of philosophy, criticism and genre-less fiction consisting of short entries or fragments by writers such as (off the top of my head) Kierkegaard, Cioran, Blanchot, Pound, David Markson, Thomas Bernhard, Jean Paulhan and Félix Fénéon – and the frequent vapidity of the chosen content suggests stunted ambition. Of course, this is a product of its inbuilt unwillingness to develop insights with defensive reason, and there is logic and merit in such a refusal: it lets the work speak for itself. However, such a lack is experienced by the reader as a discharge of authorial responsibility. That is, responsibility toward the destiny of every book: its inevitable submission to unity. This is finally what, for all its local entertainments, betrays *Reality Hunger*. No matter how many chunks of reality David Shields or anyone includes in a work, it becomes something else: literature takes possession of it.

How then is reality in art possible? Recall Joseph K. in *The Trial* seeking the commanding reality of the law in order to refute the charge that led to his arrest at the beginning of the book. The law could be said to be reality, the ultimate judgment passed on each mortal individual which, with the utmost seriousness and utmost absurdity, K. pursues to its origin. His quest ends with a terrible, half-noticed execution. Yes, absolute law is reality and perhaps *The Trial*, in its purity as pure fiction, retreats from the fatal, dominant X of reality. Kafka was not unaware of it fate. On January 19th 1922, he turned to his diaries, that space in which we try to give witness and response to our real lives, and continued the fiction:

> *What meaning have yesterday's conclusions today? They have the same meaning as yesterday's, are true, except the blood is oozing away in the chinks between the great stones of the law.*

Stepping into the Poem

The correspondence between Ingeborg Bachmann and Paul Celan translated by Wieland Hoban and presented in Seagull Books' smart, square edition is not the collection I had expected. There is little discussion of poetry and only brief references to works in progress or responses to published work. Unlike the first volume of Beckett's letters, there is little to make the reader pause to copy down lines or phrases. To mine it for quotations and anecdotes would probably discolour the character of reading the correspondence as it follows the arc of a lifelong friendship. Reading across over twenty years of haphazard communication is to share in what we may call an infinite holding-between of two lovers now separated forever. It is an uncomfortable sharing, even more than Kafka's distressed letters to Felice. For the most part, however, the letters are reticent approaches by two people who maintain long-term relationships with other partners and who express no wish to end them, yet who also remember the brief flaring of an affair as if it expressed the essence of something purer, perhaps of poetry itself. Much is discussed in the letters in a context that can only be guessed at, so impressions like mine are inevitable and, to their credit, the editors do not attempt to report the background any more than evidence allows.

Despite the lack of poetry, the first letter is in fact an original poem: Celan sends *In Ägypten* and dedicates it to Ingeborg on her twenty-second birthday. Andrea Stoll describes it as "a love poem that announces nine commandments of love and writing after the Shoah". Later Celan says: "Every time I read it, I see you step into the poem: you are the reason for living, not least because you are, and will remain, the justification for my speaking".

Perhaps we can appreciate from these words the real, physical grip of Celan's terrible bind and therefore why poetry was so important to him. Put crudely then, Bachmann, the daughter of a

110

Nazi Party member, a Heidegger scholar and German poet, represented both Celan's love for the German language and hope for its homeland's atonement. In his letters, the progress of his writing stands for the health reports one might read anywhere else. He is often afflicted by silence due to private or professional hurts. The cumulative effects of both erupt late in the correspondence and turn the book into something much more harrowing than the reader had come to expect from what had preceded it. This is what has become known as The Goll Affair, a scandal in which the widow of the poet Yvan Goll accused Celan, who had translated her husband's work into German, of plagiarism. Benjamin Ivry explains how "some postwar German literary critics took up cudgels on [Goll's] behalf, scorning Celan in reviews that reeked of subtle and not-so-subtle antisemitism, and alluding to his supposed greed for money or to his lack of originality".

Celan understood this as his personal Dreyfus Affair because he was as innocent of plagiarism as Dreyfus was of treason. It was later shown the widow had forged manuscripts to suggest direct thefts from Goll's work had gone into Celan's first collection *The Sand from the Urns*. While Bachmann moved to defend him, Celan was nonetheless deranged by the persistent accusations. It is unclear whether anyone could have counselled Celan before he too served a sentence at Devil's Island; whatever had been said by Goll and her supporters did the intended damage. Celan sees this as evidence of something perhaps worse than Nazis refusing to apologise. In 1959, he tells Bachmann:

I also think to myself, especially now, having garnered experiences with such patented anti-Nazis as [Heinrich] Böll or [Alfred] Andersch, that someone who chokes on his errors, who does not pretend he never did any wrong, who does not conceal the guilt that clings to him, is better than someone who has settled so very comfortably and profitably into the persona of a man with a spotless

> *past, so comfortably that he can now – only 'privately', of course, not in public, for that, as we all know, is harmful to one's prestige – afford to indulge in the most shameful behaviour. In other words: I can tell myself that Heidegger has perhaps realized some of his errors; but I see how much vileness there is in someone like Andersch or Böll.*

The volume ends with Gisèle Lestrange's warm letters to Bachmann following her husband's suicide aged fifty. Bachmann herself would die in tragic circumstances three years later. Thinking over my experience of reading these letters armed with such knowledge, I recognised the dangers of writing in a literary world policed by gatekeepers like Clive James who unjustly criticise Celan for "hermeticism". I also wondered if this is perhaps necessary for writing such as Celan's to make its way into our lives. Let me explain: think of Georg Bendemann writing to his Russian friend in Kafka's *The Judgement* and how this unhurried, Sunday-morning politeness is disturbed when his father questions Georg's habitual dissembling to his innocent friend and denounces his betrayal of his mother's memory by getting engaged to that "nasty creature" who lifted her skirts. Georg's only means to continue, he realises, is to throw himself from the nearest bridge and to drown in the river. By continuing, he lives on in the real world, but it is a continuation borne on the pain of terrible transformation. And this is, of course, as I now realise, Paul Celan's story.

Rainbow Shatterings

The title *What Ever Happened to Modernism?* is a question asked by a professor of English and answered by a practising novelist. Apart from Milan Kundera, no other living writer has engaged with modern fiction with such depth of learning and lightness of touch. I have been reading Gabriel Josipovici's fiction and non-fiction for over twenty years but little prepared me for the sustained focus and force of this remarkable book. Until now his literary critical works have been collections of essays, even his book on the Bible, *The Book of God*, is a series of discrete essays. Given this back catalogue which includes the lectures given at UCL and Oxford University, it's predictable that the new book has been characterised by some as an academic treatise rather than an accessible essay in the classic sense. The deception needs to be countered not only because it is wrong but because it also confirms Josipovici's verdict on English literary culture as "narrow, provincial and smug". This can be demonstrated by bitter and dishonest reactions, as well as some more respectful if condescending assessments.

However, there are rational reasons for resistance to the book's argument, even if they are expressed from the corner of the mouth. For Josipovici, Modernism reanimates the doubts and confusions about the authority of art that have been with us since the Enlightenment; doubts and confusion that he shows are present as dynamic forces in the great, paradigmatic works of Western literature and are essential to the reasons why they became great. For cultural gatekeepers, accommodating doubt and confusion rather than quelling their disruptive presence is anachronistic, the stuff of romantic legend or, worse, against the spirited positivity of modern culture. Peter Aspden says Modernism has "found its dancing shoes and lightened up". Surely literature is here to bring clarity and sense, to reveal the world in all its variety, intensity and, above all, reality?

Perhaps. But this is an understanding from a watchtower, from outside of writing. When a novel, good or bad, is complete, it creates and embodies unity – even if it relies for this impression on stories of the ultimate rupture of terror, violence and death – and gratitude is expressed by the reader. For someone then to come along to point out that it is an artificial and constructed unity, we are bound to be irritated; yes, we know it is only a novel. Except, however much common sense there is in this statement, it has always to elide the uncanny experience of reading; the sense that it is only within the ideal space of the greatest novels that we feel most engaged with the world, where the doubts and confusions of our lives abate and we become able, for the time of reading at least, to maintain understanding and equilibrium. This is our gratitude but also our guilty secret. We know it is only a novel and the world has thereby been distorted and we need more art to maintain the illusion. Bad faith kindles doublethink.

The problem for the critic is that this essential experience of reading cannot be easily discussed outside the special conditions bestowed by reading itself, removed from the pressures of commerce and fashion. The concealed problem explains why literary debate is dominated by personalities and political issues rather than an engagement with books themselves and why, as a consequence, attention turns to forms more congenial to disposable debate. Perhaps only a practising artist willing to analyse what's hidden can elaborate on the enduring presence of the forces of doubt and confusion. Josipovici's book certainly suggests that this is the case and that only by recognising and embracing their urgency for each one of us can literary fiction renew itself both on the public and personal level.

So, the book's purblind reception in England is really a symptom of an institutionalised instinct to repress and deny doubt and confusion. This is why in what follows I intend to address occasional misrepresentations of the book. Anyone who has read *What Ever Happened to Modernism?* cannot but be amazed at how some reviewers have deceived their readers in summarising the book as an attack on contemporary English novelists in favour of difficult, joyless avant-garde texts, while failing to mention the central theme of the book: the disenchantment of the world. For this reason, as best I can I shall summarise Josipovici's definition of Modernism before ending with a description of the quality or qualities of the art it seeks to encourage.

The disenchantment of the world

The phrase from Max Weber out of Schiller can lead a rough headline summary of Josipovici's genealogy of Modernism:

1. The disenchantment of the world
2. The inward debate of authority
3. The elimination of choice
4. The imitation of an action

The first point is perhaps the most difficult to discuss because the state of disenchantment excludes the possibility of knowing what enchantment is exactly. Instead we have to turn to familiar historical terms:

> *Weber argued that the Reformation was part of a historical process, 'the disenchantment of the world', whereby the sacramental religion of the Middle Ages was transformed into a transcendental and intellectualised religion, which led to the removal of the numinous from everyday life.*

What was lost in this process is, for Josipovici, the elephant in the living room of modernity. "Weber's argument is neutral", he adds, "but the assumption is that not only was this great historical shift inevitable, it was, since it ushered in the Enlightenment and helped to banish superstition, what the authors of *1066 and All That* would have called A Good Thing". For Josipovici, unlike his enlightened critics, it is not necessarily A Good Thing.

The concern to acknowledge what has been lost since the Enlightenment has long been present in Josipovici's non-fiction. *On Trust* from 1999 provides, in the opening scene of Shakespeare's *Richard II*, a literary example of Weber's disenchantment. When Richard interrupts the ritual duel between Harry of Hereford and Thomas Mowbray, he is interrupting the public spectacle which "demonstrated to a non-literate society through the forms of ceremony how things really stood, and it did so in a highly dramatic way, so as to imprint it on the memory of the community". What is overwritten here is the community ordered by ritual replaced by secular hierarchy. But, as he shows elsewhere, there is something more fundamental going on than a disintegration of divine right. In *The Mirror of Criticism* (1983), Josipovici is drawn to the art critic Meyer Schapiro's observations on a mousetrap in the Mérode Altarpiece:

> In the Middle Ages the notion that objects in the physical world were an allegory of the spiritual did not necessarily entail the representation of these objects as the signs of hidden truths. 'The mousetrap, [says Schapiro] like other household objects, had first to be interesting as part of the extended visible world, before its theological significance could justify its presence in a religious picture.' However, even as a piece of still-life, the mousetrap is more than an object in a home: 'it takes its place beside the towel and the basin of water as an instrument of cleanliness or wholeness [...]'. What Schapiro is doing here is to open our minds to the possibility that the alternatives are never simply either that objects are symbolic or that they are not: the very way the painter has brought them

together makes objects in a naturalistic painting inevitably symbolic.

This is what Weber means by the numinous: an interplay of physical and metaphysical that eliminates polarity. Transcendental and intellectualised religion polarised art and community with the consequences of a loss of heaven's guide and thereby the guarantee of a work's authority.

How and why this happened is a question for other books. Nor does Josipovici claim this is his history: as well as Weber, he points to the examples of established European thinkers such as Blumenberg, Gadamer and Erich Heller who have discussed the process and its consequences. In the main, however, *What Ever Happened to Modernism?* is a book about modern fiction. "[It] is no coincidence", he says, "that the novel emerges at the very moment when the world is growing disenchanted". The Novel dramatises the emergence of the self not under God, yet who nevertheless seeks enchantment however it is defined. The book's earliest example is Rabelais' *Gargantua & Pantagruel* but the most telling is perhaps Cervantes' *Don Quixote*. What Josipovici identifies as modern here is not only the comedic critique of the Knight's idealism but that the novel makes us aware that its critique relies on "the primal idealisation in the conception and execution of the very work in which the critique is made".

> *The profound irony of* Don Quixote *is ... that as we read about the hero's obvious delusions we believe that we are more realistic about the world than he is, less enchanted, whereas we are of course ourselves in that very moment caught in Cervantes' web and enchanted by his tale.*

The novel's overt self-reflexive awareness of its status as an invention "dramatises the way we as readers collude in this game because we want, for the duration of our reading, to be part of a realised world, a world full of meaning and adventure, an enchanted world". This is both very clear and unsettling. As soon as we believe we're on firm ground, amused at the follies of others, we find that instead we were engaged in the biggest folly of all. English critics' inability to follow Cervantes' looping paths into such uncertainty leads them to celebrate the novel in their own humanistic image. They can see the numinless utility of towels, basins and mousetraps but not what has been lost. It leads Philip Hensher to bluster that "it's absurdly naive of Josipovici to think that [Dickens'] Bleak House could have been written without a constant self-questioning". Josipovici's point, which Hensher confidently ignores, is that doubt and self-questioning are present in Cervantes as part of the narration just as they are conspicuously absent in Dickens. Hensher demonstrates the blind-spot in English fiction (with Sterne as its proving exception) and why, in turn, Josipovici defines modernism as "the coming into awareness by art of its precarious status and responsibilities". This is more or less where the inward debate of the authority of art begins.

The inward debate of authority

For all its picaresque comedy, Don Quixote is also "an exploration of the nature of novels and their ontological status". Of course, one might easily say it is an exploration because of the comedy. Laughter often relies on paradox just as melancholy relies on its absence. The latter would explain the melancholy that Proust said he experienced whilst reading a classic French story in the simple past tense, something Barthes comments on also:

> *Even engaged in the most sober realism, [the simple past tense] reassures, because, thanks to it, the verb expresses an act which is*

118

closed, definite, substantive. The story [récit] has a name, it escapes the terror of a speech without limit. Reality grows thinner and becomes familiar.

The elimination of the work's responsibility to the reality of its subject leads to "a past without density, freed of the trembling of existence". These stories, recognisable as a staple of mainstream English fiction, have nothing at stake except the mastery or otherwise of the novelist over his or her material; a mastery that is enough to convince many that what they're reading is great art. Yet, if this isn't enough, how can an artist inject the trembling of existence into art? Well, as Cervantes has demonstrated already, a very modern way is to place that question at the heart of the work itself. Josipovici uses Wordsworth's early poetry and Caspar David Friedrich's landscape paintings as further examples of where the question was raised. Both poet and painter are closely associated with the experience of nature and both can easily be categorised as comforts for aesthetes. What makes them modern and takes the story of Modernism forward is that both question the validity of turning an experience into art. They knew that the experience of nature is sublime because it overwhelms and transcends the individual consciousness, so, if one has the ability to write and to paint in response, to celebrate, to express awe, then that sublimity is thereby obscured and perhaps even neglected. How can a work of art claim authority when only its absence could do justice to what has been glimpsed while wandering lonely as a cloud? We can go further and apply the questions of art to the individual. It seems only self-annihilation can express fully what has been sensed: death is present yet beyond comprehension and direct representation. Josipovici shows how Friedrich and Wordsworth place the question of experience and the representation of nature at the centre of the work.

Friedrich's distinctive human figure within a vast landscape stands for the viewer viewing, the painter painting and thereby the limits of our vision, and Wordsworth describes the dialectical process of a vision of the moon and clouds during a late-night walk. The contrast again enables the experience to be sensed in its obscurity and distance rather than as merely a sentimental gesture toward the unknown. And again, as in *Don Quixote*, the self-consciousness and reflexivity usually associated with the insouciance of postmodernism appear here in more subtle, troubled forms. "Friedrich and Wordsworth", Josipovici says in a memorable sentence, "are not so much visionaries as explorers of what it means to see and what it means to paint or write".

By presenting diverse figures such as Rabelais and Cervantes, and Romantics like Wordsworth and Friedrich, alongside the Modernists of the 20th Century, Josipovici may seem to be diluting the radical power of Modernism. One soon begins to wonder about the unique qualities of modern art and literature. Perhaps, however, this is a positive. It emphasises the *longue durée* necessary for a proper understanding of how and why, according to Virginia Woolf, human nature changed in or about December 1910, as well as to reveal the deep tradition Modernism follows and in which we still move. An understanding such as this may thus provoke a revolutionary revision of the time in literary history – the Victorian era – that has otherwise seriously occluded English perceptions of art. Still today, as Josipovici has often lamented, English novelists wish to write like Dickens as if this were the pinnacle of literary achievement; the end of literary history. Dickens' novels are frequently used as examples of the compatibility of a mass readership and literary greatness while authors such as Amanda Craig and Ian Rankin receive widespread attention and praise for promoting fiction as a neo-Dickensian form of journalism, reporting on current affairs without the constraints of fact-checkers. The only surprise is that the major fiction awards for 2009 went to a huge historical novel instead, perhaps indicating where the true feelings of English critics lie.

Despite this, Josipovici's critique of Dickens is unexpectedly mild. After comparing the wish-fulfilling coincidences that "oil the wheels of the plot" of *Oliver Twist* with the terrifying trajectory of Kleist's *Michael Kohlhaas*, in which injustice and terror are not redeemed or resolved by God or plot, he concludes: "Whether [Dickens' coincidences] are merely a small example of bad faith and a price worth paying, or whether the cost in terms of repression and falsification is simply too great, is a question each reader has to answer for himself".

The elimination of choice

Repression and falsification, however, are not so easily noticed let alone resisted by the self. Kafka notes the "heartlessness behind [Dickens'] sentimentally overflowing style" and, as Oscar Wilde said, sentimentality is "the luxury of an emotion without paying for it". Dickens stands out as the obvious antagonist to writers who were not seduced by the guarantee of popular acclaim. Rather than the masses, they sought only to exclude repression and falsification. We need art to be, as Kafka said, the axe for the frozen sea inside us. Art's failure, its successful entry into the modern era of entertainment and commerce, spread dissatisfaction among artists with higher standards. This is why we should regard Modernism not as a period in artistic history but as a molten rock lurking beneath the surface, occasionally erupting into the landscape of culture. What causes its eruption is a big question but, in short, we may see the complacency of contemporary fiction, the fuss of its competing genres and its succumbing to commercial pressures from television, cinema and the internet, as promising potential for another explosion.

Josipovici cites Kierkegaard's opposition of possibility and necessity as key to "the troubled heart and soul of 19-C man" that led to the last great eruption, the man "who has been given freedom twice over, first by God and then by the French Revolution, but who does not know what to do with it except torment himself with the sense that he is wasting his life". For artists at the turn of the 19th and 20th Centuries, one answer was to eliminate the freedom of possibility, for the art that they made to be a necessary object in the world. By taking the constraints of art to the extreme, removing artistic choice and wish-fulfilment as much as possible, something else, something unexpected may appear. (Of course the Surrealists pursued the same end by doing the opposite, which amounts to the same thing.) Josipovici's prime examples are Mallarmé whose words in "Un Coup de Dés" are (in Malcolm Bowie's description) "a gravitational centre around which possible meanings of the entire sentence gathers", and Marcel Duchamp who presented the bare implications of art's arbitrary nature by entering a readymade "Fountain" into a show. Though neither are mentioned by Josipovici, we might add Schoenberg's development of twelve-note composition and Joyce's arrangement of *Ulysses'* diversity around Homer's *Odyssey* as if to open the everyday of 20th-Century Dublin to epic enchantment. Josipovici's favourite example is Georges Perec's *Life: A User's Manual*, the classic of OuLiPo constraint discussed at length in the 1992 collection *Text & Voice*.

The danger with these examples is that they soon become monuments for lesser artists to adopt and then claim their forerunners' radicalism as an alibi. We see this most clearly with Duchamp in contemporary visual art and in compendious novels "about" a city or a nation. While Josipovici argues that the novel emerged when the world was growing disenchanted, the implication suggesting itself to the contemporary reader is that the novel is itself irredeemably generic and that its fake enchantments have embedded themselves so firmly in familiar forms that a resurgent Modernism is almost unthinkable. The perennial debate about the exclusion of Crime, SF and Romantic fiction from literary-prize shortlists, and David Shields' call for more unpolished fact in novels and less generic invention, confirms the impression. The literary novel has itself become a genre and the room for manoeuvre pitifully limited. So what new form can Modernism take?

The imitation of an action

Josipovici's answer to this conundrum is surprisingly inclusive: it takes as many forms as there are artists. As an example of Modernism's variety of forms, he chooses Wallace Stevens' character Crispin, Kafka's horse Bucephalos and Duchamp's *The Bride Stripped Bare By Her Bachelors, Even* as "sad clowns" who each found their own ways to live within the condition of loss. Each form – poem, story, sculpture – pursues a similar awareness of failure and absence without falling into despair. Bucephalos was once Alexander the Great's warhorse but now, in Kafka's story, he's seen trotting up the steps of the courthouse in his new role as an advocate. Having no king to carry, he has studied law books by lamplight and changed his career. Perhaps, the narrator says, this is the best thing we can all do in post-heroic age. While there is no "formal experiment and linguistic daring" here, it maintains a contact with an enchanted past by means of its absence. So, in addition to Rabelais and Cervantes, these three make it all the more bizarre that *The Guardian*'s Ian Jack assumes the book wishes for punishing difficulty and Max Dunbar for "some monochrome wasteland, with a Beckett-style narrative intone of disjointed words and phrases and perhaps the odd glimpse of Afganistan [sic] drone attacks flashing up on the screen".

Another facet of Kafka's *New Advocate* is its lack of psychology. We don't enter Bucephalos' mind as it comes to terms with the change but see it from a distant observer. This is perhaps an understated element of Modernism and Josipovici addresses it in perhaps the most stirring part of the book, the chapter on Greek theatre; Sophocles and Euripedes in particular. The difference between the two forms a fascinating pattern we can recognise in our own time. Josipovici again follows Kierkegaard, this time his comparison in *Either/Or* of ancient and modern tragedy:

> *The hero of Greek tragedy was not an autonomous individual. He was caught in and made by a whole web of different interpenetrating elements. These were what led to tragedy but also what absolved him from full responsibility. Terrible things might happen to him, but he could not blame himself, or, to put it in terms of Greek tragedy itself, he might be polluted but he was not guilty. In modern tragedy, on the other hand, 'the hero stands or falls entirely on his own acts'.*

One can imagine Jack or Dunbar praising a different story in which Bucephalos is ridiculed, his absurdity held up for laughs – a horse in court, whatever next?! – or with gossip, rather than the mystery alone but for a little wistful resignation. There are reasons for these knee-jerk reactions:

> *Our age is more melancholy than that of the Greeks, and so more in despair, says Kierkegaard. The reason for this is that today each person is deemed to be entirely responsible for his actions while 'the peculiarity of ancient tragedy is that the action does not issue exclusively from character, that the action does not find its sufficient explanation in subjective reflection and decision.'*

Tragic drama, then, was, as Aristotle wrote, "an imitation not of human beings but of action and life". It's significant that Josipovici quotes here the critic John Jones on the mistranslations of the plays by Romantic scholars who could only see solitary individuals in their isolation, a tragic hero like Hamlet, at the centre of the story. Like our contemporary critics, they read what isn't there because they can see only personalities and the weighing of personal responsibility. It's a habit of mind we see in conventional fiction beginning and ending in a solitary consciousness even as it is reported in the third person, and also in the persistent contempt for the *Nouveau Roman* which presents description as an experience in itself. To receive its gifts, Josipovici urges us to abandon "our mistaken search for what lies behind instead of focusing on what lies before us" and thereby learn "to live with impenetrability, to relax and savour it".

Like the essays on the Bible in Josipovici's *The Singer on the Shore*, Greek drama begins to tell us more about modern fiction than discussion of modern fiction. From the play's descriptions in the book, I noted down features of Sophoclean drama which help to show this:

- Masking as a form of revelation rather than concealment
- A single event unfolding slowly
- Each moment has the same weight
- Not a fiction or reconstruction but a re-enactment
- Death regarded not as end-point but a sea surrounding life

When Josipovici turns to Euripides we begin to see the remarkable similarities between early Greek drama and Modernism and between its later manifestations with art from the Renaissance onward. These are the notable features of Euripidean drama:

- Inwardness replaces the mask
- Complicated plotting
- An emphasis on realism
- A fascination with those on the margins of society
- Who and what we are defines us rather than what we do

However, even this straightforward chapter causes Sam Leith in

The Sunday Times to criticise Josipovici for arguing for Euripides as a "proto-modernist" when he's doing the exact opposite. As the comparison above makes clear, Euripides was the Dickens of his time, Sophocles the Beckett. Why this kind of misreading continues is an issue worth pursuing. The dominance of reason and humanism in English culture, wedded to an awed reverence for commercial success, is one obvious cause. What cannot be said is not so much passed over in silence by contemporary culture as ignored or branded out of order. In his original lecture, Josipovici wondered if this cultural narrow-mindedness (he calls it innocence) is because since 1066, unlike most European nations, England was never invaded or occupied and is intolerant of the compromises and ambiguities occupation demands. I would add that English culture has also never appreciated what Maurice Blanchot called "the absolute event" of the Nazi holocaust; in London, the positivity of the Enlightenment still reigns. To resist this dominance, we need to isolate the alternatives that *What Ever Happened to Modernism?* suggests.

Rainbow shatterings

With the two lists of features of Greek theatre in mind, we can appreciate Nietzsche's recognition of the subtle yet drastic transitions in a culture. Our experience has always been one of being torn between the two forces of 19th- and 20th-Century art. However, dissatisfaction with the conservatism of many well-known practitioners of the novel (Ian McEwan's *Saturday* being the prime exhibit) may provoke another distinct era of destructive Modernist renewal. Not that this should concern us; individual works matter more than movements. And Josipovici's contention is that exceptional, breath-giving works are present anyway; it's just a matter of recognising them.

What should be sought instead is perhaps underplayed in *What Ever Happened to Modernism?* yet does appear as one of

Josipovici's sad clowns. Marcel Duchamp was an example of an artist who raised the problem of the arbitrary nature of creation by applying the label "art" to a urinal. The question here should not be "Is it art?" but "Can art be art?". In *The Bride Stripped Bare By Her Bachelors, Even* – also known as *The Large Glass* – we see this token to melancholy end as an "ironical self-portrait as an artist in troubled times", "a delay in glass" in which multiple artists as multiple bachelors enact "the futile, mechanical masturbation" that "will never lead to any congruence with the Bride, far less to any offspring". Duchamp spent eight years working on what, Josipovici says, is an "extremely beautiful and meticulously made" object. The length of time taken to make it indicates dissatisfaction with the freedom inherent to the form; the arbitrary choice of features to be engraved, the shape and dimensions of the panels, might all be different. What difference does it make what the artist does? Something had to intervene to bring it to life, but that something never arrived. Duchamp wrote boxes of detailed notes on physics, alchemy and metaphysics to accompany the sculpture, as if these might perform the role of animator. Eventually, however, he let the work go. It's then Josipovici adds the coda:

> In transit from Philadelphia to New York ... the two glass panels, which had been laid one on top of the other and not well enough insulated from each other, ground against each other and, when the work was removed from its packaging on arrival, both panels were found to be shattered. Duchamp was immediately summoned to see if he could repair the damage, but when he looked at it he let out a whoop of joy, for the work now had a giant rainbow of cracks on the top panel mirrored by a similar pattern on the lower one. And one can see why he was so delighted. For years he had been trying to bring chance into his work, but chance brought in by the artist is never exactly chance. Now chance had led to an unexpected copulation in the back of a van and the result was a beautiful

pattern which bound the top panel to the lower, while, amazingly, leaving all the main elements of the object perfectly visible and the whole still capable of standing up. He could not have asked for more from the gods. [...] Today far more visitors see Richard Hamilton's copy (made for the great English Duchamp exhibition of 1966, since the Large Glass could never be moved again) than ever see the original in Philadelphia. They think they are seeing it all, but of course they are not. The work they see is still very beautiful – but it is, somehow, dead. In Philadelphia, with its rainbow shatterings, it lives.

This passage is central to Josipovici's manifesto. When he made the news for saying English literary culture is permeated by "petty-bourgeois uptightness", a "terror of not being in control", and a "schoolboy desire to boast and to shock" he could also be describing Marcel Duchamp but for this element of chance, the ghost of the outside haunting the solipsism of the work. Again, one can easily imagine his smug critics giggling at the news of the panel breakage, perhaps labelling it God's wrath at the pretentions of modern art, at best an unfortunate accident that has ruined a potential masterpiece. However, for the viewer alone before the object, the experience is different to its public expression.

The experience is also different for the reader of fiction. Josipovici has spoken of the unique, living quality of fiction which, he says, "has something to do with time, with how human beings respond to time, with what time does to us, the losses it brings, and the sense of possibilities unrealized, but also the Proustian sense of sudden loops in time and the way our lives are sealed off to us but suddenly, in time, open up momentarily". While he says this in a brief interview, it features throughout his critical writing. In *What Ever Happened to Modernism?* it features as the possible re-enchantment of the world through a reckoning with what disappeared in the nightmare of reason. Always he has championed fiction that breaks through layers of self-protection – the self of the work and the self of the reader – to reveal loss without nostalgia and potential without self-deceit. Proust's *In Search of Lost Time* is Josipovici's keenest example and so it is appropriate that the first essay of his first essay collection *The World and the Book* is an essay on Proust's novel: "the most subtle, tenacious and profound exploration … ever undertaken" of the relation between the writer and what is written. Still, I feel this is aspect of fiction requires more attention than *What Ever Happened to Modernism?* is prepared or able to give it, to become the overt subject of a book rather than left to the margins. But perhaps this is why Josipovici writes fiction and why we should turn to his novels and short stories for more.

A Zone of Ghosts

In order to describe a novel to someone who has not read it, you can simply summarise the story it tells, excluding by necessity perhaps hundreds of pages presenting a unique authorial voice, rich and memorable characters, exotic locations and significant pivots of plot. Yet, if asked to describe a poem, you could merely recite the words, arriving at the destination immediately; no need for any bright signposts.

In general we can accept the failings of the former method as inevitable, perhaps even desirable because keeping distance can save time and trouble. But the distinction presents itself with unexpected urgency when charged with describing Mathias Énard's novel, his fourth book and the first to be translated into English. *Zone* needs to be recited; one needs to be submerged in the disturbing pace of its narrative and disruptive power of its detail to appreciate why a summary is both easy and impossible.

Zone is an account of a train journey between Milan and Rome made by Francis Servain Mirkovic, a Croat in the pay of French intelligence, with a view to selling an archive of documents packed in a suitcase. The documents contain "names and secrets", testimonies from the terrible history of the lands surrounding the Mediterranean – the Zone of the title; events of which Mirkovic is both part and partly responsible, as, in his youth, he fought in the civil war that tore Yugoslavia apart. In those days he was immersed in youth, in the thrilling moment of war, in violence and in comradeship, yet now, a paid informer with a false identity, he is not only friendless but separated even from himself.

Trapped in the "moving cage" of a train, he plans instead "a brilliant future paid for with the dead the disappeared the secrets in this suitcase". It's a risky strategy because, as he discovers, "everything is harder once you reach man's estate, everything rings falser a little metallic like the sound of two bronze weapons clashing they make you come back to yourself without letting you get out of anything it's a fine prison". These are the first words of the novel because writing begins in memory, when consciousness is displaced. Mirkovic is thereby exposed to a world of ghosts just as a train journey exposes him to landscapes: "two thousand killed and wounded, two thousand Hapsburgians fallen in a few hours lie strewn across the river's shore, two thousand bodies that the Lombard peasants will strip of their valuables, baptismal medals, silver or enamel snuff-boxes, in the midst of the death rattles of the dying and the wounded on that night of 21 Floreal 1796 Year IV of the Revolution two thousand ghosts two thousand shades like so many shapes behind my window". Scenes from the Zone like this, and from Mirkovic's own past, cascade into view:

you don't forget much in the end, the wrinkled hands of Harmen Gerbens the Cairo Batavian, his trembling moustache, the faces of Islamists tortured in the Qanatar Prison, the photograph of the severed heads of the Tibhirine monks, the reflections on the cupolas in Jerusalem, Marianne naked facing the sea, the squeals of Andrija's pig, the bodies piled up in the gas trucks of Chełmno, Stéphanie the sorrowful in front of Hagia Sophia, Sashka with her brushes and paints in Rome, my mother at the piano in Madrid, her Bach fugue in front of an audience of Croatian and Spanish patriots, so many images linked by an uninterrupted thread that snakes like a railroad bypassing a city, the possible connections between trains in a station

Mirkovic's voice, despite tumbling headlong onto the page in a continuous sentence, is still that of writing, both light enough to carry us forward, above the fray and relieving us of the past and future, yet also heavy with all that the words signify. The archive is heavy on the soul of Mirkovic the traveller, the escapee, because he discovers history is not temporal – not all our yesterdays – but spatial. Ghosts from innumerable wars appear and disappear like disused stations, and tortured lives and gory deaths reverberate through the cage of narrative like thousands of sleepers. It is an experience of history explored most notably by WG Sebald, as highlighted by Will Self in his brilliant essay on the author, and, if pushed to further the comparison, *Zone* has the quality of a highly fevered Sebald. But its other antecedents are clearer.

The novel's title comes from Guillaume Apollinaire's 1913 poem which shares the novel's decapitations, stream-of-consciousness narrative and drunken narrator and its 24 chapters match the number in that other great story of war, the *Iliad*. *Zone* is a literary novel because the documents themselves are literature and because the names that arise in Mirkovic's memory and are discussed throughout the novel, authors as various as Ezra Pound, Malcolm Lowry, Robert Walser, Genet, Proust, Céline and William Burroughs, are his fellow travellers. Literature is heavy because of its objectivity, the manner in which human life flares and disappears in a moment. But *Zone* is literary in a less abstract sense too. Mirkovic sits opposite a Czech businessman feverishly consulting a thick paperback, what turns out to be a catalogue of timetables giving precise details of where and when every single train stops. Like the archive, it is a record that "allows you to know what we could have done, what we could do in a few minutes, in the next few hours, even more, the little Czech man's eyes light up, all eventualities are contained in this schedule, they are all here". All eventualities will end somewhere. Everything in the world exists in order to end up in a book. The rigour of the catalogue's certainty is bracing and there are those, like the Czech, who relish the cold and those, like Mirkovic, who shiver. This is dramatised at the start of the journey by the cry of *viva la muerte*, long live death, uttered by José Millán-Astray, the one-eyed Falangist general, in his famous exchange in 1936 with

Miguel Unamuno, the Catholic philosopher and "strict high priest of culture" who, in a futile speech against the coming massacre, warns the fascist that "You will succeed, but you will not convince". Mirkovic succeeded too, surviving the civil war and with the prize of an independent Croatia, but he's not convinced.

I regret I don't know why I regret, you regret so many things in life memories that sometimes return burning, guilt regrets shame that are the weight of Western civilization

The weight of the Zone's history dragging Mirkovic down is a reminder of Nietzsche's essay *On the Use and Abuse of History for Life* that argues in favour of a history that serves life rather than binds it to memory. It's why Mirkovic's reading matter may prompt the accusation that the book is nothing more than a pathological indulgence in others' misfortunes. Nietzsche resisted monumental and antiquarian forms of history, giving equal importance to forgetting in the lives of individuals, communities and cultures. Mirkovic's nonstop narrative might then be seen as an unhealthy Schadenfreude and self-pity over what his pursuance of war and profit has cost him and others. Yet while we may take this view, we too are implicated in being provoked to prefer forgetfulness over remembrance and the repetition of history this threatens. *Zone* draws our attention to the web stories weave when its stream-of-consciousness is interrupted by chapters of another book that Mirkovic has in his possession. A writer called Rafael Kahla tells the story of Intissar, a Palestinian fighter resisting the Israeli onslaught in Lebanon. Her lover Marwan has been killed in a firefight and she has to carry on, rifle in hand, lamenting his death whilst remaining true to the cause in the tradition of warriors fighting for a nation's independence. It's a sad and dignified story written with familiar punctuation and in free indirect speech; a work of fiction within a fiction reminding the reader of the longing to make something redemptive in death that overtakes both people and novels. (In fact, Intissar's story is very similar to *From A to X*, John Berger's grossly sentimental novel celebrating the stifled lives of revolutionaries on either side of a prison wall.) However, the contrast to Mirkovic's narrative and to the *Iliad* is not in its style but in its boundless pathos. Where *Zone*'s pages leap over rows of headless bodies and the *Iliad* describes violent death with swift and terrible lyricism, Intissar does not let go, wanting to retrieve Marwan from death, going so far as to risk another firefight to recover and then bathe his stiffening body.

Mirkovic's present might be said to be one in which unresting death is faced when the attenuated husks of religious or nationalist myth have been breached. Mirkovic is the exposed core, and the choice between memory and forgetting is impossible; a brilliant future depends on both. His existence in writing – sustained, incessant, brutal, resourceful to the brink of insanity – thereby becomes necessary for survival. Everything is coursed into a recital, a unique poetic ritual of mourning to reach the destination that is itself. *Zone* is indeed soaked in trauma yet, in Mathias Énard's hands and Charlotte Mandell's fluid translation, it is exhilarating, and has to be read.

Three Steps Not Beyond:
Peter Handke's Trilogy of Thresholds

Ever since the time when he lived for almost a year with the thought
that he had lost contact with language, every sentence he managed
to write, and which in addition left him feeling that it might be
possible to go on, had been an event. Every word, not spoken but
written, that led to others, filled his lungs with air and renewed his
tie with the world. A successful notation of this kind began the day
for him; after that, or at least so he thought, nothing could happen
to him until the following morning.

The opening paragraph of Peter Handke's *Nachmittag eines*
Schriftstellers, as translated by Ralph Manheim, is a marvel in a
book of marvels. Even in English, or perhaps only in English, the
sentences, not written but spoken, verify their meaning by
enacting the same experience of renewal in the reader. *The*
Afternoon of a Writer is only 85 pages long and not a great deal
occurs in terms of narrated event, yet the same can be said of the
whole. It is a clearing in a forest of books.

When the novel was published by Methuen in 1989, with the
paperback of the translation following two years later in the
superb Minerva imprint, it completed a series of three consec-
utive clearings: preceded in 1986 by *Across* and by *Repetition* in
1988. All three are long out of print and a new work by Handke
has not been issued by a British publisher since *Absence* in 1990.
Perhaps this fact explains the reason for my sudden need to
revive attention for these books and this particular moment
decades on. The more likely reason is that I want to understand
how a reticent book like *The Afternoon of a Writer* can mean so
much more than the overtly worldly and eventful novels that are
published instead.

Until now I have not written about this unofficial trilogy

because each book's significance to me at the time of reading was apparently held in suspension beyond the expressible content of the narrative. I returned to them recently only out of nostalgia and regret following the uncertain disappointment of each subsequent novel, with only *My Year in the No-man's Bay* (1998) coming close to air. This is not to say the novels since – *On a Dark Night I Left My Silent House* (2000), *Crossing the Sierra de Gredos* (2007), *Don Juan: His Own Version* (2010) (all published in the USA by Farrar, Strauss & Giroux) – have been anything other than unique, virtuosic even, except that they seem too novelistic, fixed in facility, admirable certainly, yet only in a rhetorical understanding. And if this response appears excessively personal and limited, it is only because the trilogy appears more personal and limited itself, formed of brief moments from outside a career, moments in which the promise of a magnum opus is a threat.

Across is the testament of Andreas Loser, an amateur archaeologist and translator of ancient poetry who, while estranged from both his job and his family, begins to see images in nature, beginning with a "warming emptiness" rising from an Austrian swampland plain surrounded by mountains and low-rise housing developments, which prompts him to discover what that emptiness allows:

> *Under its impulsion, everything (every object) moved into place. "Emptiness!" The word was equivalent to the invocation of the Muse at the beginning of an epic. It provoked not a shudder but lightness and joy, and presented itself as a law: As it is now, so shall it be. In terms of image, it was a shallow river crossing.*

Successive images are then witnessed of the primordial given form in a language otherwise saturated by artificial light. Against the resistance of habit, he expresses anger at the casual, careless repetition of words bleeding images of enchantment, contrasting them to Virgil's *Georgics*, the ancient poems he translates in his rooms above a supermarket. It leads to a violent encounter, but this is a novel of attention rather than of action. Loser's patient narrative leads him to the threshold of a new knowledge of reality. He wonders if one could speak of "the possibility of repetition" as opposed to its danger:

> *Shine for me, hard hazelbush. Glide hither, lithe linden tree. Rounded elderbush, prosper under the protection of the willows. Here is my other word for repetition: "rediscovery".*

Across is full of such epiphanies and one can certainly caricature the affectations of Loser's attention to nature, yet the novel and our reading of it is a means to fuse perception and imagination without yielding to the expedience of language as public utility. To do so it must risk disdain to reach that threshold.

Die Wiederholung continues such a quest and is perhaps the most beautiful and remarkable of his novels. The connection with *Across* is explicit in Manheim's translation of the title: *Repetition*. Filip Kobal travels across the border from Austria into Slovenia to find his missing brother Gregor, whom he has never met. He travels light and often sleeps in the open, living close to the landscape of the Karst region. In his rucksack he carries two books his brother owned, a notebook from agricultural college and a German-Slovene dictionary and, instead of a person, Filip discovers a language and through it a means to write about the land in which his brother lived. By acknowledging and including the experience of absence (his brother is never found), he recovers what had apparently been lost forever. *The Guardian's* reviewer called it "one of the most dignified and moving evocations I have ever read of what it means to be alive".

The inherent paradox of storytelling – a gift dependent on withdrawal – is a dynamic throughout the trilogy. Loser's journey in his encounters with images is his narrative description of the images themselves, and Kobal ends his

narrative with a song of praise to the "all-appeasing And then ..."
of storytelling, thereby confirming that there is no crossing of the
threshold if that threshold is a portal to a transcendent realm –
such as one in which his brother is brought back to physical life
– but the patient response of helplessness before evanescence. So,
both novels imply that even if storytelling is immanent to a disenchanted world, it at least offers an acute awareness of what may
have disappeared. "Long live my storytelling!" Kobal writes. "It
must go on."

It's ironic then that Handke has become the focus of disapproval from literary conservatives for whom impatient grasping
is the sole gift of writing. They share an intolerance of reading
attentively, or even fairly, with his politically conservative critics.
The Afternoon of a Writer risks reinforcing prejudices because it is
explicitly metafictional; a novel about an unnamed writer living
in an unnamed town. The caricature of metafiction as self-
regarding, self-obsessional is countered here by an obvious but
subtle moment: the use of the third person; "Ever since the time
since *he* lived". By virtue of writing, the writer is already distant
and so is his success. This gives this opening paragraph a
peculiar status. If the notation that began the writer's day is a
success only because this distance is recognised and the writer is
able to maintain awareness of the apparent disjunct of imagination and life, then the metafictional step is the first toward
genuine fiction. The alternative is "straying beyond the frontiers
of language" into a realm where the figures of the imagination
maintain their power only in a perpetual, award-winning illusion
of presence.

This latter condition forms the nightmare from which
Handke's writer suffers: that what he had written was "irrelevant
and meaningless" and, as a result, "he had been banished from
the world for all time", a nightmare shared earlier in the century
by another great poet of alienation, Franz Kafka. The task of both
writers then becomes an exploration of the withdrawal of

writing, how it may enable a fuller life without delusion. It is a task shared by Enrique Vila-Matas who has received similar critical disdain yet, as Nick Caistor writes, for him too "the quest to create literature is a metonym for the ability to live a life that has some meaning". They begin by raising the issue.

As Handke's writer soon realises, writing is, after all, a part of our lives as much as anything else – "loving, studying, participating" – only less subject to the utile words of which it consists, a contemporary no-man's land that, for us, is redeemed only by a relation to chronology. Otherwise, it disappears into a common void. Even as we seek that relation, writing escapes and opens into a timeless solitude. Writing is something whose elements, the writer reflects, "hold one another in suspense; something open and accessible to all, which cannot be worn out by use". The utility of writing is gifted to us, uselessly. The dynamic of the paradox can be witnessed every week in the popular book review pages: a perpetual motion between celebrating the "imagination run wild" of consumer escapism and solemn concern for state-of-the-nation realism. Handke's writing is a voice from elsewhere. In this light, the knee-jerk timidity and intolerance directed toward him is less a rejection of solipsism than a fear of an uncanny force. Writing remains taboo, and recognition of the direction in which it moves is an unspeakable danger only very few writers dare pursue.

Despite this, the mystery has been acknowledged in the general current of literature of "the recent rise to prominence of the biographical-novel-about-a-writer". As this review of *A Man of Parts*, David Lodge's novel about the life of HG Wells, explains, Lodge himself has attempted to identify the reasons why this subgenre has produced fine novels from, for example, JM Coetzee (Dostoevsky), Penelope Fitzgerald (Novalis) and, Lodge's own nemesis, Colm Tóibín (Henry James). They are mixed:

Some ... echo the rationale behind the New Journalism of the 1960s and 70s; they also echo David Shields's assault on the novel in Reality Hunger *(2010). The turn towards the biographical novel ... could be a symptom of a "declining faith" in "purely fictional narrative"; or "a characteristic move of postmodernism" in its assimilation of past art; or "a sign of decadence and exhaustion" in fiction; or "a positive and ingenious way of coping with the 'anxiety of influence'."*

All are certainly plausible, particularly given that each of these novels is founded upon the recovery of the author, his time and his company, and thereby accommodates and veils the secret of writing in more writing. The recent rise in such fiction would then be a repressed return of the repressed. *The Afternoon of a Writer* fits into this subgenre but also escapes because of the writer's mysterious namelessness. Here the secret is pursued even as the work frees itself from the "purely fictional" by describing the washing on his roof terrace, the cat looking for food, the smell of sweat in his study.

[He] told himself ... not to lose himself in his work the next day, but on the contrary to use it to open up his senses. Instead of taking his mind off his work, the shadow of a bird darting across the wall should accompany and clarify his writing, and so should the barking of a dog, the whining of a chain saw, the grinding of trucks shifting gears, the constant hammering, the incessant whistle blowing and shouts of command from the schoolyards and drill grounds down in the plain.

No matter what he experiences, the shadows, the movement, the noises, writing takes possession of it, and so Handke's framing of the writer's story in the third person is necessary in order to begin an exploration of the paradox. By beginning with a celebration of writing and, at the same time, questioning its success, Handke is literally making a move to leave the house much as Descartes' Cogito leaves unreflective being. What the writer finds then is perhaps more disturbing than failure.

Beneath his letterbox he finds "advertising circulars, political flyers, free samples and invitations to art galleries or so-called town meetings", a postcard from a friend and "grey envelopes all addressed in the hand of the same unknown individual". The envelopes contain fragmentary sentences referring to a private life with no apparent relevance to the writer's. He regrets having answered the first ten years previously but had done so for a strange and telling reason: "he had mistaken the stranger's handwriting for his own". He dumps the letters unread in a wastebasket and leaves the house. But it follows him through the door. Walking by a riverbank, he bumps into an old man who introduces himself as a fellow writer and, unbidden, begins to recite a poem at a loud volume. The writer endures it and moves on. He passes a road crossing at which a man sits haranguing the traffic, his words drowned by the noise. In both cases we're reminded of Kafka, his dissimulating letter writer Georg Bendemann throwing himself from a bridge in an attempt to bind himself to the continuous stream of traffic passing overhead. The poet and shouting man, however, are indifferent to the outside; their words are of desperate opposition rather than approach. A driver asks the writer for directions; then, at the roadside, he discovers an elderly woman trapped amongst branches. She can't remember her name or address but, as paramedics place her in an ambulance, she gabbles her life story "in a few fragments, unintelligible to the others".

It is as if everyone he encounters is dealing in their own way with the polarity of dream and world. The writer's initial impulse to reply to his correspondent is a possible clue that the author of the letters is a doppelgänger, the writer-as-stranger, the person our writer is in danger of becoming. Perhaps he was initially drawn to replying to the correspondent because he felt it might begin contact with the other writer, the "he" left at the desk. But he didn't need to go that far. On the other side of the threshold, he witnesses many writers straying beyond the frontiers of language, working deeper grooves of an infernal circle.

Seeking relief, the writer takes the postcard from his pocket but is unable to decipher his friend's writing. It is covered with blots, dots and wavy lines, a "mutilated cuneiform" suggesting "the writer had repeatedly and vainly assaulted the paper". So he takes refuge in a bar and drifts off into imagining a joyful summer of writing, and so once again risks becoming one of the wandering doppelgängers imposing his fantasies on the world, except here the third person intervenes to offer rescue:

> Did such imagining in a procession of forms take him out of present reality? Or did it, on the contrary, disentangle and clarify the present, form connections between isolated particulars, and set his imprint on them all, the dripping beer tap and the steady flowing water faucet behind the bar, the unknown figures in the room and the silhouettes outside?

Yet even this doubt becomes a circular daydream as he is interrupted by a drunk who sits next to him, rambling incoherently and grabbing the writer's notebook to scrawl more dots and wavy lines over the pages.

Finally, he meets a translator of his own books, an elderly ex-writer with advice for his client. He explains how he turned to translation after suffering the same nightmare that his writing was meaningless and, worse, that his magnum opus, "the Ur-text of his innermost being", was original sin. By translating, however, he feels part of the world. "Don't cross the threshold", he cries.

Even back at home the writer cannot escape the presence of those on the other side. A newscaster reading the midnight news breaks down mid-report as if despairing of anonymous language. The writer wonders what could possibly have afflicted the poor man but the answer can only be withheld. In seeking it, the writer risks the siren call of imagination, so instead he merely airs possibilities. Except, of course, in inventing the newsreader he has already succumbed to the call.

Handke's writer began with the joy of having written, of having renewed his tie with the world, only to find when he leaves his house that the world itself is populated by other solitaries with the same delusion and imposing it on the outside. Worse, we realise by necessity that all the doppelgängers are mere characters too, workroom fantasies, and the writer is the deviser devising it all for spurious company. And he too is a fantasy. That initial separation of the time of the writer and the time of narration is a sleight of hand; renewal is a fantasy like any other work of fiction, meta- or otherwise.

The illusion of separation is exposed on the penultimate page on which the writer described retreating to his bedroom and gazing at the stars through the window. "What am I?" a voice cries:

Why am I not a bard? Or a Blind Lemon Jefferson? Who will tell me that I'm not anything?

The words appear without introduction. No "he says", no quotation marks. Who has spoken and who is asking these questions? We may answer: the writer of Handke's story, or we may go further and assume: Peter Handke himself breaking through the façade. This may take us one step closer to the aim of allowing experience to accompany and clarify writing. And as if suddenly aware of this possibility, the speaking voice regains confidence or resignation.

I started out a storyteller. Carry on. Live and let live. Portray.

Transmit. Continue to work the most ephemeral of materials, my breath; be its craftsman.

Perhaps this is how literary renewal becomes possible, but this is where the story ends.

Mehr Nichts

In an essay for the *TLS*, Tim Parks wonders what kind of literature will reach the international public after "what is now an industrialized translation process". He points out that, while authors from English-speaking nations can include meticulous detail on every aspect of everyday life, to reach a global audience a writer from, say, Serbia, the Czech Republic or Holland "must come up with something impressive and unusual in terms of content and style. Five-hundred pages of Franzen-like details about popular mores in Belgrade or Warsaw would not attract a large advance." He cites the struggles of editors in various European countries to sell foreign rights for their authors. Worse, for readers less concerned with popular mores (such as the size of advances) than discovering novels exploring content and style, what Parks calls "direct, unmediated contact between a writer and reader" may not survive such translation because "the final product will be flattened and standardized".

A case study may be *Alice*, a translation by Margot Bettauer Dembo of Judith Hermann's 2009 German novel. It is published by The Clerkenwell Press, a new imprint of Profile Books, publishers of such mainstream favourites as Alan Bennett and Susan Hill. Hermann's work is very popular in Germany, so cannot be accused of pandering to the foreign image of Germany. Her 1998 volume of short stories *Sommerhaus, später* sold a quarter of a million hardback copies and, according to *The Independent*, its translation revealed "a master storyteller". When *Alice* was published in Germany, Katy Derbyshire reported that "the press are going absolutely wild" (sic) and Irish novelist Hugo Hamilton says "Alice has the breadth of an epic novel". Might local appreciation indicate a writer of her time and place, and thereby allay Parks' disquiet?

The answer is no, probably, but this has very little to do with the translation. *Alice* is an effortlessly readable sequence of five linked stories each named after a man who is dying or dead: Misha, Conrad, Richard, Malte and Raymond. The novel itself is named after the woman to whom they are related either by love or blood. In the first three chapters, Alice visits the men on their death beds. They are almost entirely silent and their deaths occur off screen, implied in the description of a hospital room being cleared or from words in a foreign language. The narrative consists of descriptions of Alice's thoughts, actions and polite interaction with the dying men's relatives and carers. There is almost no backstory or passages of nostalgic reminiscence. A certain chill pervades:

> *That morning Alice sat at Misha's bedside until noon. First on one side of the bed, then on the other. The room was utilitarian, fitted cupboards, a sink, the door to the toilet, a bare area of painted linoleum where a second bed had stood in which another patient had been lying. Some days ago the nurses had pushed him elsewhere, without giving any reasons. To some other place.*

The abrupt division of the final sentence, which we must assume is a feature of the German original, mimics the pauses in speech; an aural semi-colon adding a peculiar stress to the banality of the information it contains. It stands for Alice's experience in general.

> *Sitting on the left-hand side of the bed, she'd be next to the IV drip stand for the morphine, but leaning back against the wall unit, she could look out of the window and see the hills when she could no longer bear to look at Misha. To look at his face. Misha slept with his eyes open. The entire time. Like a plant, he had turned to the light, towards the grey but bright day.*

The technique is soon dropped, yet the motifs hinted at here continue and begin to dominate the content: light on walls, physical and psychological distance, water for drinking and swimming in, and insects. Alice describes how, in her final days with Misha, a spider built a web between their two beer bottles, which they had to destroy in order to share a drink. Later, questions about a dead relative are described as threads of spider webs broken as soon as one seeks an answer. Back in the present, Alice moves close to the hospital and notes that she can see his room from her window: "Misha's there. And we're here." In the second story, she lies in Conrad's empty bed and watches a spot of light on the wall, realising Conrad would have seen it too. In the next story, there is more light on another bedroom wall and then later, as Alice travels to Richard's Berlin home, she thinks: "In a room in that apartment in this house on this street, a man I know is dying. Everyone else is doing something else." So, rather than Franzen-like details about popular mores in Germany, we have stories drained of the usual personal histories and emotional struggles and instead filled with the distance felt between one living on and another on the brink of a grave. The reader lives with Alice on the surface of the narrated moment like the pond skater, unsure if it is over a millennia-old ocean floor or a transient puddle.

The incommensurability of death then is the dominant theme and determines the style and content. Alice avails herself of the modern world, phoning for taxis, visiting cafés and state-of-the-art hospitals, yet these are the limits of reference. There is only one reference to literature; an unnamed science-fiction novel being read by her husband. It is as if the loss of religious context has also emptied art and literature of consolation; the fate of art has followed the fate of theology. However, while characters have bland, pan-European names and live in bland, pan-European cities, as if to emphasise the universality of the incommensurable, there is only so much that can be drained from the particulars of place and time before it disappears into silence. As well as evoking obscure pathos, such motifs and metaphors inevitably invoke a tradition.

For example, in an otherwise insignificant moment, an unidentified, "multi-legged" insect drowns in Alice's latte macchiato. The readerly impulse here is to recognise a possible allusion to Kafka's Gregor Samsa, and thereby to appreciate the implications of this absurd event. We may ask: is German literature drowning in consumer culture? Instead, or in addition, we ought to admit the tension this moment generates, when literature tries to exhaust literature by means of literature. Rather than having been flattened and standardised by translation, *Alice* is flattened and standardised in its quest for an impossible loss of meaning. The plaintive death of the insect is a small manifestation. In his review of Hermann's first book of stories, Zulfikar Abbany says that the word "Nichtssagend", meaning empty or meaningless, "describes a host of young German literary lights who, aside from a smattering of cute observations, have nothing to say". The leading light of Nichtssagend, he says, is Judith Hermann. The problem for them and their admirers is that the cute observations say more than they might wish.

In Hermann's case, North American minimalist realism is the clearest influence; Alice's husband is called Raymond. Perhaps this indicates the loss of tradition in German fiction concurrent with multinational cultural homogeny; the odd translation decision suggests as much: American-English terms such as "liquor bottles" and "fat bugs" appear alongside "centre". Yet no matter how much the stories appeal to an international audience, the contradictions within Nichtssagend are distinctly European. In October 1921, Kafka wrote about the essence of Moses' wandering in the wilderness and death before he can enter the Promised Land:

It is incredible that he should see the land only when on the verge of death. This dying vision of it can only be intended to illustrate how incomplete a moment is human life, incomplete because a life like this could last forever and still be nothing but a moment.

Alice's reticence about the past and preoccupation with the distance between herself and the dying men is a fascination with this moment.

The fourth story is unique among the five in that Malte, Alice's uncle, is already long dead and Alice never knew him. He killed himself decades ago and she seeks out Frederick, Malte's lover, to learn more about his death. He gives Alice the letters he received from Malte, which, however, she does not read: "It didn't matter what was in them – it wouldn't change anything. But it would add something – one more ring around an unknowable permanent centre." The reader is both disappointed and relieved. The centre is his death and, while an addition may be welcome, it is merely a surplus of strength. This is confirmed in a metafictional moment when Frederick, who has no contact with Malte's family since his death, asks after Malte's mother, who happens to share the protagonist's name: "Alice has been dead a long time, Alice said".

On reaching the final page of *Alice*, the reader appreciates why it has to end without epiphany, unless that epiphany is its own absence, an appreciation that neither diminishes nor improves upon re-reading. Alice is dead. It is a prime example of what the blog *Life Unfurnished* calls the Emperor's New Clothes of contemporary literature – "writing in a manner to give the appearance alone of literature" – and wishes someone would cry: "But they aren't writing anything at all!"

Reading *Alice* we can only wonder if this is the failure of living writers or a necessary characteristic of literature itself to which they are admirably faithful. Perhaps the failure is that writers do not strive more determinedly for *mehr nichts*. What does it mean to acknowledge the limits of writing? After his own wandering in the wilderness, Kafka concluded, "Moses fails to enter Canaan not because his life is too short but because it is a human life".

A World Without Feeling

I don't know how people can read an emotional novel. Unless the reader is hoodwinked into thinking the novel can deliver 'real' emotion.
–Tweet by @LeeRourke

Twitter is an unreliable arena for literary debate because terms cannot be defined – what is an emotional novel? what is a real emotion? – and one can only misunderstand by assuming answers. Better to move away. Displacement is therefore precisely Twitter's value for literary debate. Lee Rourke's rightful distaste for button-pushing novels displaced me to remember a passage in Saul Bellow's *More Die of Heartbreak* in which the narrator recalls the existential troubles of his uncle Benn Crader, a botanist, an expert in arctic lichens:

> *Benn once told me that when he landed by helicopter on the slope of Mount Erebus to collect samples, he had felt that he was very near the end of the earth, the boundary of boundaries. "Of course, there's no such thing," he said, "but there's such a feeling."*

A scientist, a rationalist, Benn appears to have been hoodwinked into distress by a combination of reality and illusion, and yet, while he knows this, the feeling haunts him. What does it mean that he can't dismiss this illusion? The question might be familiar to keen readers of novels. We are surrounded by such events teasing us with unwarranted emotion, and not just in novels. Beckett's unnamable has bitter fun at the construction of emotion:

> *They love each other, marry in order to love each other better, more conveniently, he goes to the wars, he dies at the wars, she weeps, with emotion, at having loved him, at having lost him, yep, marries*

again in order to love again, more conveniently again, they love each other, you love as many times as necessary, as necessary in order to be happy, he comes back, the other comes back, from the wars, he didn't die at the wars after all, she goes to the station, to meet him, he dies in the train, of emotion, at the thought of seeing her again, having her again, she weeps, weeps again, with emotion again, at having lost him again, yep, goes back to the house, he's dead, the other is dead, the mother-in-law takes him down, he hanged himself, with emotion, at the thought of losing her, she weeps, weeps louder, at having loved him, at having lost him, there's a story for you, that was to teach me the nature of emotion, that's called emotion, what emotion can do, given favourable conditions, what love can do, well well, so that's emotion, that's love, and trains, the nature of trains ...

Love and trains, mere mechanics. Beckett had begun writing in French in part to get away from the sentimentality of English, so this – even when translated back – and the headlong nature of the prose, begins to dismantle the mawkish tendency of story-telling. And yet the rough grains of narrative remain and so too the seeds of emotion. The fatal dangers are present in the title of Bellow's novel, taken from a passage in which Benn discusses a journalist's questioning of him over his botanical research and his sense of guilt over the death of a neighbour:

... he wanted a statement about plant life and the radiation level increasing. Also dioxin and other harmful wastes. He was challenging about it. Well – I agreed it was bad. But in the end I said, 'It's terribly serious, of course, but I think more people die of heartbreak than of radiation'.

Why do we embrace such narratives in which unhappiness is amplified? In his 1920 diary, Kafka wrote a series of entries in the third person, one of which presents a diagnosis:

The fact that there is fear, grief and desolation in the world is something he understands, but even this only in so far as these are vague, general feelings, just grazing the surface. All other feelings he denies; what we call by that name is for him mere illusion, fairy-tale, reflection of our knowledge and our memory. How could it be otherwise, he thinks, since after all our feelings can never catch up with the actual events, let alone overtake them. We experience the feelings only before and after the actual event, which flits by at an elemental, incomprehensible speed; they are dream-like fictions, restricted to ourselves alone. We live in the stillness of midnight, and experience sunrise and sunset by turning towards the east and the west. *

The distance of "he" is Kafka's freezer next to Beckett's microwave and extends Rourke's statement to affirm that we experience "real" emotion only by elective agency. We turn to books in order to have emotion in the first place. Otherwise the chimes of midnight are all that we hear.

This kind of existence is deeply unsettling – reading fiction to fabricate meaning, to provide a telos for the interminable, even if we are reading a novel like *The Unnamable*. As readers, we are like Benn later in *More Die of Heartbreak* when, stuck in an apartment away from his research, this self-proclaimed "plant visionary" seeks solace by contemplating an azalea and gains emotional stability for weeks communing with its plant nature, only to discover that it is a fake, made of silk from Japan. More comedy, more distress. Yet if we believe this reveals human gullibility, we are correct only to the extent that we too are hoodwinked, because this is only a story, made of silk from Chicago. Benn Crader is an invented character who never visited Mount Erebus, never had such a feeling and never mistook a silk plant for a real one. There is no such thing.

But there is such a story, and we condemn susceptibility in the act of succumbing. Modern writers might suggest that, once cleared of sentiment, the novel has the potential to be the ground of truth, of clinical analysis, a place in which we are no longer hoodwinked; a world without feeling. Except of course this is maintained on a contradiction: storytelling is the means to this world. Beckett's comedy confirms that even the most constricted, stripped-down story is emotional. Even the most overtly heartless, realistic novel relies on a certain kind of sentiment. Swooning under the gaze of its gritty beloved, it refuses the possibility of error or unknowing. Contemporary fiction's impatience with this paradox and its refusal to confront it in form and content actually constitutes the bulk of contemporary fiction, and might thereby trace the fate of humanism. Apparently free of heavenly abstraction, humankind still struggles to ground its story and still swims in a sea without shore, and so, to save itself, clings like Pincher Martin to one remaining outcrop, repressing its fate.

Can the novel let go? The question is the starting point of Vila-Matas' *Montano's Malady* with its epigraph: *"What will we do to disappear?"* The writer's block suffered by the title character suggests it is also necessary. He must stop writing in order to write. The author of the epigraph, Maurice Blanchot, has emphasised that there is nothing negative in "not to write": "it is intensity without mastery, without sovereignty, the obsessiveness of the utterly passive". If letting-go is then obsessive passivity, how might that be written?

Passivity is what's notable in Ágota Kristóf's *The Notebook*, a novel recently celebrated by Slavoj Žižek. What's notable in his description of the story and his wish to be like the "ethical monsters" whose words we read, the twin boys who behave with "blind spontaneity and reflexive distance" promising a world "in which sentimentality [is] replaced by a cold and cruel passion", is that he doesn't mention the form the novel takes: a notebook written by the twins in the first-person plural and the present tense. It lacks both the usual ornaments of novelistic prose, has no psychological or emotional description and offers no relief or guidance from a third person. The twins state that the notebooks consist only in what they know to be true: "We must describe what we see, what we hear, what we do". This means the writing does more than "tell the story" as Žižek says, it embodies their behaviour and becomes their passion, their obsession, their passivity. The question then becomes: what do we do with this illusion?

* Translated by Malcolm Pasley

To Set the Lost Afire

In his essay "On Reading", Proust says great writers prefer old writing, the works of the ancients, and finds two reasons: firstly because they are "more easily diverted by different ideas" and secondly because they recognise "the beauty which the mind that created them was able to put into them". Both standard observations I suppose. But, as is Proust's habit, he doesn't stop there: "They receive another beauty, more affecting still, from the fact that their substance, I mean the language in which they were written, is like a mirror of life".

He compares the experience to walking through a 15th-Century hospice that has been preserved in tact into the 20th: "its well, its wash-house, the painted panels of its wooden ceiling, the tall gabled roof, pierced by dormer windows surmounted by frail finials of beaten lead". Walking here is like reading a tragedy by Racine or Saint-Simon's memoirs because they "contain all the lovely suppressed forms of a language that preserve the memory of usages or ways of feeling which no longer exist, persistent traces of the past unlike anything in the present and whose colours time alone, as it passed over them, has been able further to enhance".*

In this sense Pascal Quignard's *The Roving Shadows* is the project of a great writer. In the first few chapters there is an extract from a letter written in Latin by Descartes, a passage from Chin P'ing Mei, a novel of the Ming Dynasty, and the story of Syagrius, the last king of the Romans, as told by Gregory of Tours. But this is not a waterfall to disrupt Proust's deeper current: each chapter is a discrete approach to suppressed forms and persistent traces, the shadows of the title. "I seek only thoughts that tremble", he writes; "a flush that belongs to the interior to the soul". This does not always require many pages, as short stories and poetry attest. *The Roving Shadows* seeks its own form – Quignard insists the book, published in 2002 as *Les Ombres errantes*, is not a novel or an essay but "a sequence of beginnings of novels, stories, landscapes, autobiographical fragments" – and yet yields similar rewards.

It is still a very Proustian quest, as the word *Ombres* suggests: to experience the presence of Time Past (he capitalises the phrase throughout) not as the past but as "a ceaselessly active actuality". Our access is frustrated by the blinding light of modernity. In chapter 15, he describes Jun'ichirō Tanizaki's 1933 work *In Praise of Shadows* which laments, of all things, the loss of old Japanese toilets; places once hidden in near darkness now illuminated with "dazzling, puritanical, imperialist … neon light". He goes on to present a list of what has passed from Japanese life: peeling paint on wood, tarnished metal objects and "freer or dulled or vacillating thought that arises in the human head when it buries itself in shadow". Suddenly a culture that seems to run ahead of modernity like sanderlings happily evading a foaming wave diminishes and becomes more pathological as one recognises the millennia of tradition from which it has been wrenched. This is a Proustian moment of universal consciousness.

The structure of *The Roving Shadows* – 55 chapters in 223 pages, with the chapters themselves divided into fragments of story, aphorism, anecdote, reference and citation – plunges the reader into open water in which one can never fully breathe nor fully drown in the comforts of narrative: "Fish that still rise to the surface", he writes. "A gulp to stave off death. That gulp: reading." The hyperbole is a necessary misstep of the form, as David Shields' *Reality Hunger* confirmed, and the two books share the goal of overcoming their book misfortune: "Books that can be said to be touched by the reflection of the sun, of which they know nothing, are even more silent than purely literary ones."

Except Quignard's predates Shields by eight years and is far more aware of the contradictions of writing towards such a goal: "One can't offer a visible counterweight to the domination of light". It is thereby more literary. What this means, and as this aphorism asserts, is that *The Roving Shadows* is in constant battle with its own accomplishment. After all, by writing in commonly intelligible French to a contemporary audience about ways of feeling which no longer exist, translated and contextualised in notes at the end of the book, he has also endangered them; risking exposure of the pale beast to imperial neon light. Chris Turner's translation, which has to accept the impossibility of containing the double meaning of *ombre* – both shadow and shade – is thus a double threat.

Alerting us to the danger, chapter 39 tells the story of the imprisonment of the Abbé de Saint-Cyran, a 17th-Century Jansenist who spoke "of the vanity of books that are merely books. Of gods that are mere phantoms. Of ideas that are merely desires." Emerging from months in darkness he wrote: "after the greed for wealth, honours and worldly pleasures has been destroyed, there arise in the soul – out of those ruins – other honours, other wealth, other pleasures that are not of this visible world, but of the invisible world". Quignard comments: "It is dreadful to think that, after destroying within us the visible world, with all its trapping, as much as it can be destroyed on this earth, another invisible one is immediately born, a world more difficult to destroy than the first". Dreadful perhaps, and of course Quignard is contributing to our sensitivity to the invisible, yet it is why Proust loved ancient works and why reading was so important in his life:

> *Often, in St Luke's Gospel, when I come upon the 'colons' which punctuate it before each of the almost canticle-like passages with which it is strewn, I have heard the silence of the worshipper who has just stopped from reading out loud so as to intone the verses following, like a psalm reminding him of the older psalms in the Bible. This silence still filled the pause in the sentence which, having been split into two so as to enclose it, had preserved its*

shape; and more than once, as I was reading, it brought to me the scent of a rose which the breeze entering by the open window had spread through the upper room which the Gathering was being held and which had not evaporated in almost two thousand years.

As with Time itself, reading gives access to what habit and the violence of modernity obscures; no phantoms or mere desires here. Even if he shares Proust's vision, he does not entirely share his optimism: "To set the lost afire with loss – this, properly speaking, is what it is to read". Yet to accept on face value the statements and assertions peppering *The Roving Shadows* is to fall back into the positivism its form and content resist. The contradiction is always present; a fish rising briefly to the surface thereby reaffirming the depths.

* Translated by Chris Turner

Paul Celan's *The Meridian*

Poetry, ladies and gentlemen: an expression of infinitude, an expression of vain death and of mere Nothing.

These were the first words I read from *The Meridian*, a speech given by Paul Celan on October 22nd 1960 in the German city of Darmstadt on reception of the Georg-Büchner-Prize, as quoted by Maurice Blanchot in *The Writing of the Disaster* and translated by Ann Smock. The excess of specification is deliberate. On a provincial train in the early 1990s I read the words in the dizziness of discovery and recognition. At that time it was fragment of a speech not readily available in full – at least not available to me – found in amongst the dizzying fragments deconstituting Blanchot's own work. Blanchot understands this enigmatic juxtaposition to mean that "the final nothingness ... occupies the same plane as the expression which comes from the infinite, wherein the infinite gives itself and resounds infinitely". This would then afford poetry an extraordinary lightness as its social weight evaporates.

The same dizziness occurred with the line of René Char's that Blanchot also quotes: "The poem is the realized love of desire still desiring". Years of familiarity may have calmed the dizziness, and the sediment of acquired understanding buried recognition, but each time I read these sentences, the vertigo of those moments returns like a jolt of a train and a green glow from the countryside.

Does it have to be these words precisely? In Carcanet's *Collected Prose*, Rosmarie Waldrop translates the line as: *Poetry, ladies and gentleman: what an externalization of nothing but mortality, and in vain.* James K. Lyon, in his study of Celan's dialogue with Heidegger, translates it in passing as: *this endless speaking of nothing but mortality and gratuitousness,* John Felstiner's

Selected Poems and Prose of Paul Celan from 2000 has: "*Poetry, ladies and gentlemen–: this speaking endlessly of mere mortality and uselessness!*". In Pierre Joris' extraordinary new edition entirely dedicated to the speech – not only a new translation of the speech but of its drafts and materials, based on the German critical edition – the line is: *Poetry, ladies and gentleman: this infinity-speaking full of mortality and to no purpose!*

When I read these new translations, the experience is one of distance. It is certainly not a problem of translation; the fidelity of each is not in question – try putting *Die Dichtung, meine Damen und Herren -: diese Unendlichsprechung von lauter Sterblichkeit und Umsonst!* into Google Translate. It happens with Char's line too: both Kevin Hart and Susan Hanson translate *Le poème est l'amour réalisé du désir demeuré désir* as *The poem is the realized love of desire that has remained desire.* Nor is it a problem of amended meaning: the lines that moved me do not necessarily assert a demonstrable, objective truth that any fair translation or paraphrase can repeat with ease. So why this distance? Is it anything other than the melancholy romance of nostalgia?

The Meridian itself may offer an answer in that it addresses specific people on a specific date and in a specific place. What follows then is an attempt to summarise the speech in all recognition of the violence of such an attempt.

The counterword

Celan begins the speech by using words and metaphors from three plays by the author after whom the prize is named to situate art as the *subject* of a conversation taking place *within* works of art. For Celan it is an eternal problem that in *Danton's Death* the French Revolutionaries Camille and Danton are able to string together word upon word just as he can in this speech: "It is easy to talk about art". Such is the complacency into which culture can fall, to be welcomed by art-peddlers – those whom

Celan compares to carnival barkers. "But whenever there is talk about art", he goes on, "there is also always someone present who ... doesn't really listen". In *Danton's Death* it is Lucile, who, upon seeing her husband led to scaffold, cries "Long live the king!" thus guaranteeing her own execution. For Celan, her cry "is the counterword, it is the word that cuts the 'string' [...] It is an act of freedom. It is a step."

This, ladies and gentlemen, has no name fixed once and for all, but I believe that this is ... poetry.

He is quick to distinguish the precise, political meaning of the words from their authenticity in face of what Lyon calls "the empty rhetoric and poetizing of the revolutionaries". The point is: "Homage is being paid to the majesty of the absurd as witness for the presence of the human".

Against mere wordplay

The speech seeks such witnessing. Celan admits one can read the words "Long live the king!" in various accents, accents one may place over or under a letter: the acute of today, the grave of history, and the circumflex of literary history. The latter places an obstacle to Celan's destination in the speech so, to follow Lucile, he says: "I give it–I have no other choice–the acute."

To explain further he turns to another work of Büchner's. In *Lenz*, the title character, in the midst of a breakdown, relates a vision of two country girls which sometimes prompts him to wish to have Medusa's power to turn the vision to stone so that others might experience it. The obstacle is how Celan may be seen to be orientating himself within the folds of a movement between Idealism to Naturalism that is present in Lenz's own words. But this is no literary-historical debate. He wonders instead if with this example Büchner may be calling art into question, the art of automata, "wooden puppets", a "stepping beyond what is human" into "an uncanny realm turned toward the human" and where art seems to be at home. The art-peddlers would be the first to call us to see the tableaux of country girls. He accepts that the idea of Büchner's intention may be far-fetched. Still, Celan asks, where, against the route of automata, can poetry instead move toward this realm without losing its humanity?

His suspicion is that it can move with Lenz himself, the person who "on 20th January walked into the mountains" and who was sometimes annoyed that "he could not walk on his head". On this date and in this state of mind, the authentic human being steps into literature. For someone who walks on his head, Celan reminds us, the sky is an abyss. The narrative itself is Lenz's "Long live the king". Reading Lenz today we notice an extraordinary modernity for a novella from 1835, perhaps thus obscuring its radical expression. However, this is an example of what moves poetic art away from elegant wordplay or social realism in favour of finding the words for an authentic human moment. The poem might then be "one person's language-become-shape ... [in its] presentness and presence". We may compare this moment with Blanchot's writing of the disaster, in which the disaster is a rare and hopeful act of communication.

It should be noted what Celan need not have: January 20th was decisive for him and so many others in that it is also the date in 1942 of the Wannsee Conference.

Towards an encounter

Despite this connection with Lucile's cry, Büchner's Lenz has, Celan says, gone a step further: "His 'Long live the king' is no longer a word, it is a terrifying falling silent, it takes away his–and our–breath and words". I presume this is because the story is one of mental breakdown and the narrative describes

Lenz's walk into such a land without authorial knowingness or narrative redemption. Celan thinks this may be where the Medusa's head shrinks and the automatons break down if only for a "single short moment". And it is here Celan introduces his famous neologism, later used for a title of a collection, to describe such a moment: *Atemwende*, breathturn. Such moments still demand a certain turning away from the self toward a certain darkness. "The poem wants to head toward some other, it needs this other, it needs an opposite". In *Under the Dome*, his memoir of his friendship with Celan, Jean Daive observed how this need affected the man and his poetry: "The impenetrable–inhuman–distance between him and the Other. A distance where the remains of the world may accumulate."

In an implicit response to the impatient reaction to his own poetry headed in the UK by Clive James, Celan says turning away is a submission for the sake of such an encounter. "Attention", he says, quoting Benjamin's essay on Kafka, "is the natural prayer of the soul". For example, read Peter Szondi's remarkable essay "Eden" on Celan's transfiguring of personal experience in an untitled poem about his brief visit to Berlin in 1967. Impatience speaks only for itself.

The route of the impossible

What Celan has argued for then is simply the inclusion of the human in poetry; that is, poetry in which the poet speaks within the puppet show of art "under the angle of inclination of his Being, the angle of inclination of his creatureliness": "The attention the poem tries to pay to everything it encounters ... is a concentration that remains mindful of all our dates". Jean Daive again: "Paul always kept his watch on his wrist. He told me: the day I take off my watch I'll have decided to die."

This emphasis on "radical individuation" leads to the end of the speech and a memorably declarative line: "Enlarge art? No.

To the contrary: go with art into your innermost narrows. And set yourself free." Public art lives on, yet inside it the breathturn is its poetry "due to the attention given to thing and being" in which "we also [come] close to something open and free. And finally, close to utopia. Poetry, ladies and gentlemen: this infinity-speaking full of mortality and to no purpose!"

Perhaps I should now see this line as slightly and cheerfully sarcastic. The purpose, after all, he suggests, is a kind of homecoming. Yet included in the new edition is a draft of a letter to the president of the prize committee with another version of the same line: Celan asks:

> *Aren't words, especially in the poem, aren't they–aren't they becoming and–decaying–names? Aren't poems exactly this: the infinite-saying of mortality and nothingness that remains mindful of its finitude? (Please excuse the emphasis: it belongs to that dust that sets free and receives us and our voiceful-voiceless souls.)*

So not sarcasm but awareness of the double movement recognised by Blanchot.

Celan ends the speech by expressing a wish to avoid misreading Büchner – something that I will have to express here with regard to *The Meridian* as I have no doubt warped the speech in trying to summarise it – and by emphasising the impossibility of talking about the breathturn. However, he adds:

> *I find something that consoles me a little for having in your presence taken this impossible route, this route of the impossible. I find something–like language–immaterial, yet terrestrial, something circular that returns to itself across both poles while–cheerfully–even crossing the tropics: I find … a meridian.*

Celan's reluctance to assert, almost to the point where hesitation, qualification and doubt undo the occasion of a prize rewarding mastery, reminds me of Blanchot's observation about Celan's poems: that however hard, strident and shrill his language, it "never comes to produce a language of violence, does not strike the other, is not animated by any aggressive or destructive intention: as if the destruction of self has already taken place so that the other is preserved, or so that *a sign borne by obscurity is maintained*".*

Pierre Joris' edition of *The Meridian*, translated over seven years, reveals to us how much learning, reflection and patience went into maintaining such a permeable presence. It is a staggering document in that regard alone. In the drafts we can read innumerable versions of familiar passages from the final speech, and many more that did not find their way there. Of the latter, in writing of the encounter with the poem:

> *It is ... the second at the core and in the casing of your desperation.– It stands with you against infamy. It stands against Goebbels and Goll.–*

The first name needs no explanation but second is Claire Goll, the woman who persecuted Celan with falsified evidence of plagiarism spelled out in a German literary magazine. It was enough to trigger the mental breakdown that led eventually to his suicide. We need not consider its deletion from the final version as ironic or contradictory because *The Meridian* is not a call for the confessional but for the pursuance of the single short moment of dizziness of discovery and recognition. What is exceptional about *The Meridian* is that it continues this work of poetry, Celan's poetry, rather than being merely an adjunct to it.

* Translated by Charlotte Mandell

"I am no longer capable of writing *about*"

Soon Beckett's stipulation that only letters with a bearing on his work can be published will be repeated as often as Kafka's request to Max Brod. The difference is that we may regret Beckett's executors were not as disloyal. Whatever the riches the letters contain, we will always wonder about those bearing on the life. However, the latest volume stresses the unavoidable and indeed necessary nature of such wonder.

The cover of volume two announces letters from 1941 to 1956, yet the first letter is dated 17th January, 1945. The missing years were those of war, most of which Beckett spent living and working in a farming community deep in the "free zone" having escaped occupied Paris on the brink of arrest. From there he sent postcards to his family in Ireland, which they didn't receive and, on January 12th 1941, he sent a "pre-printed lettercard" to James Joyce. A facsimile is shown in the introduction. Joyce died the next day.

If we cannot have direct access to what Beckett experienced in that time, it remains indirectly sensible. The anxious verve of the brilliant young writer is replaced by a quieter man, still gravely lyrical yet less prone to hyperbole, much more forgiving of third parties (unless it's Alexander Trocchi) and more focused on writing, just writing. What makes the editors' task particularly daunting (that is, in persuading the executors to publish) is Beckett's reluctance to discuss the detail of his work. When he does mention what he has written, he is excessively dismissive. So, rather than offer a review of the letters, I want to focus on this apparent oddity.

It is odd because Beckett was exceptionally learned and eloquent – the letters to Georges Duthuit, the major highlight of this collection, are proof enough of both – and before the war published critical essays, including the monograph on Proust.

There is strong evidence of diverse learning in his fiction too: Molloy likes anthropology because of "its inexhaustible faculty of negation". This is no divine innocent at work. One expects at least one letter to raise local decisions made during his famous "siege in a room" while writing *Molloy, Malone Dies* and *The Unnamable*. Yet the nearest he gets is to comment on the possibility of an overall title: "this work is a complete whole only in so far as one takes for granted the impossibility of going on". So much, at least, for Beckett's alleged pessimism. What he tells the German translator Hans Naumann suggests it was nothing new: when he knew James Joyce they "seldom talked literature, he didn't like doing it, neither did I".

He has to be more open about the plays: while *Waiting for Godot* is in production, the director Roger Blin learns "the spirit of the play ... is that nothing is more grotesque than the tragic". Otherwise he avoids all requests for insight and interviews and makes only one public statement about his relation to the play: "All that I have been able to understand I have shown". Silence, then, Beckett claims, is not due to having anything to hide, but due to ignorance. "You may put me in the dismal category of those who, if they had to act in full awareness of what they were doing, would never act." Is this disingenuous? The answer, which can be neither yes nor no, may reveal the uncommon nature of Beckett's non-method.

Once he is famous Beckett receives letters from enquirers curious about the origins of his work. Hans Naumann again: "Has the work of Kafka ever played a part in your spiritual life?" He apologises for his response: "I am not trying to seem resistant to influences. I merely note that I have always been a poor reader, incurably inattentive, on the look-out for an elsewhere. And I think I can say, in no spirit of paradox, that the reading experiences which have affected me most are those that were best at sending me to that elsewhere." Reading Kafka, he says, "I felt at home – too much so". He didn't finish *The Castle* because it did not offer this elsewhere: "I remember feeling disturbed by the imperturbable aspect of his approach. I am wary of disasters that let themselves be recorded like a statement of accounts."

As this suggests, the letters bear on the work most powerfully when Beckett is looking away. And indeed he is most expressive as only Beckett can be when talking about an entirely different art form. The painting of Bram van Velde is, he tells Duthuit, "the afterbirth of the unfeasible". His art "is new because it is the first to repudiate relation in all its forms. It is not the relation with this or that order of opposite that it refuses", he says, "but the state of being in relation as such, the state of being in front of". In this we can recognise the remove in which Beckett's narration operates and in which the reader experiences it.

*I think continually of those last paintings, miracles of frenzied impotence, streaming with beauties and splendours, like a shipwreck of phosphorescences, decidedly one is a literary all one's life, with great wide ways among which everything rushes away and comes back again, and the crushed calm of the true deep.**

Beckett admits what we suspect: "bear in mind that I who hardly ever talk about myself talk about little else". He goes as far as to call Bram van Velde his soul-mate:

The further I sink down, the more I feel right beside him, feel how much, in spite of the differences, our ventures came together, in the unthought and the heartrending.

The reason for Beckett's critical silence after the war is perhaps best expressed when he ends a letter about van Velde: "I am no longer capable of writing *about*". The contradiction inherent in making such statements cannot go unnoticed: "To write is impossible but yet impossible enough". There is also a need to speak. To Thomas MacGreevy he writes of his "feeling of helplessness ...

and of speechlessness, and of restlessness also I think, before works of art".

In contrast, Beckett's references to contemporary literature are few and far between: Salinger's *Catcher in the Rye* he liked "more than anything for a long time". For me, however, the great revelation of the letters is Beckett's occasional engagement with the work of Maurice Blanchot. As early as October 1948, he acknowledges receipt of an unspecified essay sent by Duthuit, presumably for translation. Three years later Duthuit has Beckett translate passages from what is presumed to be "Sade's Reason" and "the foreword" to *Faux Pas* which just happens to contain this passage:

> *The writer finds himself in the increasingly ludicrous condition of having nothing to write, of having no means with which to write it, and of being constrained by the utter necessity of always writing it.*

Compare this to the famous passage in Beckett's *Three Dialogues* with Duthuit:

> *There is nothing to express, nothing with which to express, nothing from which to express, no power to express, no desire to express, together with the obligation to express.*

No trace of these translations remains, not even the name of the journal for which they were intended. In April 1951, he translates another essay "The 'Sacred' Speech of Hölderlin" and complains of the "very badly translated" extracts from Heidegger. That same month *Molloy* was published and was nominated for the Prix des Critiques, for which Blanchot was a judge. He supported the novel "without reservation" and tried to persuade the jury to award it the prize. Beckett's partner Suzanne wrote to Jérôme Lindon that "[to] have been defended by a man like Blanchot is the main thing for Beckett, whatever the outcome". In 1954, when Peter Suhrkamp was preparing a journal dedicated to Beckett and requested French reviews, Beckett told him that those by Maurice Nadeau and Georges Bataille were the best "but the big thing, for me, is the recent piece by Maurice Blanchot". He means "Where Now? Who Now?" published in the *NNRF* in October 1953. This is the extent of his comment, understandable given the formality of the letter, yet he doesn't mention the review to more casual correspondents let alone responds to its analysis. If such reticence is not disingenuous, we may recognise a reason in Blanchot's words:

> *What first strikes us is that here someone is not writing for the worthy purpose of producing a good book. Nor does he write in response to the noble urge we like to call inspiration; or to say the significant things he has to say; or because this is his job; or because he hopes by writing to penetrate into the unknown. Is it then so as to get it over with? [...] What is this vacuum which becomes speech in the inwardness of he whom it engulfs?***

The vacuum may then be a stuporous passivity; an elsewhere engulfing.

> *Art requires that he who practises it should be immolated to art, should become other, not another, not transformed from the human being he was into the artist with artistic duties, satisfactions and interests, but into nobody, the empty animated space where art's summons is heard.*

What must a writer do in order to inhabit this space? If we search these letters in the hope of finding Beckett's secret, we betray our admiration and need. The question assumes the mastery it must divest to discern an answer. One of the final letters in this volume is to a young writer seeking guidance and consolation from a writer he revered: "Don't lose heart", he tells Robert Pinget, "plug yourself into despair and sing it for us".

In "Oh All to End", his obituary tribute to Beckett, Blanchot remembers *Molloy*'s failure to win the Prix des Critiques, and recognises his naïveté in trying to alert members of the literary establishment to its deserve. Beckett's early novels, he says, were after all "foreign to the resources of 'literature' ". Even today one cannot imagine such a novel winning anything but the label "unreadable". Blanchot then compares Sartre's theatrical soliciting and refusal of the Nobel Prize with Beckett's distance: "he had neither to accept nor refuse a prize that was for no particular work (there is no work in Beckett) but was simply an attempt to keep within the limits of literature that voice or rumble or murmur which is always under threat of silence". The aside prompts reassuring disquiet: there is no work in Beckett. Blanchot continues by quoting from his own work *Awaiting Oblivion* "because Beckett was willing to recognize himself in that text". Does this mean Beckett corresponded with Blanchot? How else did he find out? Perhaps volumes three and four will disabuse us.

* Translated by George Craig
** Translated by Sacha Rabinovitch

Victor Halfwit: A Winter's Tale

As a child I didn't read books. At least, I have no memory of doing so. My teacher in primary school once read to us *James & the Giant Peach*, and I enjoyed that, so why didn't I rush straight to Roald Dahl's other books? I don't know. Still, it can't be true that I didn't read because, a few years ago browsing in a small shop dedicated to children's books, I found a display of Ladybird Books' Well Loved Tales, reprints of editions I recognised as part of my childhood.

The moment I saw the cover of *The Gingerbread Boy*, involuntary memory washed over me. Fascination with the image of the gingerbread boy himself is particularly distinct. I can see now that he is running away but then, as a child, it wasn't so clear. I could see only a two-dimensional figure, though of course "two-dimensional" meant nothing to me. His odd way of running must have made me wonder what he was doing exactly; it didn't look like running. And why is he smiling? I'm sure I didn't know, and this is why I found it mysterious and captivating. But the distance between the content of my innocence then and my knowledge now is almost impossible to close outside of that momentary wash.

Other features in the series have a similar if slightly dimmer aura: the size of the elves against the shoes in *The Elves and the Shoemaker*, the presence of the pea beneath the layers of blankets in *The Princess and the Pea*, the contemplative demeanor of the ape in *The Beauty and the Beast* and the disdainful remove of the black goat in *The Three Billy-Goats Gruff*. I should be clear: these are not Proustian reveries in which remote times and places merge into one, but something less grand, a fleeting sensation, a shadow of memory. I have no memory of the stories, only the images and the fascination they summoned then returns to me in placeless, wordless memory.

I am now fascinated by this fascination: what is its cause? If the gingerbread boy's oddness stands out, the others are not so clear. With adult knowing one may apply Freudian analysis to the blankets, aligning perhaps with Kafka's disgust at his parents' unmade bed, but I think the explanation is much simpler: they each manifest the part of the story that writing cannot contain. That is, the fascination created by storytelling itself, the inexplicable enchantment of the imagined world. Perhaps this is why graphic novels are so popular now, and my own puzzlement at this popularity – and inability to share in it – is due precisely to my lack of childhood reading. This is no doubt true, but I think there's a deeper reason.

In 1837, Soren Kierkegaard wrote there were two ways of telling stories to children with "a multitude of false paths in between".

*The first is the way unconsciously adopted by the nanny, and whoever can be included in that category. Here a whole fantasy world dawns for the child and the nannies are themselves deeply convinced the stories are true [...] which, however fantastic the content, can't help bestowing a beneficial calm on the child. Only when the child gets a hint of the fact that the person doesn't believe her own stories are there ill-effects – not from the content but because of the narrator's insincerity – from the lack of confidence and suspicion that gradually develops in the child. The second way is possible only for someone who with full transparency reproduces the life of childhood, knows what it demands, what is good for it, and from his higher standpoint offers the children a spiritual suste-nance that is good for them.**

I suspect with graphic novels the problem for me is that the graphical content cannot bestow a beneficial calm, and this is because, put as simply as possible, the novels that drew me into reading (and thereby bestowed calm) were adult novels aware of what they cannot contain, an awareness necessary to form and content (*In Search of Lost Time* would be the first example) which nevertheless sought that lack against nature. And the addition of graphics to a text is a shortcut, an unwitting act of insincerity. Perhaps I was too far from childhood fascination to maintain ready access to it, while those readers with an uninterrupted passage from the freedom of childhood books to reading for social integration and acceptance feel drawn to the beneficial calm afforded by the gesture of sincerity implicit in graphic novels, even if that means they are told, inevitably, by someone who knows the stories are not true.

Kierkegaard contrasts the two paths of storytelling to the false paths which "crop up by coming beyond the nanny position but not staying the whole course and stopping half-way". But how can modern writers stay the whole course if full transparency means knowingness inimical to fascination? It can't be a coincidence that the most popular children's books of recent years – JK Rowling's and Philip Pullman's – are enjoyed by many of the same readers, albeit "ironically". Postmodernists need sincerity too.

Thomas Bernhard's story for children, *Victor Halfwit: A Winter's Tale*, first published in Austria in 1966 with the subtitle "a winter's tale not just for kids", and now translated by Martin Chalmers and published by Seagull Books in an extraordinarily extravagant illustrated book, may be an example of Kierkegaard's false path. Had it been closer to a graphic novel, it may have found one of the other two.

The story itself is typical Bernhard: dark and charming, brutal and funny, moving and disturbing, all at the same time. That is, not each of these in turn but *all at the same time*. A doctor in Traich is walking to Föding through the "high forest" late one night – "this is what you have to picture" he says, the time of night is important – on his way to see a patient with "an ailment of the head", when he stumbles upon a man lying in the snow, unable to move. From his prone position he introduces himself as Victor Halfwit, a man with two wooden legs: "the locomotive tore them from my body!" Victor is delighted as, had the doctor not arrived just then, he would surely have died of the cold and, "as you know, the most horrible death occurs when one freezes to death". You can expect children to love this. The rest of the very short story is taken up with Victor's explanation of how he came to be trapped in the high forest and what the doctor does to help him.

Interrupted routines recur in Bernhard's fiction, especially interrupted walking routines: the novels *Gargoyles* and *The Cheap-Eaters* suit comparison with *Victor Halfwit*. The first features a doctor on his rounds meeting grotesque characters, the second a scientist missing one leg changing restaurants on a whim. So what difference does having illustrations make to the Bernhardian experience? One particularly effective feature is emphasis of the comedy. The doctor notices that Victor is even more delighted when he learns of his rescuer's profession. He is happier than if he had been a plumber, an electrician, a baker or a farmer. In a normal book, this information would take up two lines of text, three at most, which one would scan without pause. Here it covers ten pages! Two pages count for the doctor's comments, then there are two for each profession mentioned. On first reading, each page provokes smile upon smile as the unnecessary excess increases. Each page-turning pause is a perfectly-timed caesura. Yet while the collages representing each profession in the abstract are impressive and fun, they seem more decorative than illustrative. Had each been related directly to the story and the interaction of characters, I wonder how much more captivating they would be. A regular graphic novel reader, one for whom illustration itself is a narrative, would be a better judge. Perhaps they would be enchanted by the illustrations just as I was by the Ladybird books. However, I longed for the straightforward representation offered by the latter. In the former, nowhere is the doctor or Victor Halfwit depicted. Sometimes there was little compulsion to look at anything but the words before turning the page. Perhaps, however, if they had been depicted, each caesura would have been missed as one studied the relation of one character to the other before reading the text.

Late on, there is a two-page spread featuring eight wooden grotesques in a distinctly medieval Germanic style, one of whom I decided looks like Victor Halfwit. This emphasised to me what the rest refuses and which I missed. Perhaps though, as the doctor says: "this is what you have to picture".

* Translated by Alastair Hannay

Apostle of Impassioned Sincerity

"It is not every day one is sent a masterpiece to review", wrote Gabriel Josipovici in reviewing WG Sebald's *The Emigrants*; "(I suppose one is lucky if it happens more than once or twice in a lifetime)".

I started writing reviews in the year Josipovici's review was published (1996) and had not read a book by an author entirely new to me that I thought might be a masterpiece. As I read Karl Ove Knausgaard's *My Struggle*, I thought that this is perhaps the closest I will ever get. Such is the reach of the word *masterpiece* beyond craft and industry considerations, my instinct was not to review at all and instead to tell people in person. But I must write something. Reading *My Struggle* was often like reliving fragments of my own life – an intensity resonating in a void – and a review would mean explicating this in formal terms, and that wouldn't be right. Yet the terms available seemed too personal, something to be shared only in person. How then to continue? This is perhaps the gift of reading: others can open doors. Josipovici spends most of his Sebald review describing a twenty-page short story rather than racing through a summary of all four:

> *Like all good art, the form and the style bring into being what would otherwise have remained in darkness and silence for ever, so that a mere account of what the story was 'about' would not have begun to do it justice.*

This is good advice for any critic: stick to what you believe is important. Volume one of *My Struggle* is 471 pages long and is "about" the relatively normal, middle-class life of a Norwegian male born in 1968, so even an extended account would say very little, and while Knausgaard's ability to make the unremarkable resound means the detail is vital, it is its framing that brings the book to vivid life.

Knausgaard has explained how his difficulty in writing led to the specific form of the book: "I was looking for language ... to tell the story about my father". His father had left his family, begun a new relationship and then become an alcoholic. Before Knausgaard had "tried to write a kind of regular, realistic but fictional work about his death. Nothing worked." Then he found the solution: "Eventually I just started to write it as it was. I gave up all ambition, I didn't try to be clever or anything: I just tried to write as fast as I could." Except the book does not begin with regular memories nor, as in so many careless novels nowadays, drop the reader *in medias res* into a voice-world providing its own alibi. Instead it begins with a confrontational prologue about dead bodies in modern society. Death, he writes, is all around us and we even consume media in which violent death is the main attraction, yet its physical reality is repressed.

A town that does not keep its dead out of sight, that leaves people where they died, on highways and byways, in parks and car parks, is not a town but a hell. The fact that this hell reflects our life-experience in a more realistic and essentially truer way is of no consequence. We know this is how it is, but we do not want to face it. Hence the collective act of repression symbolised by the concealment of our dead. What exactly it is that is being repressed, however, is not so easy to say.

He contrasts the physical reality of bodies in basement mortuaries with their digital abstraction: "One is associated with concealment and gravity, earth and darkness, the other with openness and airiness, ether and light". The images of death, no matter how graphic, "have no weight, no depth, no time and no place, and nor do they have any connection to the bodies that spawned them. They are nowhere and everywhere." What is the purpose of this severe opening full of examples with which we are all familiar? Knausgaard finally includes one we're unlikely to know, a news report of a fishing boat lost off the coast of Norway in which the crew of seven drown, which he then blends seamlessly into a childhood episode because he saw news footage from a helicopter flying over the scene [with his emphasis]:

> *I stare at the surface of the sea without listening to what the reporter says,* and suddenly the outline of a face emerges. *I don't know how long it stays there, a few seconds perhaps, but long enough for it to have a huge impact on me. The moment the face disappears I go to find someone I can tell.*

The only person nearby at the time is his father, a stern man, a head teacher after all, who tells him not to give it another thought. For many, not giving it another thought is no problem, and *My Struggle* will probably leave them nonplussed (the allusive title is likely meant for those who may regard the whole enterprise as arrogant and self-indulgent), but for Karl Ove Knausgaard it is the beginning of thought. What did he see?

Throughout the book there are variations of the face-in-the-sea incident and for Knausgaard and the reader each one has the promise and terror of an imminent revelation, which never in fact occurs. From a distance, they can appear banal. Sometimes he is able to identify windows on the experience and provide an interpretation. Looking at a book of Constable's paintings for instance:

> *I didn't need to do any more than let my eyes skim over them before I was moved to tears. So great was the impression some of the pictures made on me. Others left me cold. That was my only parameter with art, the feeling it aroused. The feeling of inexhaustibility. The feeling of beauty. The feeling of presence. All*

compressed into such acute moments that sometimes they could be difficult to endure.

Another is when the elderly poet Olav H. Hauge reads a poem on his driveway to a youthful Knausgaard and his mates. He finds it in music, having at one time a poster of John Lennon – "the apostle of impassioned sincerity" – over his desk. The epithet suits Knausgaard himself and Don Bartlett's translation is especially convincing and memorable in evoking such passion and sincerity.

The immense, visceral detail describing Karl Ove's family and friends has contributed to the news media controversy surrounding the book and will no doubt detract from the necessity of its form, as will summarising the face-in-the-sea experience as "religious" or "mystical". Like his *grand amour* for a girl called Hanne, it is the everyday unknown. Also in the same movement of distraction, Proust is invoked as the main precursor, though only Boyd Tonkin has singled out the reason as Knausgaard's "microscopically detailed account of how [the book] came to be written". Another influence would seem to be Thomas Bernhard, whose father also died in mysterious circumstances and who also describes each turn of his life with preternatural precision. The collective title of *his* great five-book memoir *Gathering Evidence* is a good pointer as to why, as well as Knausgaard's expressed admiration. The author's need to understand his father's trajectory from family man to squalid drunk requires access to the unknowable, to the physically dead, and the only alternative he discovers is to piece together evidence of his own experience – experience of his father and of everything else – and, now, as his father's equal in age and social position – to try to pinpoint the origin of the descent. Only then might something remarkable emerge from darkness and silence. And it does.

Easter Island, the Book

The moai of Easter Island offer proof of the signal quality of art. For whatever reason they were constructed, with art being the first to be refused, their multiple and identical existence transfigures the known world.

What race of people carved them? Why were so many constructed? How was each statue moved to where it stands? Why were they toppled? For many decades our fascination has been diverted by such questions, perhaps out of necessity. Indeed, the initial question was asked by the Dutch seafarers who first encountered the islanders, struck as they were by the lack of timber and rope. Later the question was answered by the likes of Erich Von Daniken who claimed extraterrestrials carved the stone using advanced tools before disappearing, and more serious investigators like Thor Heyerdahl, who promoted the theory of the migration of traditions from South America over Polynesian colonisation. In more recent years their answers have been demoted as Easter Island has become a symbol of man-made environmental catastrophe. The trees that once covered the island are said to have been chopped down to provide rollers to move the statues from the volcanic quarry to platforms on the coast, leaving the landscape a barren steppe. The image of a man cutting down the last tree has infused modern studies with horror. In 1992 *Easter Island, Earth Island* confronted us with "the specter of a civilization destroyed by reckless plundering of the environment", a specter reprojected in *Collapse* by Jared Diamond. The story has also featured in recent novels including Jennifer Vanderbes' feminist potboiler *Easter Island* and Jeanette Winterson's fantasy *The Stone Gods*. Winterston herself puts Easter Island's demise down to "the pointless obsession with carving". When the resources to feed it declined, internecine violence flared and an entire culture was razed. Is then Easter

Island a microcosm of global disaster?

Nicolas Cauwe's spectacularly illustrated new study *Easter Island: The Great Taboo* challenges this narrative with evidence drawn from ten years of archaeological work. He argues that the moai lying incomplete in the quarry were not abandoned as previously assumed but carved deliberately to prevent further exploitation, and those on the roads between the quarry and the coast were placed there to discourage approach to the volcano. The quarry thereby became taboo, reflecting "a profound change in the religious system". While the change has long been visible via the toppling of the moai, it has been assumed this happened much like the violence attending the English Reformation. Cauwe refutes this by demonstrating how each toppled statue does not have damage consistent with revolutionary iconoclasm. In fact, they appear to have been lain down with as much care as they were raised.

For those unfamiliar with the island's history and theories surrounding it, *The Great Taboo* recounts and then revises what is known to those who are familiar. For example, it looks at the competing hypotheses for deforestation: newly introduced domestic farm animals, climate change and the use of rollers, and suggests they each played a part. Cauwe's opinion is more forthright when dismissing the mystery of the rongorongo tablets that have long been assumed to be an untranslated script. He argues instead that they are stylised aids to oral storytelling whose meaning disappeared with the voices of the storytellers.

Cauwe's address of the issue of the moai themselves is more noteworthy and requires some background. In his 1774 visit, Captain Cook's naturalist George Forster asked a native what the statues were for and was told they were deified clan chiefs. The platforms or "ahu" contain their bones and ashes and were often constructed using moai from earlier, deconstructed ahu. The coral eyes of their moai overlook agricultural land. The reason for their ultimate abandonment, we're told, cannot be easily reconstructed as there were no witnesses once Westerners came to interview islanders a century or more after the events; only legends remained. However, Cauwe argues that rather than being destroyed, the ahu were transformed from altars for statues to altars for the dead, much like Christian cemeteries, with the moai helping to seal the ashes; a transformation that took generations while the power of the statues diminished. According to Cauwe, this would explain why Captain Cook saw both standing and toppled statues, while in 1864 a French missionary saw only ruins. So, the archaeology reveals not a populace in thrall to the command of all-powerful gods but a traditional community supplicating to ancestral spirits for good harvests.

Easter Island is now little more than a tourist destination, its sacred sites reconstructed without any religious intent, making the island's given name ironic as Christianity supplants another religion based on the continuing life of the dead. Nicolas Cauwe's narrative, originally published in French and, from a certain stiffness of expression, apparently self-translated, has none of the lyric effusions of Pierre Loti's account of 1872 or the indulgence of other personal narratives such as Katherine Routledge's *The Mystery of Easter Island* (1919) or Heyerdahl's *Aku-Aku* (1958), which is perhaps inevitable given the exhaustion of Easter Island's enchantment. The stunning colour photographs at least offer a glimmer of an aura now faded; a glimmer, however, that still fascinates.

In 1990, John Banville published an essay that begins by comparing James Joyce to "a great looming Easter Island effigy of the Father" before which the writer stands "gnawing his knuckles, not a son, but a survivor". Joyce, he says, is not an artist one can use to learn one's trade:

> *the methods of production are well-nigh invisible, buried so deeply inside the work that we cannot get at them without dismantling the*

parts. The greatness, or part of the greatness, of an Aeneid, *of a*
View of Delft, *of a* Don Giovanni, *of a* Ulysses, *rests in the fact
that they are, in an essential way, closed. By this I do not mean to
say that these works of art are difficult, or obscure – what could be
more limpid than the light that hovers over Delft? – but that they are
mysterious at their core.*

He goes on to say that he thinks all great works of art have this
"quality of reticence, of being somehow turned away from us
gazing off, like nature itself, into another sphere of things,
another reality". With this comparison, Easter Island's profound
shift from erecting auratic monoliths to sealed necropoli bounds
me to think of the modern literary novel, boxing with the
shadows of looming effigies of statuesque classics, always
appealing to equivalence, contemptuous of sealed necropoli, yet
never convinced of its own capacities and unable to acknowledge
the implications.

Banville precedes his essay with a quotation from Nietzsche's
Human, All Too Human: "Every great phenomenon is followed by
degeneration, especially in the domain of art" and, following
Nicolas Cauwe's study, we might correlate fiction, specifically
anachronistic 800-page state-of-the-nation novels, to reconstructed platforms without bones, without ashes; mere fodder for
tourists. While Nietzsche ascribes degeneration to "vainer
natures" imitating one-in-a-million greats, the degeneration of
art in our time cannot be attributed to a lack of craft mastery or
objective lessons of novels, but rather to the experience of the
phenomenon itself.

The experience of the moai is not an experience at all but,
following Banville, a presence incommensurate with formal
properties. Compare the hundreds of impassive statues staring
without eyes covering a fragment of earth in a vast ocean with the
overwhelming affluence of accessible art and fiction in our time,
heedless of an exhausted quarry and the great taboo of

Modernism. Banville offers no solution except to express a condition that "half the time ... feels like drowning". But who knows what drowning feel like?

On His Back in the Dark

A "self-indulgent, ill-conceived, and poorly-edited disaster" is how J. Robert Lennon sums up Paul Auster's *Winter Journal*, a companion piece to *The Invention of Solitude*, that remarkable book from 1982 comprising two brief biographical pieces by a novelist still to make his name, in contrast to the new book which is (Lennon again) "a rambling, informal collection of memories, musings, and minutiae" written by a prolific, internationally renowned bestselling author. It has to be said that Lennon's review is entirely fair and utterly misses the value of the book.

> *You think it will never happen to you, that it cannot happen to you, that you are the only person in the world to whom none of these things will ever happen, and then, one by one, they all begin to happen to you, in the same way they happen to everyone else.*

Winter Journal begins in the manner of the two earlier with a general statement, a valedictory welcome as it were, the first on the random event of death – his father's – the second on the passing of the moment – his own:

> *He lays out a piece of paper on the table before him and writes these words with his pen. It was. It will never be again.*

Actually, more than that: "The Book of Memory" – part two of *The Invention of Solitude* – is written in the third person as if to mark the passing of the moment against the guile of memoir. By becoming "He" and later "A.", Auster enacts the implications of the statement. We can see how the peculiarity of his profession, which then included translation, prefigures the fiction he will go on to write.

Every book is an image of solitude. It is a tangible object that one can pick up, put down, open, and close, and its words represent many months, if not years, of one man's solitude, so that with each word one reads in a book one might say to himself that he is confronting a particle of that solitude. A man sits alone in a room and writes. Whether the book speaks of loneliness or companionship, it is necessarily a product of solitude. A. sits down in his room to translate another man's book, and it is as though he were entering that man's solitude and making it his own. But surely that is impossible. For once a solitude has been breached, once a solitude has been taken on by another, it is no longer solitude, but a kind of companionship. Even though there is only one man in the room, there are two. A. imagines himself as a kind of ghost of that other man, who is both there and not there, and whose book is both the same and not the same as the one he is translating.

Auster writes *Winter Journal* in the second person and so becomes his own translator – his own ghost writer, the second man reasserting the solitude of the subject; a kind of paranormal activity we recognise from *Oracle Night* when Sidney Orr disappears into his study with the blue notebook and breaks his writer's block. The proliferation of interrelated stories and digressions and the fascination with the act of writing are undoubtedly the most distinctive features of Auster's fiction, the former attracting wide appreciation, the latter perhaps allowed as a concession to Auster's European inheritance (*The Invention of Solitude* contains extracts from his translation of Mallarmé's "A Tomb for Anatole" and Blanchot's fiction, equivalents of which are disappointingly lacking in *Winter Journal*, the most notable memory of France here being an affair with a prostitute). The focus on the everyday and corporeal, which Lennon labels self-indulgent, is then a necessary recourse for the ghost, however uncomfortable and unliterary it is.

"You would like to know who you are" Auster writes as a

question to both ghost and subject, with only the latter able to reveal himself. The ghost must remain elusive for as long as the book is written. Auster is aware of this problem in "The Book of Memory" because he cites a line from Blanchot's fiction: "What is extraordinary begins at the moment I stop". But here the choice is either not to write or to write too much. The proliferating memories engage yet lack the mystique and sense of possibility innate to fiction, and instead rely on the mystique of the author who writes it. As, inevitably, we associate what is written with the life of a flesh-and-blood individual suffering family bereavements and panic attacks in Brooklyn, New York, there is a need to relate it to the fiction that appears to redeem it. The reader will thereby feel most at home when reading what Lennon calls "a pointless 10-page précis of an obscure 1950s movie", which reads very much like a plot from an Auster novel. But this is secondary to the subject of the book.

The catch-22 of *Winter Journal* is outlined in "The Book of Memory" when Auster discusses the story of Jonah. Ordered by God to go to Nineveh to prophesy the city's destruction, Jonah instead sails to Tarshish, a journey that leads to what makes his story one of the most famous in the Bible. Eventually he does prophesy to the inhabitants and they save themselves with profound repentance. Thus Jonah complains that since God is merciful there was no need for him to prophesy, have his warning heeded and thereby be exposed as a false prophet. Whatever Jonah does, he is condemned to isolation, trapped in the belly of the whale: "the shipwreck of the singular" as Auster describes it. So whereas *The Invention of Solitude* speaks of a singular life swimming in the ocean of human experience and stories, the new book is more Crusoe patrolling his island.

The shipwreck of *Winter Journal* is salvaged when Auster describes "the scalding, epiphanic moment of clarity that pushed [him] through a crack in the universe", one that marks the transition between jobbing translator and cramped poet to prolific and popular storyteller. He attends the rehearsals for a dance choreographed by a friend and watches the dancers perform without the usual accompanying music:

> [At] a certain point something began to open inside you, you found yourself falling through the rift between world and word, the chasm that divides human life from our capacity to understand or express the truth of human life, and for reasons that still confound you, this sudden fall through the empty, unbounded air filled you with a sensation of freedom and happiness, and by the time the performance was over, you were no longer blocked, no longer burdened by the doubts that had been weighing down on you for the past year.

While this provokes thrills by offering possibilities for our own personal release, the hyperbole prompts the readers to wish for a prolonged meditation on this experience; what doubts were these and how does it affect the writing of his novels? What is this crack in the universe and where might we squint through it? Perhaps it is fiction itself, into which *Winter Journal* by definition cannot venture. Perhaps the clue as to why the epiphany forms only a climax to the book rather than its core is in Lennon's summary of *Winter Journal* which I did not quote in full: "a rambling, informal collection of memories, musings, and minutiae presented in the second person". The inclusion of the form as incidental, as if equivalent to the colour of the dust jacket, is surprising because it is the formal challenge that distinguishes Auster's narrative and aligns it with another of those European inheritors unmentioned by Lennon: Samuel Beckett's *Company* (1980), which John Pilling says, "gravitates more openly towards the genre of autobiography than anything before".

> A voice comes to one in the dark. Imagine.
> To one on his back in the dark. This he can tell by the pressure on

his hind parts and by how the dark changes when he shuts his eyes and again when he opens them again. Only a small part of what is said can be verified. As for example when he hears, You are on your back in the dark. Then he must acknowledge the truth of what is said. But by far the greater part of what is said cannot be verified. As for example when he hears, You first saw the light on such and such a day. Sometimes the two are combined as for example, You first saw the light on such and such a day and now you are on your back in the dark. A device perhaps from the incontrovertibility of the one to win credence for the other. That then is the proposition. To one on his back in the dark a voice tells of a past. With occasional allusion to a present and more rarely to a future as for example, You will end as you now are.

The connection is most explicit when Auster describes how he recalls his past during bouts of insomnia on his back in the dark: "For it is only in the darkness of solitude that the work of memory begins". But, as *The Invention of Solitude* attests, the work of memory requires the distance between writing and what is written to be brought to life and, here, the second person eventually becomes a tic, employed as a device to win credence for straightforward memoir. The ghost and the subject become too cosy in each other's company. However, while *Company* focuses more on the veracity or otherwise of the voice in the dark and *Winter Journal* its sentimental revelations, both have in common the pursuit not of what is behind the writer but what lies in front of us all.

"But why call it a novel?"

In August 1987 I cycled to a small seaside town to check out its small library. These were the days when shelves lined with free-to-borrow books arose like the New World. The mental image is of a bright Western sky. On the fiction shelves was a pristine hardback of VS Naipaul's novel *The Enigma of Arrival*, published only weeks before. I had not read Naipaul and the book attracted me, perhaps only because its black spine shined new. The object seemed enough in itself. But I did read all its 318 pages and have never forgotten Naipaul's evocation of walks over the Wiltshire countryside around Stonehenge – not because the narrative is effusive or eventful but because it is so restrained. The narrator is seen only at an oblique angle, like the Rückenfigur in one of Caspar David Friedrich's landscapes. Wanting to find out how others responded I looked for reviews and found one in a now long-defunct magazine:

> [*Naipaul*] *makes us aware that most writing hurries much too much, and so misses what is essential: that nothing seems to alter, yet everything is in flux. Though this is a book almost without incident it catches unforgettably the transformation of rural England in our time* [...] *It is a moving and beautiful piece of work, unlike any other book I know.*

These lines corroborated my innocent enthusiasm and helped me to recognise and articulate what I had experienced. However, the review ends with a question I hadn't considered: "But why call it a novel?" Last month I considered it for the first time.

With no patience for any new novel, I reread *The Enigma of Arrival* and the response was the same, although Naipaul's delicate self-exposure was far more impressive and moving this time round and darkened by a better appreciation that death is the motif of his story. In 1987 I had followed Naipaul; twenty-five years later I walked beside him.

Death is also the motif of Karl Ove Knausgaard's *My Struggle*, which I read earlier in the year with equivalent pleasure and was perhaps the cause of Naipaul's novel floating back into my memory. The title of the British edition – *A Death in the Family* – makes the motif explicit. Both books are overtly autobiographical and rely on the life of the writer to infuse their narratives with authority, an authority that itself relies on a unique encounter with time, existence and non-existence. This suggests such authority has been depleted, perhaps because fiction relies too heavily on distance. What these books possess in contrast is a pressing proximity. A novel is anchored on generic safe ground even as the writer's imagination flies high or plumbs the depths, but now that ground is loose and barren. So why is Naipaul's book subtitled "A novel in five sections" and *My Struggle* identified as a novel?

There are clear differences in each author's approach, suggesting a lack of generic clarity, which is not given to autobi-ography but is familiar to the novel form. Where Naipaul's focus is on his journey from colonial province to imperial centre in classic bildungsroman fashion, Knausgaard is more concerned with the density of the moment; and where Naipaul is selective and respectful in his exposure of himself and others, never mentioning that his cottage has another occupant, his wife, or that the landlord he refers to throughout is the legendary Stephen Tennant, Knausgaard is famously inclusive. "[He] seems unable to leave anything out", James Wood appeared to complain, quoting a novella-length description of a New Year's Eve party: "After a few hundred pages of this, I started to grumble: I understood that this was 'My Struggle,' but did it also have to be my struggle?" He soon turns around and acknowl-edges that "the banality is so extreme that it turns into its opposite, and becomes distinctive, curious in its radical transparency".

> *The need for totality that brings pages about playing the guitar,*
> *about drinking tea, about wearing his Doc Martens and listening to*
> *his Walkman [...] also brings superb, lingering, celestial passages,*
> *like the one in which Knausgaard cannot sleep, and paces his*
> *apartment.*

This is the insomniac passage I quoted in my comparatively
feeble review and is worth returning to. It also returns us to the
similarities with Naipaul. Knausgaard is moved to tears by a
cloud formation he sees in a book of Constable's paintings:

> *I kept flicking back to the picture of the greenish clouds, every time*
> *it called forth the same emotions in me. It was as if two different*
> *forms of reflection rose and fell in my consciousness, one with its*
> *thoughts and reasoning, the other with its feelings and impressions,*
> *which, even though they were juxtaposed, excluded each other's*
> *insights. It was a fantastic picture, it filled me with all the feelings*
> *that fantastic pictures do, but when I had to explain why, what*
> *constituted the "fantastic," I was at a loss to do so.*
>
> *The picture made my insides tremble, but for what? The picture*
> *filled me with longing, but for what? There were plenty of clouds*
> *around. There were plenty of colors around. There were enough*
> *particular historical moments. There were also plenty of combina-*
> *tions of all three. Contemporary art, in other words, the art which*
> *in principle ought to be of relevance to me, did not consider the*
> *feelings a work of art generated as valuable. Feelings were of inferior*
> *value, or perhaps even an undesirable by-product, a kind of waste*
> *product, or at best, malleable material, open to manipulation.*
> *Naturalistic depictions of reality had no value either, but were*
> *viewed as naïve and a stage of development that had been super-*
> *seded long ago. There was not much meaning left in that. But the*
> *moment I focused my gaze on the painting again all my reasoning*

*vanished in the surge of energy and beauty that arose in me. Yes, yes, yes, I heard. That's where it is. That's where I have to go. But what was it I had said yes to? Where was it I had to go?**

This experience relates back to the beginning of the book in the narrator's childhood, when watching a news report he sees a face in the sea. He rushes to tell the nearest person, his father, who says: "Don't give it another thought". Now you, the reader, become the author's nearest person and you might respond in the same way as the father did or, like me, suffer an intense identification.

This latter division is probably key to the original question: why call it a novel? The experience Knausgaard describes is both very personal and fascinatingly impersonal; that is, it draws attention and resists accommodation in narrative whether autobiographical or fictional because it is what is promised by narrative or what underlies it. The lengthy descriptions of the everyday in *My Struggle* become necessary to frame the urgency of the questions he puts to himself, much as the longueurs of Proust's *In Search of Lost Time* are necessary to enable the magical phenomena of time's absence. The indulgence and disruption of habit is a constant in both. *My Struggle* rides high on such experiences, of which Constable's cloud study is the incarnation; profound or prosaic yet always promising or threatening a climatic event or revelation. This is why both Knausgaard and Proust differ from generic autobiography and novel.

Naipaul himself ascribes the beginnings of his novel to a painting by Giorgio de Chirico called *The Enigma of Arrival*:

I felt that in an indirect, poetical way the title referred to something in my own experience [...] The scene is of desolation and mystery: it speaks of the mystery of arrival [...] And in the winter gray of the manor grounds in Wiltshire, in those first four days of mist and rain, when so little was clear to me, an idea—floating lightly above the book I was working on — came to me of a story I might one day write about that scene in the Chirico picture.

Later he expands on the content of that narrative – a man on a journey to a Mediterranean city in classical times, although he didn't think of it as an historical story "but more as a free ride of the imagination" – and explains why it never got written. It occurred to him that the story was "an attempt to find a story for, to give coherence to, a dream or nightmare" in which he was living through his own death. This is negative equivalent of Knausgaard's bewildered affirmation before the clouds.

A dream is much like a painting in that it consists entirely of resemblance. A self-portrait is the self as experienced in a dream: oneself and another, impossible to reconcile and infinitely beguiling; an eternally evanescent memory. Yet to write out a description of a painting is not only futile but as crushingly dull as telling the story of a dream. It can never be the thing itself, the experience which makes it essential to the self is impossible to convey; "A sponge, suffering because it cannot saturate itself", as Miłosz wrote, "a river, suffering because reflections of clouds and trees are not clouds and trees".

For the writer, whether positive or negative, the encounter demands a response. He becomes a writer in order to respond. Naipaul's resort to autobiographical material in *The Enigma of Arrival* was characterised by Salman Rushdie as a failure of strength for fiction, to which Naipaul replied with brahminical disdain: "I think it is possible that talent has moved to other things and that real writing is occurring elsewhere, rather than in novels. You have to be very clear about the material that possesses you, and you've got to find the correct form for it."

But what if that form is not open? Robert Lowell's famous poem "Epilogue" comes as you would expect at the end of the confessional volume *Day by Day* in which his experience of manic depression is laid bare, a fact that troubles him. He asks two rhetorical questions:

> *Those blessèd structures, plot and rhyme —*
> *why are they no help to me now*
> *I want to make*
> *something imagined, not recalled?*

Before the second question appears, he compares his poetry to a garish photographic snapshot in contrast to a painter's eye that "trembles to caress the light". Something imagined in writing, however, is "paralyzed by fact".

Yet why not say what happened?

Until I re-read the poem today I had assumed this line was Lowell's decisive call for "life writing", for attention to be paid to the everyday rather than, as it seems now, a reluctant concession, an admission of defeat. In writing of what happened one must only "Pray for the grace of accuracy / Vermeer gave to the sun's illumination". Reading yet again, however, the comparison with the visual arts seems to express less the poet's anxiety over the superiority of imagination than anxiety over writing itself; even if he were to produce the most exquisite work of the imagination, it would be a failure. Indeed, by referring to the "poet's anxiety" and by an urge to reproduce the paintings cited so far here I confirm this fallen state.

Paintings can of course be appreciated by anyone with vision. Whether it is a surreal harbour scene or bucolic landscape, each painting is merely there: a unique object in the world. There is no fact or fiction to decipher; a painting merely is. An abstract painting does not provoke impatience in the same way as a so-called experimental novel does precisely because it is before the viewer in the same arena as a classical landscape. The dynamic relationship of the object to what it ostensibly represents or expresses is the encounter we displace only by means of the polite discourse lamented by Knausgaard.

By contrast, the poem or novel is immediately assumed to be the voice of one standing before the world, between us and its world; it is already a part of that polite discourse. As a poem, "Epilogue" is removed *a priori* from the relation enjoyed by painting; the process of understanding and interpretation is not only the foreground, it is the poem itself.

What recommends itself then is silence or denial, and the latter does indeed constitute the bulk of literary output: the willed infantilism of popular fiction, the prissy connoisseurship of fine prose in literary fiction, and the po-faced empiricism of reality hunger. Each is after the Lord Mayor's Show of television, film and print journalism, such that the proposition that "crime novels can be used to analyse shifts in society" is recommended without irony.

Silence has less of a profile of course, but it remain present. It's present in the 800 pages of the two books discussed here. What distinguishes them from other famous novelists' autobiographical excursions – JM Coetzee's *Scenes from Provincial Life* and Thomas Bernhard's *Gathering Evidence* being two outstanding examples – is a fascination with moments that resist narrative and a preoccupation with finding a way to make them present in narrative; moments experienced before paintings, in music, in a walkable landscapes and, in Knausgaard's case, in a TV news report. But not in writing. Writing in fact dilutes these moments presenting to the writer not only a paradoxical inspiration but a destructive one. The task for the writer then isn't a matter of genre but of rinsing genre.

The common assumption in literary reception is that the novel is the noise of mastery, a story well-told and constructed with craft and good judgement. In public we can affirm this of any given work as we know others will understand as a public does. A recent example is Peter Stothard's Man Booker Prize speech recommending a genre novel to win what used to be a literary award. Except the encounter with a novel, a short story or a poem is not a public experience but one of solitude and silence. Hence the violence of corralling reviews, good and bad, hence the popularity of book clubs, hence the national obsession with prizes. There is a need to mitigate or sublimate seclusion, rarely to explore. What I found that day of blue, empty sky and VS Naipaul's *The Enigma of Arrival* and this summer with Karl Ove Knausgaard's *My Struggle* were such explorations, attempts to open onto the space that makes narrative possible, the singularities that inscribe themselves on a life and agitate a certain enchantment, opening the past as much as the present and future, yet which cannot be made present to the work itself. For this reason, I would answer that both books are more novels than most novels, willing as they are to listen to the silence.

* Translated by Don Bartlett

His Books of the Year

This is the part of a "books of the year" entry you don't read because you're scanning to find the titles this writer has chosen. You haven't noticed his name but you'll check it once your own good judgement has been confirmed.

The first is Karl O. Knausgaard's *My Struggle*, a popular one this year – you've registered the title already because he was chosen in that other list in that other place by that other guy – who was it? Visceral realism blah scandal in Norway blah full of profound insights blah. Oh look, there are the names of Marcel Proust and Thomas Bernhard again, the authors Knausgaard is already being compared to, neither of which you've read, though you keep meaning to. It makes you feel alienated and demoralised. Look, there are so many translations and editions of Proust to choose from. What was the title again? And which Thomas Bernhard novel is a good place to start?

You see there are still three paragraphs to go and you're thinking: enough with the summaries already! You relax a little because the next choice is Enrique Vila-Matas' *Dublinesque*. The title is so warm and attractive. You see that it's set around Bloomsday, which is something you've wanted to attend for years. Admittedly, you tried and failed to read *Ulysses* for a university course, but you prefer Radio 4's dramatisation because it cut through all the verbiage and made the book accessible. Anyway, the novel is about Dublin isn't it? That should be enough. You had a city break there a few years back and had such a good time in the pubs. Everyone is so friendly! But what's that he's saying? It's about the end of the Gutenberg Era, the end of literature as we know it? What nonsense: has he seen my shelf of Ian Rankin first editions?

You skip the third paragraph because he's chosen Quentin Meillassoux's *The Number and the Siren*, a book by a French philosopher about a French poet Stéphane Mallarmé, specifically his poem "Un Coup de Dés", which you've never heard of let alone read. Hey, it's in French! What if it is a revelation and not what you might expect – a momentous study of the place and meaning of poetry in post-religious society? That's just pretentious.

The final paragraph intrigues you and is the only one that you read in full because it is the shortest and the chooser is obviously passionate about *Infinity: The Story of a Moment*, Gabriel Josipovici's novel based on the life of a real composer. That sounds more your kind of thing: you like biographies.

An Everyday Afterlife

A question arises from my breathless response to volume one of Karl Ove Knausgaard's *My Struggle*: have I contradicted my exasperated review of David Shields' *Reality Hunger*? At least, this is a question I ask myself. After all, as the author explained, this autobiographical work was written only when fiction failed him. He had published two novels but:

> *I wanted to write something completely different, and I wanted to write about my father ... About his fall, how he somehow changed from being a father, a perfectly ordinary teacher, a local politician, to a divorced, dead alcoholic. For three years I tried to write a kind of regular, realistic but fictional work about his death. Nothing worked ... And [then] I started just writing it as it was: the truth, no artifice, no cleverness. Reality.*

Perhaps my enthusiasm was relief at the abolition of the generic niceties that even the most impressive novels observe and, like David Shields, I mistook disillusionment for truth. Here was something elemental, I thought, the word Thomas Bernhard used to describe Dostoevsky's *The Demons* after he had read the novel on his teenage deathbed. But in my review of *Reality Hunger* I argued that such reality cannot enter into the work without conforming to the pressure of the conceptual unity imposed by a book, and that writing plainly about plain things is no more a guarantee of realism than – following Wittgenstein – rain experienced in a dream is a guarantee of its wetness, even if it is connected to noise on the bedroom window.

Of course dream rain does mean something: meaning fills the dreamworld like sunlight, even when it is dark. We can only speculate on the meaning. This is our experience of dreams, and our speculation never feels quite enough, never proportionate to the generic purity of the dream. The quality of *My Struggle* I perceived is precisely a persistent analysis that maintains a propulsive force because it is aware that is never enough. Had Knausgaard written a regular, realistic novel instead, it might have appeared to be enough: a function of mastery and controlled distance, hence his writer's block and compulsion toward "no artifice, no cleverness". However, *My Struggle* is something other than reportage and, as I argue, the fundamental error of *Reality Hunger* is to conflate the aims of journalism with those of literature.

For this reason, Mark Thwaite makes a very good case for treating *My Struggle* as a novel, arguing that the relentless focus on "quotidian dreariness" is its method of seeking the meaning of its dream, to engage with the presence of "something numinous [that] lies just beyond sight, beneath grief, [what] lies always beyond language". He aligns this with Freud's shifting definition of the uncanny: "He finds something deeply strange, something Unheimliches, during this work: secretly, heimlich is not the antonym of unheimlich at all, but rather its sometime synonym". Words are thereby always in excess of themselves and "the yearned-for *mot juste* doesn't get us any further than just our everyday yearning". This is well put. Knausgaard must focus on "the stink, the misery, the pain, the boredom, the embarrassment" of everyday life in order to open up onto what it cannot name. "The subject here", he continues, "is death and whether writing/language has anything to say about this commonplace disaster that haunts and harries and shapes us everywhere we turn". Knausgaard himself is explicit that this can happen only when writing yields to literature's demand:

> *everything has to submit to form. If any of literature's other elements are stronger than form, such as style, plot, theme, if any of these overtake form, the result suffers. That is why writers with a strong style often write bad books. That is also why writers with*

strong themes so often write bad books. Strong themes and styles
have to be broken down before literature can come into being. It is
this breaking down that is called "writing." Writing is more about
destroying than creating.

Writing as destruction is a striking contradiction and serves
Mark's reading well, but "bad books" is vague and self-serving.
He names no names here but *My Struggle* inevitably provokes
comparisons with at least two. Who has stronger styles than
Proust and Bernhard and what books have stronger themes than
In Search of Lost Time and *Gathering Evidence*? (They are also
named in *My Struggle*, Knausgaard having "virtually imbibed"
one.) I regret mentioning them in my review, not because Proust
and Bernhard cannot be usefully discussed in comparison but
because, in my case, they weren't usefully discussed and because
doing so threatens the error that Marcel himself describes: when
one hears of a great book, one can imagine only an assemblage of
the great books one has already imbibed. It is only when one
reads the new book that one becomes aware of its otherness and
perhaps also its weakness in comparison. This has happened
with three friends of mine who have read *My Struggle*, and
caused me consternation.

To compound this error, I shall now compare Karl Ove
Knausgaard's *My Struggle* to the work of Franz Kafka.

We can say Kafka's work has more in common with
Knausgaard's in terms of style, that is, in its comparative
disconnect from style. In both we are drawn more to the specific
events described, their curious and horrific banality, than to
immersion in aesthetic bliss, while at the same time we feel
compelled to draw back and seek an organising principle, to
imagine such events as part of a containable world view, and
then to resubmerge in a newly configured aesthetic bliss.
However, Kafka's is the prime example of a body of work that is
never quite enough, a lack into which it is impossible to

submerge. The deluge of secondary texts does this for us. Maurice Blanchot asks what needs to done to rescue Kafka from this fate, one to which Kafka himself contributed, and his answer is to recommend regarding his work as Kafka had wanted: in its absence. He observes that, with the publication of the diaries, Kafka the writer was placed in the foreground and he is the one we look for in the work. He wonders if Kafka foresaw such a disaster and that is why he wanted his work destroyed. The opposite is true of *My Struggle*: knowledge of Knausgaard life saturates the page, and the interviews and reports of the scandalised response in Norway offer no room to move away in relief: there is nowhere else to look but the work. But what then is the work?

It certainly isn't the everyday content of life. This is as much the subject of *My Struggle* as ice is the subject of Scott's journey to the South Pole. An overwhelming sense of imminence is evoked by Knausgaard so that its banality becomes, as James Wood says, celestial. For example, walking home in the dark after a day of writing, he describes his route with such precision that only an event of great significance would seem to justify it. As the event doesn't occur, another world makes itself felt instead; a possible world, just out of reach. This imminence has itself been promised by occasional epiphanies, which appear to open the work to its final destination, as well to align the author with the experience of Proust. But they are frustrated epiphanies, without message, each a scintillating blank. The face in the sea and the inexplicable tears evoked by a patch of sky in an old painting appear as offerings of transcendence, but not an affirmative transcendence. Why not?

Blanchot places Kafka's work squarely in the era after the death of God: his stories are "among the darkest in literature, the most rooted in absolute disaster". Only it is not an anguished expression of lament but one of uncertainty and anxiety. "God is dead, which may signify this harder truth: death is not possible."

We think of *The Hunter Gracchus* fallen into a ravine and happy to wait for death: "Then the accident happened". Not the accident of death but that of not dying: "I am here. I don't know any more than that. There's nothing more I can do. My boat is without a helm—it journeys with the wind which blows in the deepest regions of death."

The theme is also clear in *Metamorphosis*: like Gracchus, Gregor cannot die even as his body transforms and disintegrates. Despite the utter misery and solitude of his condition, he still seeks moments of reprieve – food from his sister Grete, protecting the portrait on the wall – until, finally, he does die, only for Grete, free at last from the burden of looking after her brother, to then stretch her young body, signalling life's revival; one more metamorphosis. "There is no end", Blanchot writes, "there is no possibility of being done with the day, with the meaning of things, with hope". God is thereby not deprived of his infinite authority: "dead, he is even more terrible, more invulnerable, in a combat in which there is no longer a possibility of defeating him".

We are battling a dead transcendence, Blanchot says, and notes the prevalence of the powerful dead in Kafka's stories: the emperor in *The Great Wall of China* and the former Commandant in *In the Penal Colony*. We might add Knausgaard's father. An absurd battle perhaps, something embodied in the comedy of Kafka's stories and by Knausgaard's solemn attention to the mundane. Yet it could be the only battle left worth fighting; a combat of passivity. Blanchot believed that Kafka recognised his presentation of death had instead dimmed and erased it, and that our reading "revolves anxiously around a misunderstanding": we think we have witnessed what has in fact been hidden. Kafka wanted to destroy his writing because it hadn't failed enough.

Similarly, *My Struggle* has been welcomed with astonishment and great sales, much to the author's horror: "I have given away my soul". He must also wish to recommend his own absence. Western man, Blanchot observes, has tried to make this bearable by focusing on the positive: immortality, of an afterlife that would compensate for this life, perhaps the afterlife of fine writing: "But this afterlife is our actual life".

* Translated by Ian Johnston

Book of Forgotten Dreams

For eighteen years I have wanted the English translation of Georges Bataille's book *La Peinture Préhistorique: Lascaux ou la naissance de l'art*, ever since Maurice Blanchot's review essay appeared in the collection *Friendship* published in 1997. A strange yearning because Blanchot had summarised the content, so there was apparently nothing to gain and, what's more, I have never been a big Bataille-reader, much preferring at university Blanchot's unparalleled prose to the jargon-scarred theory beloved of my fellow students who thought "transgression" meant wearing rubber.

Still, there was something withheld by this book, the actual thing, the physical object, in its absence. Unfortunately, the edition from Albert Skira's *Great Centuries of Painting* series, described by one scholar as a "highbrow coffee table book", has been out of print since 1955 and secondhand copies have always been too expensive, often approaching three figures. Until late one night last November when desultory book-searching revealed one in good condition for under £50. In a moment of madness, I clicked *Buy Now* and sat back to dwell on the extravagance.

Taking delivery of a desired book often signals the end of possibility and the settling of melancholy in the prospect of the real thing finally arriving and dissolving the aura. And then there are the heavy demands of procedural content. Reading is bound to kill the possible book, the Platonic form revolving in your head, the edition of Bolaño's *2666* Kirsty Logan described a few years ago. So it was my good fortune that *Prehistoric Paintings: Lascaux or the Birth of Art* got lost in the post. For two weeks I waited, anticipating each furtive visit from the postman and panicking once he had left. How could I have been so careless to waste fifty quid?! Wasn't this punishment for transgressing the line between desire and its realisation?

In hope I walked to the post office depot to enquire. A queue lined the pavement outside. After fifteen minutes of standing around and shuffling forward in the cold, they said, Yes, they had a package for me but they couldn't hand it over because I didn't have a red card from the postman. What? But I'm here, now, so why not hand it over? No, that can't be done. At least let me see the parcel to prove to myself that it exists. No, that wasn't possible. They said they would have to redeliver it. Would tomorrow be OK? Yes, it would. This was good news, and I went home happy. Of course, the following day nothing arrived. I walked to the post office depot again. The queue was even longer and, after half an hour of standing around and shuffling forward in the cold, the man behind the counter just shrugged. I went home unhappy and eventually gave up caring.

A few days later the bell rang and the postman handed over an A3-sized package. I had my doubts about what it contained and tore at the parcel carefully. The first thing exposed was the spine of a book. So just look at it for a moment, shining there.

The bright colours suggested a brand new book rather than one published sixty years ago. So this is what its absence withheld! On removing the cardboard slipcase and opening the book, five black and white postcards with serrated edges fell out and pasted on the inside cover were three visitor tickets to three different caves. Souvenirs of another life. When the previous owner visited is unclear, but Lascaux was closed to visitors in 1963.

These small discoveries were the prelude to the content.

A miracle occurred at Lascaux, Bataille says, a miracle that remains before us in the "clear and burning presence" of these paintings. His rapture is evident, and it is rare for a world-weary reader to feel he shares in the author's wonder, *lifting* the pages to see what's next and reading the words so large and clear that they could have been typed directly onto the page. A similar edition written by Captain Cook or Neil Armstrong might compare. The production values are such that the illustrations are separate items, pasted onto the page.

*"What transfixes us is the vision, present before our very eyes, of all that is most remote. Of **our** presence in the real world."*

The paradox in the words of the caption, that being close to ourselves whilst in proximity to what is most remote, is explained here as the "strong and intimate emotion" of religion or, better, "the sacred", to which the cave paintings are "more solidly attached to than it has ever been since". This is not religion as one more additional theory but as the catalyst of humankind, when the creature wandering the icy plains descended into the caves and, in the remove of darkness and solitude, set itself apart from the animal kingdom and discovered itself, codifying the cosmos with paint. As Richard White puts it, this is "not the sacred as the beyond, another realm of being that exists in opposition to this one—but the sacred as

the deep reality of this life that we are typically alienated from".
So we shouldn't include these moments perusing the book with
the usual "Oh I like that" pleasures of the art gallery but as the
kindling of the effects of art was it when born; that is, when *we*
were born, and perhaps also the deeper feeling we have in
galleries that we have since been socialised to restrain. Whatever,
the miracle is foundational.

Bataille says that in looking at the cave paintings in Lascaux
"we are left painfully in suspense by this incomparable beauty
and the sympathy it awakens in us", and something close to this
is what I experience looking at the book, if this can be called an
experience. One is not transported in awe towards fantastical
otherness but toward a fog-bound interior, as comforting as it is
alien. "It is as though paradoxically our essential self clung to the
nostalgia of attaining what our reasoning self had judged
unattainable, impossible." This is where I ask: what can be done
with this suspense and sympathy if our reasoning self is how we
measure experience?

The remainder of *Prehistoric Paintings* examines each area of
the cave to elaborate on the author's theory that art served as a
channel for the animality enduring in the human community
provoked by the taboos of death and sexuality. One reader,
stepping forth with good reason, describes the book as "a lot of
flowery writing that implies interpretations not necessarily
supported by evidence", and it is this inevitable doubt and the
scientific innocence that seems to me where the book is worthwhile. In his review, Blanchot suggests that it is from this subterranean overflow that humankind appears, because it reveals our
separation from animals, over which we now recognise our
power of life and death, and yet, at the same time, exposes us to
a death blissfully unknown to animals, thereby weakening us.
However, we modern humans value this unique quality over
everything, so much that what Blanchot says weakened us is now
what we believe makes us stronger.

"The marvelous never loses its impact."

Bataille criticises the "timidity" of scholars who speak "with undue reserve" of what they see in the caves and thereby neutralise the effect of the marvelous on their studies. The "marvelous" then is that which is "not necessarily supported by evidence", and it is only an accredited scholar's book, such as *The Mind in the Cave* (2002) that can provide such evidence. However, while David Lewis-Williams is a professor emeritus of the Rock Art Research Institute in Johannesburg, his book suggests Bataille's wonderment is vital for appreciating the caves, or at least to get closer to their creation. He explains that they were not created in sober rationality, not in the light of day but in states of consciousness we have devalued.

He prefaces his study by presenting "the greatest riddle of archeology – how we became human and *in the process* began to make art" [my italics], so we see that *becoming human* is the lacuna. There were Neanderthals in the Middle Paleolithic era who did not make art and then there are Homo sapiens in the Upper Paleolithic who did. What caused the transition between animal consciousness and that of Homo sapiens?

Lewis-Williams runs through the intellectual history of attempts to explain the transition – Darwinian, Marxist, Structuralist and Evolutionary Psychological, though not Bataille's – before setting out studies of the art and beliefs of the San of southern Africa that were made before they were swallowed up by modernity. Homo sapiens have a higher consciousness than that of the Neanderthals, which allowed us to develop a fully modern language system, enabling us to "fashion ... individual identities and mental 'scenes' of past, present and future events". But, crucially, we also have access to the lower end of the spectrum, altered states of consciousness such as dreams and trance states, brought on by communal rituals, dance and hallucinogens. Language enabled us to see these alternative realities, to hear inner voices and to articulate them to others. The cave paintings, Lewis-Williams argues, are attempts to fix these visions, to enable those who made them to touch "what was already there" in the spirit world. *They are not representations of spirits but the spirits themselves.*

These dreams, sounds and visions revealed a cosmological order. Humanity's creation of the sacred was thereby possible only because of altered states of consciousness. And while Lewis-Williams' prefatory sentence implicitly rejects Bataille's thesis that art as practised by early humans precipitated its own emergence, he is as critical of Western scientists as Bataille for neglecting what he calls "the autistic end" of the spectrum of consciousness. As a result, their studies follow a positivist route in which intelligence and rationality become the defining charac-teristics of humanity and the manifest destiny of early people was grow to become "more and more like Western scientists". They are made in their own image.

Yet we have the same neurological structure as early humans

and, as Bataille reports, we respond with a curious, even painful sympathy to an art that transcends aesthetic pleasure. Cave painting, according to both Bataille and Lewis-Williams, is then not *an addition* to human society but *constitutive* of it. Lewis-Williams writes of the San that hierarchies developed according to those who had better access to the spirit world governing all life: "Art and religion were therefore socially divisive". Each member of a community had access to dreams and were keen to learn more, so were influenced by male and female "shamans" and took part in their rituals. Art and religion, art and the sacred, were indistinguishable and "image-making did not merely take place in the spirit world: it also shaped and created the world".

It is a world we have long left behind, with commonsense and the insomnia of scientific method having replaced superstition and shamanic dreams in shaping our universe. To most modern minds, this is an unquestionable good. But it leads to a troubling question: if humankind emerged and grew to be itself out of reverence for what was revealed in realms of consciousness we now not only neglect but regard with suspicion, even as intellectual taboo, is our existence vitally impoverished?

Perhaps my unaccountable wish to own a copy of Bataille's *highbrow coffee table book* reveals a buried giant of a need for the elemental in art more generally sublimated into gushing about "the wonder of nature". Such eruptions of the old fascination with dreams to be found in our confused response to art and artists, books and writers, movies and directors, and invariably contained by the intervention of biographical exposés, won't go away even in their diminished state, and indeed occasionally break through into polite society. It is implicitly approached in what has been recently labelled the Hard Problem of consciousness, itself a controversial outgrowth of cognitive science, and the explicit paradox of a debate dependent on its own immaterial space yet able to address it only in the autism of empirical discourse is the elephant in the room. However, to continue to the wildlife theme, it is suppressed, like moles on a bowling green, with the back of a humanist's spade. With this proscription of the sacred – however it is defined – deeply in place, it would seem a new kind of transgression is required. Except this is precisely the realm of true art. As Bataille writes: "only art expresses the prohibition with beseeming gravity, and only art resolves the dilemma [of proscription]. It is the state of transgression that promotes the desire, the need for a more profound, a richer, a marvelous world, the need, in a word, for a sacred world."

Extratemporal Meditations

Since its publication, David Shields' manifesto *Reality Hunger* has helped focus my thoughts on writing: why it still matters, why anyone should still read or write beyond daily utility. That is, the premise of the title and the author's brief commentary have helped, rather than the pinched miscellany of the book's content. In fact, to renew that help I need go no further than the very first line, written by the compiler before he expresses his celebrated disillusionment with the routine gestures of contemporary fiction:

> *Every artistic movement from the beginning of time is an attempt to figure out a way to smuggle more of what the artist thinks is reality into the work of art.*

Let us pause before prose so rich in cliché and poor in soul.

At first I questioned the assumptions embedded in this line and then presented miscellaneous examples indicating that the hunger is not for reality as such and that Shields' disillusion is the dismal light shining through the twin cataracts of modernity – journalism and scientific positivism – both impermeable to deep history, philosophy, theology and art. "Reality Hunger" as a movement is thereby the literary correlate of New Atheism, a displacement of monotheism mitigated only by its failure to attract the heresiographers infecting the latter phenomenon.

It has to be said my efforts to resist outweigh anything a refutation might bring forth, no matter how fine the examples. They are untimely. Despite *Reality Hunger* comprising quotations and brief reflections that might have easily fallen into a Tumblr void, it commands influence precisely because it is a book. The form of a book, any book, transcends the sum of its contents by appealing to a coherent unity and the promised land of truth.

The title is that unity. Corporate journalists found the premise congenial of course and the common reader was thereby tuned in to the buzz. A student correspondent of mine reported "energised" discussions on the library steps as his fellows passed the book around; after all, the food metaphor of writing's relation to the world is a tasty, bite-sized morsel.

This power to influence so many with what is effectively a literary gesture is intriguing because "Reality Hunger" as an idea relies on an apparent contradiction more or less identical to that of New Atheism. Implicit in both is a suppressed relation to its zone and manner of expression. In both, radical materialism is demanded from the immaterial space of mind and word, with expression demanding an *a priori* sufferance of the contradiction. For example, Shields pursues without irony the non-book in the one form that provides an aura of weight and promise to the demand. You may say this is a mere point of order perhaps, one casually set aside as one reads and thinks in pursuit of worldly answers to worldly concerns, and easily dismissed as a product of art-for-art's-sake aestheticism or ignorant of recent theories of consciousness. Except the point remains because of how these responses are expressed; the light of consciousness does not illuminate itself.

What all this reveals is that the ancient objection to writing remains embedded in Western literary culture. In the *Phaedrus*, Plato reports how Socrates compared written language to figurative painting, impersonal and with no guarantee of a living speaker.

The productions of painting look like living beings, but if you ask them a question they maintain a solemn silence. The same holds true of written words; you might suppose that they understand what they are saying, but if you ask them what they mean by anything they simply return the same answer over and over again.

Writing is thereby aligned with the uncanny authority of sacred places and objects. Both refer to an existence more original than themselves yet all the while pronouncing on the most pressing issues of everyday life, thereby posing problems for those promoting faith in reason and realism. The original has no presence. The premise of *Reality Hunger* merely echoes Socrates' anxiety about the silence of writing and, moreover, what provides Shields' solution is the same too: a physical guarantee. The cultural phenomenon we are witnessing is the laboured repetition of an attempt to reconcile our expectations with profound uncertainty.

This is why I keep returning to *Reality Hunger*. Like any obsessive oppositional stance, it is too close for comfort. I share Shields' disillusionment with contemporary literary fiction, especially its ossification into a Booker-winning genre. The difference is that while Shields recommends that novels seek "deliberate unartiness" and include "raw material, seemingly unprocessed, unfiltered", I believe the only way to go is through literature, by becoming apparently more literary, to provoke perhaps even more anxiety, which is why the books I've written about in the last few years confront the remove of writing within the works themselves, a risk invariably condemned by conservative critics as self-indulgent theorising.

So what we appear to have is competition between demands differing on mere matters of taste. However, I know my shudder over for the first line of *Reality Hunger* quoted above is more than a connoisseur's disdain for commonplace phrases and metaphors; sentences affect my experience of the world. *Beginning of time; figure out; what the artist thinks* – these are cold, shallow words evoking a cold, shallow world. And while this may seem unduly subjective and impressionistic, Socrates' objection to writing suggests a deeper reason, something fundamental to the impulse to read and write and the paradoxical gifts of the novel. What recommends itself then is an alternative model for the relation of writing to the world.

Miguel de Beistegui's book *Proust as Philosopher* offers just that. Set aside the dry title for now. It is an unfortunate consequence of the title of the French original, *Jouissance de Proust*. A literal translation – The Joy of Proust – conjures an image of a bearded man grappling sweatily with a curvaceous fountain pen, and those involved were right to reconsider the title. However, jouissance is key because for Proust's narrator the proper search is for a relation to reality that might enable essential knowledge and genuine happiness, even.

The book begins by outlining the fundamental problem of Marcel's life, which may seem familiar: a present of disappointment, frustration and suffering with a future of profundity and joy promised in the form of romantic love, great art and the natural world. When fulfilment appears imminent, disappointment, frustration and suffering remain, only in different forms: the object of his love provokes intense jealousy, what he understood as great art fails to lead him into the world of truth he had awaited so keenly, and the beautiful, fragrant hawthorn bushes he adores give him asthma attacks. Worse, when he wants to requite this condition by producing a work of "infinite philosophical meaning", everything he writes, whether richly imaginative or solidly realistic, dies on the page.

In Search of Lost Time takes its form in the revelation that a key reason for such a condition is that Marcel neglected to include the failure of infinite philosophical meaning as part of infinite philosophical meaning. Fantastic and realistic modes of creativity are both provisional, merely epiphenomenal, and always trumped by solitude and the external world. Once Marcel begins to explore and animate the space opened by experience and the expectations it refuses to fulfil then a different world begins to unfurl and, what's more, enables him to write something of infinite philosophical meaning. The exploration is embodied in the opening scene of the novel as Marcel wakes up and negotiates the boundary between dream and reality, much like Gregor Samsa in *Metamorphosis*. Waking to change then becomes a constant.

De Beistegui presents Marcel's discovery in philosophical terms: there is a lack at the heart of being – "an ontological deficiency" – that is original and fundamental to the structure of experience. The actual world escapes us because such distance is constitutive of human experience, with the real being "its very own self-absence". What Marcel experiences as hunger are the signals of what lies beyond this condition. The epiphanic moments we all know from the "petite madeleine" episode enable Marcel to realise his unhappiness is a form of inattention to these signals and impatience to grasp what they indicate. The signals correspond to a unity much like rhymes in a poem and the deficiency can be redeemed only by attention to rhymes across time and space. What made Marcel unhappy were the attempts to fill the lack by "a strategy of compensation" – physical possession, genre craft or Dionysian indulgence – or by "recapturing or reproducing the 'thing' that's lacking" – reality, realism. Joy is possible only in searching for the enchanted experience of time's absence, as presented in the book we are reading, which takes time.

De Beistegui follows Maurice Blanchot in the uncontroversial claim that the main subject of *In Search of Lost Time* is the possibility of writing, but offers a less hazardous reason. While for Blanchot writing is situated in the lack and the novel's content is a translucent density penetrated very occasionally by rapturous singularities that make such density possible, for de Beistegui writing is a means of seeing reality differently. It "transfigures life, reversing it, not into its opposite but into its other or flip side":

Literature is the flip side of the side that coincides with reality, the wrong side or the inside of the real and the sign of another meaning of experience. Far from fleeing the real ... literature actually tracks it and weaves it, spinning and following its thread. The threads that make up its text or its fabric ... are the threads of the real itself, and its mission is to trace and disentangle them. In the process, literature lets itself be carried off to where the real flees its own self-presence.*

From this we can see that to respond to the signals of the real requires a certain kind of writing, not one of lyric reverie or bureaucratic notation but precarious combinations of both. If the real is its own self-absence, it is not self-sufficient and thereby reliant on the literary project. This is why de Beistegui highlights the art of metaphor in Proust, with a wonderfully provocative rider: "Metaphor is not fancy or mistress of error and falsehood but the figure of the real in its self-transposition or transfiguration. The conversion of matter into spirit but only as an implicit dimension of matter itself."

It is a paradoxical situation, one that worries at habitual common sense: life is elsewhere, or, in Marcel's terms: the only true paradise is a paradise lost. Marcel's life is pierced by signals that, enabled by metaphor, set off a chain of correspondences opening to a unified experience. However, if metaphor is "rooted in the very structure of experience and not simply a rhetorical trope" then the quality of that life resides in the quality of those metaphors, the quality of attention and the quality of writing. It makes literature all the more demanding. *In Search of Lost Time* is a kind of bildungsroman leading to the challenge of this discovery. Marcel shows that the true paradise relies less on formal memory than on chance recognition, those rapturous singularities. It is not a direct product of masterful agency and is therefore always on the brink of falling back into petrifying genres. It's why the novel does not follow the overt facts of Proust's life, and explains why he did not publish the 800-page *Jean Santeuil* and why one reader quoted in *Reality Hunger* insists

Proust is "at base an essayist" and *In Search of Lost Time* is "not fiction".

If we recognise metaphor as the key to unlocking the temporal prison cell, we can then also appreciate why the central stories of *In Search of Lost Time* concern romantic love: Swann's pathetic obsession with Odette, Saint-Loup's for Rachel, and Marcel's own for Gilberte and Albertine. "The real significance of love", de Beistegui writes, "is epistemological: it drives us to imagine what we're unable to know". But, as a character in John McGahern's *Amongst Women* says: "Nothing is so bad as having to imagine". Marcel first meets Albertine as part of a "little gang" of young women he watches from afar in the seaside town Balbec. In fact, it is the gang that attracts him; he wants to be amongst young women in flower. They exist for him like the summer landscape of beach, sea and sky: a larger existence he cannot attain. Eventually Albertine becomes his lover but "the vague and non-existent universe" of her other life, her excursions with Andrée, another member of the little gang, provoke jealousy so that she becomes the title of the fifth volume: *The Captive*.

Some of the most rhapsodic passages in *In Search of Lost Time* are dedicated to Marcel's fascination with the distance at which Albertine holds herself, even when he has her within his four walls. It is here that Proust's unique blend of lyricism and intellectual reflection is especially powerful. These passages are also problematic for contemporary readers. De Beistegui highlights one in particular in which Marcel watches Albertine asleep:

> *Stretched out at full length upon my bed, in an attitude so natural that no art could have devised it, she reminded me of a long blossoming stem that had been laid there, and so in a sense she was: the faculty of dreaming, which I possessed only in her absence, I recovered at such moments in her presence, as though by falling asleep she had become a plant. In this way her sleep realised to a*

certain extent the possibility of love. Alone, I could think of her, but I missed her; I did not possess her. When she was present, I spoke to her, but I was too far absent from myself to be able to think. When she was asleep, I no longer needed to talk. I knew that I was no longer observed by her. I no longer needed to live on the surface of myself.

*By shutting her eyes, by losing consciousness, Albertine had stripped off, one after another, the different personalities with which she had deceived me ever since the day when I had first made her acquaintance. She had called back into herself everything that lay outside, had withdrawn, enclosed, reabsorbed herself into her body. In keeping it in front of my eyes, in my hands, I had an impression of possessing her entirely, which I never had when she was awake. Her life was subjected to me, exhaled towards me its gentle breath. I listened to this murmuring, mysterious emanation, soft as a sea breeze, magical as a gleam of moonlight ... What I felt then was a love as pure, as immaterial, as mysterious as if I had been in the presence of those inanimate creatures that are the beauties of nature. And indeed, as soon as her sleep became at all deep, she ceased to be merely the plant that she had been. Her sleep ... was to me a whole landscape.***

Recently Anne Carson had fun at Marcel's expense, with the audience appreciative of the comedy of Marcel's apparently sexist solipsism, treating Albertine as an object of play in his fantasy. But we can see in this passage how Albertine changes from plant to breeze, from moonlight to landscape, and how then she is like everyone, separate, herself, and yet part of a larger universe. Encountering her escape is as important for Marcel as anything else. For him, the possibility of love appears in the revelation of the correspondences her deep self exhibits:

Albertine's complete throughout all her metamorphoses; she's a bird, a plant, a landscape, she's Odette, Andrée, Marcel, all of them at once and even simultaneously, while we can never say what she truly is, essentially. Like the world in general she's always in a state of becoming, a composition of matter that connects with others and, doing so, becomes something else entirely.

This is what de Beistegui means by "the conversion of matter into spirit but only as an implicit dimension of matter itself". The real is always revealed in something else with no need to privilege one over the other and no need to rage for one order or the other. In this sense, the transcendent is immanent to our own lives, so much as we can write, and write well.

I'm aware that de Beistegui's ontology and theory of metaphor have their own genealogy in European thought; for example Gilles Deleuze – another philosopher who wrote on Proust – and Hans Blumenberg. But this is a review not a patent office and I shall leave tracking those threads to others. Reading *Proust as Philosopher* reminded me of the personal value of critical analysis of single works, how it can crack open the carapace of a classic work of art without bleeding it dry: adding rather than cancelling. It stands alongside Quentin Meillassoux's *The Number and the Siren* as a work that corresponds to what is apparently most untimely.

* Translated by Dorothée Katz and Simon Sparks
** Translated by Scott Moncrieff

The Horizon of Narrative

The first time Hans Henny Jahnn's trilogy *Fluß ohne Ufer* came to my attention was in Reiner Stach's biography of Kafka. I noted that of the "five monumental unfinished ruins of modern German-language prose" that include two by his subject, *River Without Shore* is the only one still to be translated into English. A few years later, China Miéville recommended *The Ship*, the first part of the trilogy that had been translated over forty years ago. Imagine a longer, more expressionistic version of Kafka's *The Stoker* and you have a good idea of what it's like. It made me wish the rest was available in English, not out of some generalised curiosity but an unfocused yearning, as if the German volumes resting on a bookstall stood for the generalised promise of all unread books, the fulfilment of which also remains untranslated.

It wasn't until I read "Landscape as the Origin of Music", Noor de Winter's essay published in the first edition of *Reliquiae*, that the content of the trilogy revealed itself and suggested in part why it remains untranslated: "full of reflections on music, nature and the creation of art", *Fluß ohne Ufer* "tells the story of fictional composer Gustav Anias Horn and his friend Tutein, their travels and friendship". This is a long way from an uncanny thriller and much closer to Thomas Mann's *Doctor Faustus*. No wonder publishers have shied away. "Anias", the essay explains, "is haunted by the possibility of permanent pain without salvation" to the extent that, on a trip to Norway, he empathises with the suffering of birch trees whose leaves are used to feed livestock. He develops "a supernatural longing" to "capture the melody of the soil, the song of the gravel on which the birches grew".

De Winter describes Anias as an artist-as-listener rather than "someone who imprints his vision upon his surroundings"; he is "someone through whom a vision of something else can be transported, translated, transformed". In this way the landscape is an unread book whose translation takes another form. The literal nature of this transformation is revealed when Anias discovers that birch bark looks very much like mechanical piano rolls whose growth rings can be transliterated into written music.

> *Ever-changing interpretations braided themselves into each other, appeared like a deluge of strange harmonies suddenly dissolving, falling apart to lamenting antiphonies [...] When I had played this music I knew it didn't originate in me, it came to me. A miraculous telluric power of disclosure had used me.*

However miraculous, the essay concludes by acknowledging that such music "can express only something of the wonder that [Anias] experienced in the birch grove" and that it is "perhaps the lot of the artist-as-listener to acknowledge the deficiency of any particular realisation of their theme".

This final point reminds us of the closeness we have to the book and the distance we have from its object. While we read of Anias' project and perhaps become enchanted by his example and practice, what we read is the opposite of any epiphanic vertigo we might experience before a landscape or listening to a piece of music. Any lyricism the narrative might have is a result of the animation of the distance between itself and its subject. Music is its own unmediated presence; literature is entirely mediation. We are like Anias himself with the only difference being that our realisation of deficiency is itself the experience of art. An impoverished experience, we might think. So what does this mean for the novel if, as Walter Pater wrote, "all art constantly aspires towards the condition of music"?

The difference between the novel and music appears like that between sociology and sleep: the first only a matter of comprehension and density, and the second a matter of their absence. The curious thing about "the condition of music" is its lack of content. Music can lead one to sense an elemental pressure irreducible to notation or lyric sheet. If we compare it to a vision of nature, the condition is equivalent to where a landscape leads: the blank horizon. From stoney escarpment and dense copse to lush meadow and glistening stream, the eye is drawn to the empty sky in the distance; an epiphany without manifestation. The urge to capture the experience can be seen in the incessant and forlorn posting of heavily filtered nature photographs.

In contrast, there is no visible horizon of the novel. The reader experiences the book by descending into a literary landscape: walking along a dirt path, sheltering in a dappled grove, paddling in a stream. The horizon is obscured. Poetry, which may be thought more tuneful, is elevated by being set to music – think of Blake's "Jerusalem" – while a novel turned into an opera has no bearing on the original. What's closer might be the Proustian epiphany in which time opens and collapses like a concertina, except, again, this is narrated like Anias' experience of telluric power. We might therefore assume that even closer is dreamlike, automatic writing taking precedence over conscious mastery, allowing the chance effects of music to occur. But this would seem to diminish the form, at best subordinate it to music and nature. Notice that the distance between *Ulysses* and *Finnegans Wake* is immeasurably greater than that between a Bach fugue and a Schoenberg piano piece. Yet what if you read novels to approach that horizon? Where is the horizon of narrative?

Perhaps merely asking these questions defines a particular experience of reading and indicates a fundamental disconnection with the prevailing mode of reading fiction, which focuses on the foreground and, if it is aware of something more, misplaces the horizon, like Bach-admirers seeking the true Goldberg among all his variations. What's lacking from literary criticism is the expression and investigation of this experience even though, for me, this must be its primary purpose. It's why Knausgaard's *My Struggle* is such a remarkable work. He is able to unite the banality of a life with the unaccountable experience of art. So perhaps indirection is the necessary future of the form, although, as *Fluß ohne Ufer* demonstrates, it has always been the form, waiting to be translated, a song waiting to be heard, a clearing waiting for daylight.

How Does Writing Fulfil Itself?

Jesus was not your everyday literary critic. Luke tells of his teaching in a synagogue:

> And he came to Nazareth, where he had been brought up: and, as his custom was, he went into the synagogue on the sabbath day, and stood up for to read. And there was delivered unto him the book of the prophet Esaias. And when he had opened the book, he found the place where it was written,
>
> The Spirit of the Lord is upon me, because he hath anointed me to preach the gospel to the poor; he hath sent me to heal the broken-hearted, to preach deliverance to the captives, and recovering of sight to the blind, to set at liberty them that are bruised,
>
> To preach the acceptable year of the Lord.
>
> And he closed the book, and he gave it again to the minister, and sat down. And the eyes of all them that were in the synagogue were fastened on him. And he began to say unto them, This day is this scripture fulfilled in your ears.

We're so used to commentary on literature as secondary, basking in the glow of the object's aura, that the idea of fulfilment is almost impossible to comprehend. This day is this scripture fulfilled in your ears. How does writing fulfil itself?

The question relates to Slavoj Žižek's wish to act like the characters in Ágota Kristóf's *The Notebook*, reading the novel as a guidebook or thought-experiment. Imagine instead Žižek proclaiming himself the ethical monster the novel embodies: this day this novel is fulfilled in your daily paper. If we did, we'd see something other than a "Book that changed me" article. Actually, we'd see something like *The Notebook*. This is why I expressed surprise that Žižek chose not to include any discussion of the form taken by the novel.

We regard Jesus' pronouncement as a given, an act fundamental to Western culture, and we regard Kristóf's novel as part
of an endless footnote to the main work, or we would if it were
not a footnote now so vast that it has broken free to bob along on
a sea without shore. We can no longer see the continent from
which contemporary fiction and critical discourse embarked and
from which it mined ballast to keep it afloat. In other words, our
reading is an evolved model of that sabbath ritual. Despite the
claims of escapism and education, the assumption of healing the
brokenhearted, offering deliverance to captives, sight to the
blind and liberty to the bruised can be found everywhere in
literary discussion, for instance that *Guardian* series title: "A book
that changed me".

I have approached the problem of this reading evolution
before with the question: where is the horizon of narrative? The
premise was that in a landscape our eyes are drawn to the
horizon and this somehow guarantees the presence of what we
see and delivers its gift of possibility in an infinity of light. For
Christians, the landscape might be Jesus' death on the cross and
the horizon his resurrection. However, it's that word "light" I
want to focus on, as it invokes Heidegger's *Lichtung*, commonly
translated as "clearing", an open space you might wish for while
traversing an otherwise impassable forest and, in Heidegger's
terms, a metaphor for where beings are revealed, for truth to
emerge from concealment. In terms of narrative rather than
Christology or ontology, the horizon or clearing is obscured by
solid facts, the trees and foliage, allowing us to bury ourselves in
dendrology: who among us prefers the sycamore over the horse
chestnut, and why? Or should we be more open to the boabab
and the gingko biloba now admirably transplanted into our
woods? But most of all, where is the next Great American
Sequoia?

So, instead, to rephrase the question, where is the clearing in
a novel? Each new book has the clearing as its potential and its

self-evidence might explain why I am drawn to a certain reading experience that otherwise goes unexamined in routine reviewing and criticism, mainly because it is both haphazard and subjective. Fortunately online reviewing and criticism has the freedom to bring the work into the orbit of the reader as a body and a life rather than as a consumer.

The experience seems to occur at the level of the sentence rather than the story, though it occurs only within a narrative. Many years ago, I was too early for an interrogation over my unemployment and, passing time browsing a bookshop in the least cosmopolitan city in England, I chanced upon two novels by an Austrian author whose work I was interested in reading but who was then difficult to find in translation. (It was so long ago that both paperbacks were priced £3.95.)

In the gloom and tension of the situation, I opened Peter Handke's *Across* and read the first lines:

> *I shut my eyes and out of the black letters the city lights took shape. Not the lights of the Old City, but the streetlamps that had just gone on in one of the many housing developments on the southern periphery. The development, consisting of two-storey single-family houses, is situated on the big plain at the foot of the Untersberg.**

And, as I did so, the gloom lifted and the tension disappeared, replaced by calm and relaxed concentration. At least, that's the story. At the time, a miraculous one. So why did this passage have this effect? The three sentences are straightforward and do not state anything profoundly meaningful about life. Not even close. Apart from the opening sentence, they could be from a local council planning document. Of course, it is the first sentence that makes it fiction: that odd, contradictory movement of eyes shutting to blackness and light taking shape as a result (there it is again, Knausgaard's light), which might explain the transformation of my state into a story: the sense that narrative is parallel rather than subordinate to the conditions of life and one can easily step aside without abandoning one or the other. Among other things. This is how a modern novel might fulfil itself, by creating a clearing for this to be absorbed by the reader.

The effect appears to be a combination of chance and design, which should offer anyone an excuse to start writing. No need for a story. Milan Kundera says "dramatic tension is the real curse of the novel, because it transforms every thing, even the most beautiful pages, even the most surprising scenes and observations merely into steps leading to the final resolution". For a clearing, resolution is hacked away and a path opened. This has happened for me in many places, and these examples come from my early days of reading fiction (the dates are when I first read them). First from Kundera himself and *The Unbearable Lightness of Being* (1986):

*I have been thinking about Tomas for many years. But only in the light of these reflections [on the opposition of lightness and weight] did I see him clearly. I saw him standing at the window of his flat and looking across the court-yard at the opposite walls, not knowing what to do.***

Second, in the preface to the first volume of Jacques Roubaud's *The Great Fire of London* (1995):

*By consigning to paper today the first lines of this prose (manifold in imagination) I am perfectly aware of administering a mortal, definitive blow to what I conceived on turning thirty as an alternative to self-chosen extinction, and which served for over two decades as the project of my existence.****

Certainly there is a quality of valediction here but at the beginning, which surely changes matters. In Kundera's paragraph the narrative is set forth on uncertainty, intellect and imagination. And third in Gabriel Josipovici's novel *Distances* (published in *In the Fertile Land*, 1988):

> *A woman.*
> *The sea.*
> *She begins to walk.*
> *She walks.*
> *She walks.*

The staccato rhythm here was like nothing I'd read before and, as each sentence and section built in length, it became like breathing itself. Reading, breathing, walking, clearing. This might be how writing fulfils itself.

* Translated by Ralph Manheim
** Translated by Michael Henry Heim
*** Translated by Dominic di Bernardi

Kafka: Not an Authority of Power

You have made me unhappy. I bought your "Metamorphosis" as a present for my cousin, but she doesn't know what to make of the story. My cousin gave it to her mother, who doesn't know what to make of it either.

So begins a letter to Franz Kafka written in 1917 by Dr Siegfried Wolff, a veteran of the trenches. He goes on to list other family members equally perplexed by the story and pleads for some help to protect his reputation: "Only you can help me". Apparently there is no evidence of a reply. Not that possession would help much: perplexity towards Kafka's fiction hasn't ceased despite the deluge of secondary material. Sometimes it is expressed with Wolff's politeness, sometimes with a journalist's boorish impatience. "Great antipathy towards Metamorphosis", was Kafka's own response. "Unreadable ending. Imperfect almost to its very marrow."

The problem with Kafka's fiction is that while in general the surface presents a generic world, recognisable even to those of us living a century later, the content is not familiar; it does not counsel the reader with wise observations on the human condition or provide practical information and descriptions of places for the reader to absorb and use in their lives; there isn't even a happy ending in sight. The only resort for the reader is critical: "What do I make of this?"

On a personal level the answer takes the regular form of what to say in discussion with friends on the common ground of "a good read" but, in the public and more private arenas, this is more problematic. Over the decades there have been innumerable readings of Kafka's fiction named under various scholarly disciplines, each one underwriting his stories with a theoretical rigour lacking in everyday communication. This guarantees at least three things: that Kafka's fiction can be contained by structured analysis; that it has value only insofar as it confirms the premises of that analysis; and that the stories are capacious enough to accommodate an infinite number of disciplines. The first and second are full of promise for the reader keen to learn and use fiction as proof of theoretical authority. They also nullify the superstitious power of the object while allowing it to live like an insect quivering in a spider's web. However, these guarantees are possible only as far as one is able to deal with the inherent bad faith of the third: why choose the Freudian reading over the Marxist? Or, if you think the Existentialist reading fails, what do you think of the Gnostic one? In bringing social esteem to the daydream of fiction, analysis raises fiction to new heights or depths of impenetrability, leaving the third guarantee full of despair because the number and variety of readings demands a decision, sending the reader back to the beginning of the search, only this time in the shadow of an entire library. Who is quivering now?

Biography offers a compromise in that it is a craft requiring certain constraints yet without the rigidity of a theoretical armature: it is both authoritative and curious. *The Years of Insight*, Shelley Frisch's translation of the third and final volume of Reiner Stach's definitive life of Kafka, begins with a scene-setter of Prague at the outbreak of the First World War and the crowd-pulling recreation of a trench from the frontline, which Kafka visited and which of course immediately suggests inspiration for *The Burrow*. We are on familiar ground here. But this is no series of suggestive coincidences. Instead Stach allows the reader to sense the free play of contingent conditions of Kafka's life, enlarging the picture when events such as the war intervene, or switching the focus to characters like the actor Ludwig Hardt, the journalist Milena Jesenská and the agricultural adventures of his sister Ottla when their influence is entertaining (as in Hardt's case) or profound (as in the other two). This means there is much less of the prurient conjecture of Saul Friedländer's recent study. Stach continues with Kafka's magical reunion with Felice Bauer in Marienbad before the relationship ended for good, the postwar epidemic of Spanish flu, which Kafka caught and miraculously survived, the creative burst he found in his sister's tiny cottage beneath Hradčany castle and, finally, the discovery of his tuberculosis and the years of convalescence in various sanatoria; a time that included living on a farm in Zurau, writing *The Castle*, another fraught engagement, the affair with Milena and moving to Berlin with Dora Diamant.

Stach argues that such contingency troubled Kafka, which in turn infuriated his closest friend, Max Brod. Whereas Brod was constantly publishing in multiple genres, performing at readings, making a public stand for Zionism, his friend was fastidious in the extreme, preferring not to push himself, commit to a movement or even pursue a living by writing. However, there is a brief glimpse of Kafka's possible other life when in 1916 he was invited by an art gallery in Munich to present "a literary evening" using his own work. He would be mixing with the German avant-garde including Rainer Maria Rilke. But it was in the midst of war and Kafka's reading of *In the Penal Colony* did not rouse the audience. As always, Kafka accepted the criticism and apparently was not distraught by the poor reviews in the Munich press. Stach writes that for Kafka "the concept of twists of fate stood for the absolutely unendurable" and, despite its apparently failure to convince others, this event at least convinced him this was necessary: he was a writer in essence and not a celebrity cruising the social whirl.

We know how important the act of writing was to Kafka in regard to those twists of fate from the letter to his father written two years later. That it was unsent is less important than that it was written. Stach argues that Kafka was "impervious to abstract reproofs" but was "receptive to prelinguistic gestural, spontaneous outbursts", and presents a list of an eclectic treasury where "absolute authenticity" could be found, so we might see the gesture of the letter as primary. It becomes clearer in the first line of the letter: he is unable to answer his father's question as to why he is so afraid of him precisely because he is afraid. He can not contain the answer in his head in order to answer. Silence is the answer. This makes writing all the more challenging because it is always threatened by the gravity of rhetoric and overt content. Silence is the proof that cannot be admitted to court. So how to at least approach the prelinguistic in writing? We can see how Kafka tries in other first lines, this time of the diaries:

> The onlookers go rigid when the train goes past. 'If he should forever ahsk me.' The ah, released from the sentence, flew off like a ball on the meadow.

Plain observations were it not for the uncomfortable presence of what they release in meaning, or lack of it. In March 1912, after writing part of a story in his diary, he stops and reveals his dissatisfaction:

> Nothing, nothing. This is the way I raise up ghosts before me. I was involved, even if only superficially, only in the passage, 'Later he had....' mostly in the 'pour'. For a moment I thought I saw something real in the description of the landscape.

These moments had their equivalents in his life. He regarded the eruption of tuberculosis as an outburst of authority and wrote in order to appreciate the meaning. More happily, in a letter from Marienbad, he tells Brod of Felice Bauer's trusting gaze in the time they spent alone: "I got my bearings somewhat while she, who had always held out her hands into the utter void to help, helped again, and with her I arrived at a human relationship of a kind that I had never known before". "This gaze remained the symbol of everything good", Stach writes, "the assurance that redemption was only conceivable but feasible". Just a gaze; nothing said. Four years earlier he had noticed Felice's "bony, empty face that wore its emptiness openly" and, no matter how suspiciously unromantic it may read to modern eyes like Friedländer's, he was immediately attracted to her and the possibility of a marriage in which "harmony ... runs beneath any opinions" and "cannot be analyzed but only felt". Marriage was otherwise the false, abstract, oppressive realm of the father. Their subsequent correspondence eroded that potential for harmony, the ghosts of rhetoric drinking their written kisses. He felt it again in Marienbad when he joined the Rabbi of Belz and his entourage inspecting the sights of the spa town, writing in detail to Brod about that too, fascinated by the "serene, happy faith" of the man and his followers yet not convinced he was in the presence of mystic knowledge: "I think that the deeper meaning is that there is none and in my opinion this is quite enough".

Reading the letter, one can't help but wonder what a biography might be like if the subject could be observed like the Rabbi of Belz, without interrogation and judgment. What might we see instead? This may be the province of another genre but the virtue of *The Years of Insight* is that it contains so many small details like Dr Wolff's letter and the Munich expedition that one is able to sense Kafka as a living presence rather than a repository of secrets emitting evidence for the prosecution. But this is why Kafka has such renown: his stories hurtle forward, embodying what can only be felt not analysed: the pressure driving Georg Bendemann to throw himself from a bridge minutes after quietly sitting at a desk writing; the interruption of routine when Gregor Samsa is transformed into an insect and descends quickly toward death, continuing with his sister Grete stretching her young body on the family's celebratory picnic. What can we make of this terrible momentum? Perhaps Kafka felt *Metamorphosis* imperfect because its length obscured the overall gesture of the story and the short, aphoristic writings in the Bohemian countryside attempted a resistance to this tendency – sentences as gestures ("A cage went in search of a bird"). Writing seems to usurp metamorphosis and while at first its abstract definitions offer a defence from change, it then becomes a tormenting, unfulfilled promise of freedom ("My prison-cell – My fortress"). Writing's remoteness drives the perverse enthusiasm of the penal colony's officer for a form of execution in which writing is engraved in living flesh, guaranteeing its authority but, in this case, killing the one who values it so highly. In the opposite way, what kills the hunger artist is an absence of nourishment. Starvation is the truth misconstrued as art. For this reason it would have made no difference to Kafka had the audience in Munich been more enthusiastic about his story; it was not about confirmation of a writer's mastery.

The unfortunate irony then is that Kafka's own authority as a writer largely rests on Dr Wolff's misapprehension that there is a deeper meaning requiring more than the movement of the stories and which only the author or sundry experts can impart. While readers of *The Years of Insight* receive a rich and moving account of the pressures of one man's life in a certain time and place, the true authority of the biography is felt in what is glimpsed around the accumulated detail, and even more so in what gets lost: photographs taken with Felice Bauer ruined because she inserted the film back to front, the stash of notebooks written in Berlin confiscated by the Gestapo, the life not lived because it was ended prematurely by a disease that would soon be curable and, most of all, what happened to his friends and family years later. It is not an authority of power.

Death stalks the reading of any biography, even that of a living subject, but this one more than most. For seven years Kafka endured the tuberculosis that would kill him soon after he found domestic contentment with Dora Diamant. This makes for desperately sad reading. But nine years later the Nazis took power in Germany, and the three-page epilogue registering without elaboration the fate of his family and friends is an exceptionally desolate space. Reiner Stach concludes by reiterating the fact that Kafka's world was thereby erased and all that remains is his language. This is true enough, yet his request to Brod to destroy all his papers was a necessary gesture in keeping with a deep mistrust of language, and a final gesture we should appreciate in kind.

The Munro Doctrine

Two years ago, walking by the sea, I listened to the *New Yorker*'s fiction podcast in which the writer Lauren Groff read aloud her choice of story from the magazine's history: Alice Munro's *Axis*. It was pleasant company for three-quarters of an hour, telling the story of two women, Grace and Avie, as they reach adulthood in the post-war years, go to college and begin relationships. For Groff, reading an earlier story by Munro was an epiphany and changed her mind about fiction. As a young writer, the writers she wanted to emulate were "very experimental, the breakers of the form". "I didn't scorn but I didn't love the realists", she says, but, after reading the story, she "looked up and the whole world had changed". Munro is "a revolutionary" in what she does with time and structure, "but it's not super flashy; it's very deep". "Alice Munro does time and structure better than almost anyone", seeing time as "layers of tissue as opposed to a linear way", which is "incredibly interesting in a short story format".

The narrative twist of *Axis* is that the fictional events are narrated from the perspective of fifty years in the future when the past re-enters the present via a chance meeting, something that's bound to resonate with readers of a certain age, as it did with me. Nevertheless, two years on and surprised that Munro had been awarded the Nobel Prize, I listened again hoping to appreciate why the committee chose this "master of the contemporary short story" over other living writers. In the end, it helped me to appreciate a lot more.

Axis was doubly resonant with me because I was reminded of all the John Updike novels I'd read when I started reading fiction in the late 1980s, but perhaps not for the reasons you might assume. While *Axis* traverses the same landscape of lower-middle-class sexual politics as Updike's work, it is above all the sentences that evoke that time; sentences in which the narrator has no qualms in explaining why, for example, Avie decided to have sex with her boyfriend:

> *She thought it would make him seem more manly, more assured. He was a nice-looking, eager boy with dark hair flopping over his forehead, and he had a tendency to pick out people he could worship: a professor, a brilliant older student, a girl: Avie. If they slept together, she thought, she might fall in love with him.*

Sentences like this appear throughout. When Grace and her boyfriend Royce are in dialogue, she expresses her preference for Acacia trees while he holds his tongue and thinks:

> *Favorite trees? What next: favorite flower, favorite star, favorite windmill? Did she have a favorite fence post? About to inquire, he figured it would hurt her feelings.*

There is something peculiarly North American in these sentences – witty, wistful, above all *knowing* – perhaps because every week on Michael Silverblatt's BookWorm podcast, I listen to extracts reporting the inner lives and experience of people narrated in the third person. In the movie *Wonder Boys*, Tobey Maguire's contribution to Michael Douglas' creative writing class begins in exactly this way. Updike's fiction is exemplary in its reliance on these reports, something Gore Vidal noted, if for different reasons. Summarising the plot of the 1996 novel *In the Beauty of the Lilies*, he quotes a typical line:

> *Clark is in rebellion against the Communism of his mother and her friends pinks if not reds [sic] and, worse, unabashed enemies of the United States in the long, long, war against the Satanic Ho Chi Minh. "Mom, too, wanted North Vietnam to win, which seemed strange to Clark, since America had been pretty good to her." As irony, this might have been telling, but irony is an arrow that the*

Good Fiction Fairy withheld from the Updike quiver. Consequently, this non sequitur can only make perfect sense to a writer who believes that no matter how misguided, tyrannous and barbarous the rulers of one's own country have become, they must be obeyed; and if one has actually made money and achieved a nice place in the country they have hijacked, then one must be doubly obedient, grateful, too.

For Vidal, the non sequitur is solely political but the sentence also enables us to recognise how Updike uses fictional characters as vehicles for comment, with their inner lives as accessible as mustard in a jar. Yet how did the narrator know Clark found anything strange? And, in Axis, how can anyone but Avie and Royce know what they thought?

In those early days of reading, I would not have questioned such narration and I suspect the vast majority of common readers will be nonplussed by such difficulties; this is what fiction does, after all, isn't it? Perhaps their happy innocence reveals what is after all ideological – that narration is imperial in nature, demanding that writers colonise minds as an empire colonises the world and calls it freedom. The ideology of power infects the reception of literature too, so that mastery is the guarantee of literary value. Note the prevalence of the word "tackle" in newspapers' description of what an author does to their subject matter.

What Lauren Groff sees as revolutionary appears then to be merely the condensation into a short story of what Proust or Sebald do in the novel. But, in their works, the narration is for the most part first-person or telescoped through that first person, so the kind of sentences Munro uses would never appear without qualification. In this way the literary project is borne on uncertainty in the way life, as seen in the conclusion to *Axis*, is determined by either chance or necessity. The impact of this revelation in *Axis* is certainly moving in context, but hardly deep or revolutionary.

The alternative in the US, those "very experimental" writers, those "breakers of the form", might be the school of Gordon Lish, whose writing "represents the US's answer to Samuel Beckett and Thomas Bernhard". His creative writing classes advanced "a distinctive and demanding approach to the craft of fiction", preaching "what his student Gary Lutz has called a 'poetics of the sentence' – an almost mystical attunement to language's hidden rhythms and resonances". So let's sample some of Lutz's sentences from his short story *Loo* narrated by an unnamed sibling:

> *She supposed that it helped her to be far from the center of anything and uninfluenced by what went on in any thicker populations.*
> *Her private life was not so much private as simply witnessless.*
> *Her life did not so much advance as narrow itself out unamelioratingly.*

In isolation the contrast to the work of Munro is not subtle, but the epistemological certainty here and throughout is identical.

Kafka recognised the danger of such sentences in a diary entry from 1911 in which he says the "special nature" of his inspiration is that, as a writer, he can do everything: "When I arbitrarily write a single sentence, for instance, 'He looked out of the window', it already has perfection". On first glance this appears to be uncharacteristic hubris, but "perfection" here is the mastery Georg Bendemann exercises as he gazes through his window high over Prague and writes to his Russian friend before being condemned to death by drowning by forces without and within the domain of writing. Georg's real life begins only when the sentence has been carried out and the story ends. The rest is fantasy.

I have been thinking about Tomas for many years [...] I saw him

standing at the window of his flat and looking across the court-yard
at the opposite walls, not knowing what to do.

Milan Kundera's *Unbearable Lightness of Being* begins by presenting the main character as both a product of imagination and independent of it, with the effect of foregrounding the work and responsibility of the imagination rather than indulging its freedom to noodle with language. (The claim to know Tomas' uncertainty exists under this effect.) What Beckett and Bernhard, Kafka and Kundera have in common then is very different to what is shared by Munro and Lutz.

While thinking about the differences, I remembered an essay in *The Modern English Novel* (1975) by John Mepham on narrative and fictional time in Woolf's *To the Lighthouse*. It might help here. He begins by acknowledging that for a story to be told at all there must be "the voice of one who knows". Writing would then be a means of creating order by way of an independent framework much like those provided by political or religious values. "But", Mepham writes, "what if we lack this sense of epistemological certainty? What if our experience seems fragmented, partial, incomplete, disordered?" The reader is then asked to think about the memory of a person they have loved, an act perhaps similar to Munro and Lutz writing about Grace, Avie and Loo. Without the means of thought and expression provided by an independent framework "we might have the feeling that the remembered person escapes us, is ungraspable, cannot be contained in our minds except as a disordered flow of particular fragments of memory". We might still feel there is a unity in these memories if only we could use them as raw materials to "work on, condense, assemble into a form of speech worthy of their object":

If writing could be the means of completing the half-finished phrase,
or bringing together and thereby enriching the fragments, then

writing would not be primarily the telling of a story but the search for a voice. Narration would not be the embodiment of some pre-existing knowledge but the satisfaction of the desire to speak with appropriate intensity about things of which our knowledge is most uncertain.

Does the search for a voice define what is unique about contemporary European fiction in that the sense of epistemological certainty is certainly lacking? Mepham goes on to examine the relationship between the narration of *To the Lighthouse* and the fictional story told within that narration. I was struck by a quotation in which parts of words are emboldened to emphasise the narrative's own search for a form worthy of its object, while also reminding me of Lish's demand for an attunement to the hidden rhythms and resonances of language:

Standing between her knees, very stiff, James felt all her strength flaring up to be drunk and quenched by the beak of brass, the arid scimitar of the make, which smote mercilessly, again and again, demanding sympathy … James as he stood stiff between her knees, felt her rise in a rose-flowered fruit tree laid with leaves and dancing boughs into which the beak of brass, the arid scimitar of his father, the egotistical man, plunged and smote, demanding sympathy.

In this [Mepham writes] *we suddenly hear the narration trans-formed into poetry. We hear repetitions of metrically striking phrases. It is as if the narrative space and time are multiplying themselves. Things which are singular and short-lived in the fiction become multiple and protracted in the narration, as if their fictional intensity were forcing an expansion of narrative dimensions. Repetition slows down fictional time for us, and opens up its pores and allows its full force to swell through into the narration.*

The word "repetition" reminds me of the most alluring feature of Thomas Bernhard's prose which is, however, used less in his short stories, suggesting that the short story itself is less amenable to the slowing down necessary to be worthy of its object. Of course, Woolf also uses the kind of sentences of which I have been suspicious, but here the attunement is to another's experience sensed in the swell of wandering words. The short story instead tends to display a confidence in form, of the strength of a long-practised voice, and the dominance of narrative time. It is appropriate then that the Nobel committee chose the word "master". Contrast this to Woolf's creative letting go.

Thomas Bernhard's Prizes

After days of inert wondering why Thomas Bernhard's *My Prizes* felt like more than what Geoff Dyer calls "a weakish book" (and thereby, according to the dictates of professional reception, valuable only for throwing the so-called greatness of his novels into finer relief) or, rather, why it felt that this so-called weakness was in fact *a strength* in the same way that the illness (or, to be more precise, the *double illness*) that I was enduring was fortunate in that it demanded the choice of an episodic book to read, as it enabled me to consider *basic questions* rather than suffering to read another product of industry-friendly dilettantism, I read Ingeborg Bachmann's brilliant short essay on her friend and discovered she had asked questions about Thomas Bernhard that had also nagged at me:

> *The fact that a certain person writes at a distance from contemporary literature and increases this distance through solitude ... is already a reason for not knowing how to begin to do him justice. Where does he belong, what does he want, where are his points of reference (to what end?), in which conversation, hence in which non-conversation, does this monologue of his participate, what does he have to say and to whom?**

Yes, I thought, what makes Bernhard uniquely disturbing appears to have something to do with his personal reticence, a silence reminiscent of the terrible solitude out of which his characters begin to speak and yet which seems to have been Bernhard's only way of speaking, a kind of self-stifling game, or something to do with how his work emphasises the solitude necessary to all writing, its remove from Sunday Supplement profiles, bookshop signings and prize ceremonies, and why it is best to go, like Bernhard, in the opposite direction, even if that means reinforcing exceptional solitude.

After reading Bernhard, one is left with the impossibility of doing justice to the silence behind the game. Clearly this is due to the moderating activity of the critical act and its tendency to orchestrate traditions rather than self-blinding before singularities, but this is also present in the malady of existence, as brought forth by Thomas Bernhard so clearly in his narratives. So, yes, *My Prizes* is a minor work, a collection dredged from the publisher's bottom drawer and diluted compared to the novels, and, yes, while the anecdotes expose the grotesque vanity and philistine violence of municipal art culture so brilliantly that it is probably enough only to celebrate the comedy, the anger and the excess of the collection, none of this would express anything new or worth saying. Every week someone announces to a startled world how funny and dark Bernhard is or how unfunny and dark Bernhard is, and everything they say is true or not true and not worth saying again.

But what might be worth saying again is the significance of the recurring ambiguity of the reckless acts in Bernhard's fiction, something repeated throughout *My Prizes*. In the first essay he needs a suit for a ceremony and at very short notice chooses one from the rack of a posh menswear store. After the event he decides it's too small and takes it back to demand a replacement, which, to his surprise, he receives. For the next prize he decides the money should go towards buying a house, so an estate agent lines up twelve farmhouses in upper Austria for a full day's viewing. The first is mouse-infested, has damp-rotted floors and is much too big, but, before he's seen the second, let alone the twelfth, he decides to buy it there and then. Days follow in which he frets over the decision: the prize money will pay only an installment – so where will he find the money to pay the remainder let alone refurbish the building? We don't find out but we know from elsewhere the farmhouse became his country retreat for the rest of his life. Later, another prize pays for "storm windows".

Another prize prompts him to buy a car despite having never driven one. In a showroom he sees a Triumph Herald and once again buys it on the spot, demanding the display car to drive away immediately. He drives to Croatia where he and his "aunt" had rented a villa. In his room he writes the terrifying novella *Amras*, sends it to his publisher and, to clear his head, goes for a drive along the coast and promptly has a life-threatening accident. Back in Vienna, he hires the best and most expensive solicitor to deal with the case and frets about the extravagance given the regular ill-fortune of cross-border justice. But once again things work out and he gets more money in compensation than he had ever hoped for.

These are just a few examples of reckless behaviour from the nine essays but, as I said, they appear throughout his work. There's the famous bike ride in *Gathering Evidence* and the abrupt changes in habit that recur in various novels, such as the beginning of *Gehen*, translated as *Walking*, apparently his break-through work stylistically. Except in *My Prizes* he doesn't talk about his work! The car and the crash are discussed in detail but *Amras* itself, this extraordinary work whose fiftieth anniversary it is this year, is mentioned only in passing and almost dismissively as "romantic, something born of a young man who'd been reading Novalis for months".

The most notable example of behavioural change comes at the beginning of the valedictory novel *Extinction*, with perhaps the greatest opening sentence in modern literature.

On the twenty-ninth, having returned from Wolfsegg, I met my pupil Gambetti on the Pincio to discuss arrangements for the lessons he was to receive in May, writes Franz-Josef Murau, and impressed once again by his high intelligence, I was so refreshed and exhilarated, so glad to be living in Rome and not in Austria, that instead of walking home along the Via Condotti, as I usually do, I crossed the Flaminia and the Piazza del Popolo and walked the whole length of the Corso before returning to my apartment in the Piazza Minerva, where at about two o'clock I received the telegram informing me that my parents and my brother, Johannes, had died. Parents and Johannes killed in accident. Caecilia, Amalia, it read.**

The implicit connection of the change in Franz-Josef's routine to the change in his fortune comes from the excess of detail within the proliferating clauses and the desolate two-sentence telegram that follows immediately. But how can they be connected? The connection is both obvious and absurd. However, rather than seek cause and effect, we need only see this perplexity as the birth of the narratives we are reading and the voices of individuals rising from the predicament of "exigency, necessity, inexorability", as Bachmann describes it.

This is the key to Bernhard's radicalism and why he is more than a scourge of bourgeois pretensions, or whatever else the critics say, and why it's impossible to pin him down. His prose soars, exploding like fireworks illuminating the landscape for a moment before plummeting to earth in darkness. If he knew where he belonged, what he wanted, what he had to say and to what end, in what conversation or non-conversation he might participate, his work would be very different; *das gewöhnliche Zeug*, to borrow Kafka's uncle's phrase: the usual stuff.

In the Summer of 1970 Bernhard starred in *Drei Tage*, a filmed monologue in which he suggests why his style of writing does not escape what is written about:

The thing I find most terrifying is writing prose ... it's pretty much the most difficult thing for me ... And the moment I realized this and became conscious of it, I swore to myself that from then on I would do nothing but write prose. Of course I could have done something completely different. I have studied many other disciplines, but none of them are terrifying.***

* Translated by Flowerville
** Translated by David McLintock
*** Translated by Douglas Robertson

Two Paths for Writing

It's been said that *Boyhood Island* is "the most Proustian" of Karl Ove Knausgaard's *My Struggle* series, and while it is true that both Proust and Knausgaard present intense remembrances of childhood, the same could be said of many other novels, for example Tomas Bennerhed's *The Ravens*, published at the same time by the Clerkenwell Press and, like *Boyhood Island*, a novel of a 1970s childhood set in Scandinavia. Both Proust's and Knausgaard's would surely be lost among them were it not for what sets them apart.

What sets them apart might best be summarised as the lingering uncertainty of their generic status. These are both presented as novels, but we know they are *not quite* novels. This has a profound impact. For all the differences between the authors that are finally destructive to the casual comparison, there is a common pressure exerted by the formal quality of each narrative voice: an essayistic spirit set within a distinct, first-person predicament refusing the comfortable distance of the knowing third person and, because of that, demanding that the reader participates in the questing nature of the narration.

While the overture to *In Search of Lost Time* emerges from the uncertain place between dreaming and wakefulness, *Boyhood Island* merely introduces a discussion of the status of childhood memory. After a traditional family scene of moving into a new house on a Norwegian island narrated with objective confidence, Knausgaard interrupts the nostalgic flow and admits that he doesn't remember any of it himself: the action and dialogue are inventions based on family legend. As the distance is made explicit, there is no blurring of generic edges.

Memory is pragmatic, it is sly and artful, but not in any hostile or malicious way; on the contrary, it does everything it can to keep its *host satisfied. Something pushes a memory into the great void of oblivion, something distorts it beyond recognition, something misunderstands it totally, something, and this something is as good as nothing, recalls it with sharpness, clarity and accuracy. That which is remembered accurately is never given to you to determine.**

This is certainly a truism yet, placed before a narrative explicitly based on the author's own life, it introduces anxiety to the mournful dejection that personal memories invariably provoke, making what proceeds less an indulgence than a nervous exploration of what remains. As a writer then, Knausgaard, like Proust, must navigate a path between the total freedom offered by the constraints of genre – amply demonstrated by Tomas Bennerhed's reliance on heavily descriptive prose to dissemble its lack of truth and necessity – and the silence of terminal uncertainty. It is here that Knausgaard retreats from Marcel's quest to recover the living presence of the past and instead sticks to a straightforward narration of everyday life. There are only two brief, vertiginous diversions that resemble anything like those in the first two volumes and what elevates them beyond fictionalised memoir, and, as a result, the sly and artful come to the fore.

He writes that young Karl Ove took great pleasure in not defecating when he felt the need, sticking his fingers up his backside to smell what he held back, which means we have the author of a six-part autobiographical work reporting that he was anally retentive as a child! He then enjoyed the relief of letting go, a feeling perhaps similar to completing the sixth and final volume of *My Struggle*. Moreover, he is told off by his teacher for revealing in class the reasons for a classmate's broken home and is instructed that he should learn some social decorum. Are these anecdotal precursors of later life too good to be true? Sometimes it seems that way, especially as much less trivial events are later pushed toward the void.

Where Knausgaard might become realigned with Proust is the

tension in the book created by opposing ways of life. In *Swann's Way*, the child Marcel walks two paths in the country surrounding his home: going in opposite directions and accessed by different gates, the Méséglise Way is full of lower-class sexuality and sensuous nature, while the Guermantes Way presents the aura of history, nobility and the glamour of high society. Each represents a core example for Marcel's understanding in later life and the potential for happiness – what Deleuze called his "apprenticeship to signs". Each has its appeals but they are apparently irreconcilable. Which should he choose? Knausgaard has similar paths: the island's wooded landscape full of schoolmates, adventure and exciting temptations, and the one provided at home under the panoptic gaze of his tyrannical father. How will the boy deal with such competing pressures? Outside he behaves recklessly, testing the limits of his freedom, while at home he cringes with fear at the probable consequences. Knausgaard has acknowledged that the "dynamic force in this book" is:

> *the difference between the freedom outside and the prison-like state inside, and how the latter very slowly influences the former, and in the end changes it fundamentally. Another word for that would be integration, I think. The eye of God ends up inside, so that, in the end, you take care of judgment and punishment yourself.*

Perhaps a supplication to greater powers sums up the reckoning with the past and present that the book sequence displays and why it began with the death of his father. However, in *Time Regained*, the adult Marcel takes the Méséglise Way again and discovers it is in fact physically linked to the Guermantes Way; there wasn't such a profound opposition and, in revising his assumptions, he becomes more aware of continuities and possibilities for revising ongoing assumptions. The proximity of separate paths turns out to be true of Karl Ove's paths too, leading us to a better comparison than with Proust's novel – that of Kafka and his father, or, more specifically, Georg Bendemann and *his* father.

The Judgment begins with Georg's self-assurance that he can write about his life to his friend in Russia without worrying too much about the consequences. Writing is freedom. But this is soon ended by his father when he reveals that the Russian friend knows all about Georg's self-serving behaviour because he, the father, has been in contact with him all along. Georg's suicide then is a submission to the power that reveals itself to be present in writing too. His suicide is the murder of writing by means of writing. Compare this with Karl Ove's actions as his family prepares to leave the island idyll. The teenager finds himself out of God's sight and, at a school camp, he and other boys pursue girls and behave in ways that readers will have to read and judge for themselves, if indeed they notice it all, so cursory is the description. Collusion with other boys is significant here because it dilutes responsibility, allowing the brute instincts of teenagers to stand in for the "suicide" of the oppressed little Karl Ove; these girls disappear into the distance like a roadkill in a rearview mirror. Writing is as pragmatic as memory.

> *I guess I have a talent for humiliation, a place within me that experience can't reach, which is terrible in real life, but something that comes in handy in writing. It seems as though humiliation has become a career for me.*

Behind this confession is perhaps what is most disturbing about *Boyhood Island*: the possibility that father's tyranny is growing in the little boy even as he appears to resist it, or, to be less personal and less judgmental, the manifestation of the manipulative power that secretes itself within even the most open, honest, self-abasing act.

* Translated by Don Bartlett

A Silhouette of Itself

Some novels offer the perfect opportunity for reviewers to palliate otherwise desolate and sundered lives. Notable examples in recent years include Vila-Matas' *Montano's Malady*, Jonathan Littell's *The Kindly Ones* and Tao Lin's first novel *Eeeee Eee Eeee*. There are many others but Tao Lin's *Taipei*, published last year, is an extreme case. One reviewer found relief in the "vapid stupidity" of its prose, another in its "massive discharge of waste matter", a third in its "mindless kitsch". As we watch them scurry in haste to the well-furnished bunkers of polite literary society, we can infer each reviewer found clarity and meaning in the apophatic trial of the real thing, leaving only smeared pages of abandoned review copies fluttering on the waste land above.

Meanwhile, those still exposed to the breeze might be better able to recognise the gifts of subjecting experience to writing, or perhaps that should be subjecting writing to experience. The two are often difficult to tell apart, which might be why such hacking is routinely accepted as the task of critics: everything must be kept clear and fiction must remain a desirable product for consumers. But just as the words *Taipei* and *Tao Lin* run into each on the outer cover of this novel, so the artist's struggle to articulate a relation to the world disappears into the work of writing so that neither can maintain a discrete identity.

The meeting of life and art is a familiar theme in fiction of course, and while some are content play with biographical fact and bibliographical fiction in order to run amusing rings around an audience – for example Philip Roth, whose fiction Adam Thirwell characterises as "daring the reader to confuse [fictional] doubles for the original" by "making the life and the art seem like disguises for each other" – Tao Lin approaches it more anxiously and without the distance of mastery. The novel is narrated in traditional third-person omniscience reporting the thoughts and actions of Paul, a 26-year-old New York writer with a family in Asia, with specific attention on his relationships with soon-to-be departed girlfriend Michelle and new girlfriend, soon-to-be wife Erin. They go to literary events, visit his parents in Taipei, "ingest" prescription painkillers and Ecstacy, mention how "depleted" they feel, watch movies on their MacBooks, *make* movies on their MacBooks, but nothing ever generates an event to disrupt the core of their existence or the narration of their existence. If there is nothing especially radical here in literary terms, it does generate a mix of blankness and disquiet in the reader. The repetition of "ingest" and "depleted" throughout blows air between word and experience to the point where neither has any weight, so we read them without gaining what reviewers persuade us to expect in terms of narrative development. Disquiet then is the impossibility of anything happy emerging in our otherwise pleasurable habit of reading. We are not *moving forward*. So while *Taipei* evokes the apparent insignificance of our modern lives, what might be dismissed as literary posturing and provocation is instead realism become tragically unreal.

Critics are also suspicious of the social-media references as indicative of a cynical contemporaneity, spurred on by the author's persona presented in the same social media. It is true that Paul and his friends are embedded in contemporary American culture to an alarming degree – there is only one novel mentioned to compare to the learned references to philosophy and literature in *Montano's Malady* and *The Kindly Ones* – and yet, as a result, the friends float free of any contact, like despairing ghosts in the machine. Their culture is a given, a plateau of distraction and superficial interaction – fast-food restaurants, chain stores, electronic goods, movies on Netflix – but, like a plateau, lacking any decline or elevation. Seeking relief, Paul notes that he has just sent his longest email via iPhone and then listens to his favourite music track on high volume and repeat, concentrating on the drums or the bass "so that he becomes memoryless". The reason why it is his favourite is as inconsequential as the iPhone email record and the track appears to be his favourite only because it comes closest to enabling the condition whereby he loses the self compelled to make such distinctions. While for Estragon and Vladimir everything is promised in the form of Godot, in *Taipei*, there is only the promise of nothing. All of which leaves the status of this novel in question. What kind of relief does yet another novel about relationship issues and existential gloom offer?

The reason why the works of Marcel Proust and Karl Ove Knausgaard maintain a fascination with readers is not due to the extreme length of their books or similarities in subject matter but instead the ambiguity of their genre: both are presented as novels yet are so closely aligned to the reality of the authors' own lives that we read them more aware of everyday mystery and chance than in a traditional memoir, and far more so than in "gritty" realism. While the coy name-change moves *Taipei* closer to Roth/Zuckerman territory than to the same-name first person of Proust and Knausgaard, this is a necessary function of the condition of interchangeable signs without meaning from which the novel emerges: Paul is barely himself, and it is no joke. So while *Taipei* might not gain the aura of Proust and Knausgaard, it shares their struggle.

Going beyond the insouciance overt in his earlier novels, *Taipei* both enacts a fundamental alienation and seeks a cure within its means. While considering the state of their relationship:

> *Paul thought that he would stop thinking about himself and focus on Erin, but instead, almost reflexively, as a method of therapy, began thinking about suicide, then became aware of himself, a few minutes later, earnestly considering—or maybe only imagining—trying to convince Erin that they should commit suicide together. [...]*

Paul began to feel, in a way he hadn't before, like he compre-
hended double suicide — the free and mysterious activity of it, like a
roller coaster descending only into darkness, but accessible from
anywhere, on the theme park of Earth, always open.

Comprehension is only a moment, only "like" and never itself, and occurs so rarely that it flares like fireworks of dark matter, promising, much like writing, much like reading, the presence of mass where mass cannot be seen. The novel resolves without resolution as darkness is pondered again by Paul, in bed with Erin sleeping beside him, thinking of the "glistening, black, mound-shaped mass" of a monkfish she ate in a restaurant and whose picture he then looked up on Wikipedia to show her. He feels emotional contemplating "the light-absorbing mass of it, a silhouette of itself", just as we might contemplating this novel. It helps to palliate otherwise desolate and sundered lives.

The Lawn of Genre

In the relaxed confines of the LRB Bookshop on a warm August evening, Lars Iyer marked the publication of his fourth novel by telling an audience that as a youngster he had been drawn to philosophy rather than fiction as a means to find a way to live, to *think* his way to life. It's an old question – how to live? – and one often so pressing that philosophers have made it central to their lives. This indeed used to be the definition of a philosopher: someone who lived consistently with their beliefs. Ludwig Wittgenstein is one example. For his character Wittgenstein Jr, Iyer says philosophy is also "a kind of spiritual progress", with Socrates and Augustine as his own key figures. So why did Iyer himself turn from philosophy to writing fiction?

How to live? is a simple question too of course, as light as a falling leaf and easily brushed aside as you join a queue to have your copy signed. Without noticing, you're soon dealing with ephemeral demands and the question is answered for you. Iyer said that by the time he was established as an academic in the subject, teaching and supervising, researching and presenting papers at conferences, publishing books, philosophy itself had been displaced. The pressure of having to justify every turn in an argument with references and footnotes covering all contributions and all angles meant the youthful quest was replaced by bureaucracy and career concerns in which "spiritual progress" equalled redundancy. How then to ask the question again?

Fiction marks his answer, a form defined by a lack of pressure, by freedom, so we shouldn't be surprised that the drama of each novel he has written persists in the distressing absence of a philosophy by which to live; a certain weight. In the *Spurious* trilogy, it is found in the double-act despair of W. and Lars as they float like schlubby cherubim in search of God's anchor while, in *Wittgenstein Jr*, the drama emerges from the asymmetry of a troubled Cambridge philosophy tutor and his lightweight, hedonistic students. The philosopher perplexes, irritates and fascinates them in equal measure with his silences and gnomic remarks. *I will teach you differences. Philosophy stands between us and salvation.* They decide he has modelled himself on the real Ludwig Wittgenstein, and so the fun begins. "When will he present an *actual argument*? – Mulberry's taking bets."

After a while the stand-in Wittgenstein becomes more talkative. He implores his students to dispense with *Cambridge cleverness* and *Cambridge pride* in order to face the challenge of his philosophical lesson. The anxious silences are due to paranoia. He believes the Cambridge dons are out to destroy him, as he seeks a utopia of "after philosophy" in which "the light on a particular afternoon will be as rich as the collected works of Kant". Cambridge University stands for what obscures such light, it stands for the hegemony of English philistinism, English parochialism, for a landscape flattened by the English steamroller.

All of England was once a lawn, *Wittgenstein says. The whole of the country, with its uplands and lowlands, with its suburbs and towns, was once the* quintessence of lawn. *[...]*

And it was in the name of the English lawn that the enemy within *was kept down, Wittgenstein says. The Peasants' Revolt was crushed for seeking equality on the English lawn. The Diggers were transported for declaring that the English lawn was part of the commons. [...]*

But never was the English lawn so lush as in the great *univer*sities of England! *Wittgenstein says. Old expanses of lawn, strewn with meadowsweet and buttercups in high summer. Crocuses blooming in spring.*

The numbers soon dwindle to the handful of students whose comments and exchanges narrate the novel, including the aristocratic Ede, convinced of his own destiny, the sore-thumb Benwell, a working-class boy from up north, the Kirwin twins lost without a war in which to die a futile death and who instead throw themselves into vigorous sports, Mulberry in his obscene T-shirts and the self-effacing Peters, the shy Yorkshire boy with a crush on his tutor who records what everyone says. His cartoon of campus life is one of the joys of Iyer's new-found freedom. Wittgenstein Jr takes a walk on the lawn:

> Posh students everywhere. Rah boys in gilets and flip-flops, with piles of bed-head hair. Rugby types, as big as fridges, all red-cheeked health, their voices booming. Rah girls dressed in gym gear and pony-tails. English roses in horse-and-hound clothing, as though fresh from the gymkhana. Yummy-not-yet-mummies in fur-lined Barbour. Ethno-sloanes, with string tops and slouch bags. Sloane-ingénues with big cups of coffee, sweater sleeves half pulled over their hands.

But why is it so pleasurable? At first this sounds like the classic and contemptible English light comedy in which characters are ridiculed for the Schadenfreude of harassed commuters, generic personas dancing on the end of the author's strings before a garishly painted state-of-the-nation backcloth. Perhaps because such hyperbole is counterbalanced by Wittgenstein Jr's apocalyptic vision of philosophical rapture. Combined and in opposition they have a peculiar effect on the reader, both ecstatic and deflating, so that even as one savours the possibility of another life, another world, there is also the absurd present. While Iyer convinces us of Wittgenstein Jr's spiritual yearning and captures the aura of his namesake with minimal brush strokes, the madcap students remind us it is of course *only a novel* and that the characters are inventions, that the stifling conformity of Cambridge is an exaggeration and that Wittgenstein Jr is not Ludwig Wittgenstein. Everything is weightless. But this is also necessary, because lightness enables flight. When Tibor Fischer judged the book "too long" he might have added that such airborne hyperbole is *always* too long and even one excessive, declaratory fictional sentence might already be too much, popping up like a molehill on the lawn over which the donnish greenkeeper might then stand, tutting.

Wittgenstein Jr comes to an end as the carefree life of a student comes to an end. Salvation of a sort is offered to Wittgenstein Jr, but he disappears. A clue to his whereabouts is seen earlier when students go to his room to check on his well-being and spy scraps of paper tacked to the wall with only one word visible: APERION, Anaximander's word for the eternal or cosmological infinity (also spelled "apeiron" but this is how it appears in the novel). Perhaps this is an additional mark of excess to the one Derrida says signifies the participation in a genre without membership, a mark that is itself not part of the genre yet necessary for its distinction and recognition. *Aperion* then is the mark of a universal principle of existence, an abstraction *outside* of life that nevertheless makes life possible and is apparently sensible only in the light of a particular afternoon and in the freedom, lightness and excess of writing, and yet which, as Fischer's cavil confirms, must also succumb to the ever-encroaching English lawn.

Back in the LRB Bookshop, the event drawing to a close, the audience was given a chance to ask questions. As hands went up and a microphone passed around, I wondered what it would mean for the lightness of fiction to become as heavy as academic philosophy, with its own bureaucracy and career demands, for it to be a kind of spiritual regression, for *aperion* to be only a word tacked to a wall, and then how a writer might evade the lawn of genre. But I didn't ask the question. Perhaps Wittgenstein Jr's disappearance is the answer.

Fear of Reading

In the monochrome sunlight of a January afternoon in the Sussex countryside, someone was involved in a road traffic accident. He sustained two obvious injuries: a cracked bone in his wrist and a whack on the back of the head a smile's width from his right ear. He says he has no memory of the accident, no memory indeed of the next four days in hospital. The cold air of the car park on the final day is all he feels now.

Since then, including another nine days in hospital after the skull fracture was discovered, I have wondered how to slough off this thick critical skin in order to … in order to …

And that is the problem, if there is one. There is no clear object of this wondering. In order, perhaps, to write differently. So what would it mean to write as one imagines writing rather than in this hesitant, potholed manner? As I waited in a hospital bed, I imagined this other life of writing in which the word disappears.

Little has changed.

I have thought often about those nine days, and how I was unable to watch a documentary on the pharaoh Akhenaten but listening caused an obscure epiphany which later I assumed was due to the morphine. However, recent events have challenged that assumption.

Akhenaten had ordered that the capital city be moved from Thebes into the desert 200 miles away. The documentary featured new archaeological discoveries that revealed the disastrous consequences for his subjects. What stirred me was not these human facts but the glorious and terrifying absurdity of Akhenaten's project. It demonstrates the same impressive or horrendous folly as those in fictional works: William Golding's *The Spire* for example, and Herzog's *Fitzcarraldo* and, more familiar to me, those of the many characters created by Bernhard: Roithamer who builds a cone-shaped house in the middle of a forest, Reger who studies every masterpiece in the Kunsthistoriches Museum in Vienna until he finds a flaw in each, even Bernhard himself aged eight deciding to cycle to his aunt's house in Salzburg, twenty-two miles away. A creative writer may respond by sketching a novel idea based on the crazy plans of an individual – perhaps Naguib Mahfouz's *Akhenaten: Dweller in Truth* is it as far as the pharaoh is concerned – but, in my sedated condition, I imagined a writing project that would itself be the absurdity, something itself animated by impossibility.

Nothing specific came of my epiphany. Since then I have wanted to write about the accident and this strange time in hospital but have also felt uncomfortable about discussing an experience that seems hopelessly subjective. The details of the accident were also *sub judice*. The police were unable to release the witness statements until the case was resolved. I had to wait an indefinite period before I could find out what a buckled rear wheel couldn't tell me. Seventeen months later, out of the blue, the case was concluded and, soon after, I received the statements in the post. This was a reality I had been unable to anticipate. It was unreal. Every day for over a year I had imagined the permutations of what may have happened, but had failed. I couldn't imagine anything. Perhaps one day, I thought, I will experience a flashback to the shock of the impact. But no, nothing beyond the memory of an uncertain point in the road. (If this is what death is like, I thought, then it's fine; it's nothing.) And then I became uncomfortable about the possibility of the reports triggering such memories or, if they did not, then planting indelible images in my head. This would be experience without experience, I thought; history without event. But, really, it already is. All I could do was to submit to more.

As I opened the envelope and flipped A4 sheets over and over to get through the formal police checklists and onto the handwritten and typed statements, I felt a slight derangement, an almost physical vertigo. This is the fear of reading. This is why I cannot read crime or horror novels; books that bring great suffering into being for no other reason than generic necessity. It is a terrible addition to actuality. Actuality occurs once but literature never ends; every moment in a novel is eternal, every character immortal. Fiction makes something happen forever. This is what stirred me when I heard the story of Akhenaten's new city: the real presence of the imagination.

Worse still, the addition to actuality – the repetition of what's not there – is never enough. No matter how resourceful the writer, the writing is never enough. Jonathan Littell's *The Kindly Ones*, one of the most remarkable novels published in our belated lifetime, was roundly condemned for its doubling of real massacres yet, in their industrial haste, the staff reviewers mistook the narrator's descriptive restraint, its reserve towards empathy, for the author's callousness toward others' suffering and, much worse, capitalising on it. Except Max Aue is clear that his experience of the massacres is itself not enough and that the suffering and death he witnesses, and then inflicts, reveal an unavowable space he cannot traverse. It haunts him and his story. Aue describes a mass killing to his colleague Hohenegg: "the spectator can never fully grasp the experience of the deceased". Hohenegg replies: "But this gap exists only for the person who watches". Aue's narrative is the revelation of that gap; the reader watches. His punishment by those seeking vengeance might be said to be the narrative itself in which his crime and punishment recurs eternally.

So I submitted and looked at the witness statements. One saw the cyclist fly into the air still holding the handlebars, then land to lie stock-still across the tarmac. The other witness got out of his car and ran over. After a minute or so the cyclist opened his eyes, sat up straight but did not respond to questions: his eyes open "but nobody at home". Blood ran out of his right ear. Then he insisted on moving to the side of the road.

That was it really. I read the words with a forensic attention, as if each was an unrequited love letter, yet what I really wanted wasn't there. I wanted to see what was not seen. Why was the fracture below the overhang of the skull? If my head struck the tarmac (there is no curb), how was this part damaged rather than the crown? Perhaps it hit the frame of the car, but wouldn't that have been more damaging at such speed? Reading the statements has not been enough; answers have become questions.

What remains? The legacy of traumatic brain injury for one. My inner ear was damaged so I have had to retrain my sense of balance. This also has a weird side-effect that mimics chronic fatigue syndrome. My sense of smell has gone and may never return – which thereby also diminishes the sense of taste – while concentration and short-term memory levels are challenged. On the plus side, I think my writing has improved; that is, has become more closely attuned to what concerns me and renews the fascination with books with which I began over twenty years ago. This beginning and the time in hospital tell me that, while reading and writing are not enough, life isn't, either.

Acknowledgements

While a blog is a solitary pursuit beholden to no one but the writer, this book would not have been possible without the generosity and friendship of Flowerville, Victoria Harding, Lars Iyer, Gabriel Josipovici, Charlotte Mandell and Mark Thwaite.

Contemporary culture has eliminated both the concept of the
public and the figure of the intellectual. Former public spaces –
both physical and cultural – are now either derelict or colonized
by advertising. A cretinous anti-intellectualism presides,
cheerled by expensively educated hacks in the pay of
multinational corporations who reassure their bored readers
that there is no need to rouse themselves from their interpassive
stupor. The informal censorship internalized and propagated by
the cultural workers of late capitalism generates a banal
conformity that the propaganda chiefs of Stalinism could only
ever have dreamt of imposing. Zer0 Books knows that another
kind of discourse – intellectual without being academic, popular
without being populist – is not only possible: it is already
flourishing, in the regions beyond the striplit malls of so-called
mass media and the neurotically bureaucratic halls of the
academy. Zer0 is committed to the idea of publishing as a
making public of the intellectual. It is convinced that in
the unthinking, blandly consensual culture in which we live,
critical and engaged theoretical reflection is more important
than ever before.